CULTURAL PATTERNS IN URBAN SCHOOLS

CULTURAL PATTERNS IN URBAN SCHOOLS

A MANUAL FOR
TEACHERS, COUNSELORS, AND ADMINISTRATORS

Written under the direction of
JOSEPH D. LOHMAN

UNIVERSITY OF CALIFORNIA PRESS
Berkeley and Los Angeles   1969

University of California Press
Berkeley and Los Angeles, California

University of California Press, Ltd.
London, England

Copyright © 1967, by
The Regents of the University of California

Second Printing, 1969
Library of Congress Catalog Card Number: 67-21846

A Joint Project of the School of Criminology and the School of Education, University of California, Berkeley, California. Prepared through the assistance of Grant No. 63228 of the U. S. Department of Health, Education and Welfare.

PREFACE

The purpose of this book is to help teachers to understand and accept the subcultures from which an increasing number of their students come. It is our premise that in this way teachers can learn to bring out untapped strengths and enthusiasms among their students and open the door to communication with them.

The content of this book was developed from the experience of many teachers working at the elementary, junior-high, and senior-high school levels. The teachers were drawn from schools with a large proportion of minority youth and were identified by their colleagues as having shown sensitivity, insight, and skill in engaging alienated youth.

Our task, as researchers, was to draw out these insights and this we did through a series of panel discussions and group interviews conducted during the course of the school year, 1963-64. During these sessions problem situations—partially based on the teachers' own experience—were presented in such a way as to elicit discussion and analysis of various coping strategies.

The manual is particularly suitable for group training, since the materials can be used as starting points for further discussion. It is, however, equally suited for individual use since analytical questions and guiding commentaries are included in each section.

The project was carried out and written by cooperating members of the Schools of Criminology and of Education, University of California, Berkeley. The principal contributors were John Ablon, James T. Carey, T. Bentley Edwards, Dorothy Hansen, Elizabeth Lacy, Eugene McCreary, Joseph Reid, and Michael Rowe. Considerable assistance was also rendered by Karl Anselm, Margot Dashiell, William Green, Marie Kroger, Neil Ross, Joyce Scott, and Elizabeth Waterman. Horace Cayton and Marianne Pennekamp served as consultants. Through the efforts of these persons, a manual in mimeographed form was produced. We have been extremely gratified by the enthusiastic response with which the manual has been received. The present volume is a revision of that document. I want to thank the University of California Press and Fannia Weingartner for editorial assistance. Steve Talbot of the School of Criminology assisted with the revision and other matters requisite to the completion of the present text.

I want to express my thanks to the President's Committee on Juvenile Delinquency and Youth Crime, the President and Regents of the University of California, and the Dean of the School of Education, Berkeley Campus. The authors of this volume wish also to express their gratitude to the superintendents and cooperating school districts of Berkeley, Oakland, and Richmond, California. Above all, we wish to thank the teachers who so willingly cooperated and generously gave of their time, their wisdom and their talent for dealing with culturally diverse youth. This manual is, in the wider sense their contribution to both new and experienced teachers who are confronting the challenge of teaching in these highly significant years.

JOSEPH D. LOHMAN, *Dean*
School of Criminology
University of California, Berkeley

GENERAL INTRODUCTION

In the course of the last twenty years there has been a radical change in the color and character of the great metropolitan centers of the United States. This change is most dramatically demonstrated in our public schools. A recent newspaper headline read:

> PUBLIC SCHOOLS OF CHICAGO FOR THE FIRST
> TIME IN HISTORY NOW 51% NONWHITE.

And this in spite of the fact that of the total population of Chicago only 23 percent are nonwhite. The situation in Philadelphia is similar. The same paper reported that while 31 percent of the total population are nonwhite, a full 63 percent of the students in the Philadelphia schools are in this category. These examples are typical of many of the large cities of the Northeast, Midwest, and West Coast.

Within these urban centers a "new city" is rapidly growing, one whose population has predominantly rural roots. In more than one way this "new city" is in conflict with the "old city" which still holds the reins of government and public affairs. It is not surprising that the newer population forms subcultural groups marked by customs and modes of behavior which differ sharply from those of the established "old city" population. If we are to understand, let alone solve, the problems of our urban centers we must focus our attention on the lives led by these newer arrivals in our cities.

We, the educators and teachers in these urban centers are predominantly creatures of the "old city": white, middle class, habituated to pursuing long-range goals. We tend to regard the patterns of behavior of the newer subcultures as unusual, even deviant and bizarre. Almost always we evaluate them from our own stance, usually negatively. Thus, when we attempt to cope with the problems that inevitably result from the juxtaposition of the "old" and the "new" cities we use the only means we know, means that are appropriate to our own culture and hence seldom effective when applied to the newer subcultures.

Our immersion in our own middle-class culture blinds us to the fundamental problem: our assumption that the conflict between the new subcultures and our own culture is to be attributed solely to the character of the weaker, newer subcultures. Our first step in solving our problems must be to understand the new subcultures and in this way to change the perspective from which we view the conflict between the established and the new.

This problem of perspective is intensified when teachers confront the subculture of youth. In working with all children teachers find themselves dealing with customs, habits, and even a language different not only from those of their own age group but different as well from those of the youth of their own generation. Youth in general might be considered as forming a subculture of its own. In the case of children who come from a different socioeconomic and often racial subculture as well, the existing age and generation barrier is raised even higher.

It has become clear that our past approach to these problems has been unsuccessful. Our customary test procedures and disciplinary methods have proved ineffective. The very structure and organization of our institutions have proved unsuitable for dealing with the increasing number of "problem" children. Nor has this failure necessarily been because of a lack of empathy, good will, or individual insight. Most often it has been a failure of the kind of understanding that must be based on knowledge.

A progress report on educational research and development prepared for the United States Commissioner of Education in March 1964, noted:

By all known criteria, the majority of urban and rural slum schools are failures. In neighborhood after neighborhood across the country, more than half of each age group fails to complete high school, and 5 percent or fewer go on to some form of higher education. In many schools the average measured IQ is under 85, and it drops steadily as the children grow older. Adolescents depart from these schools ill-prepared to lead a satisfying, useful life or to participate successfully in the community.[1]

Instead of looking at this merely as an indictment — which it certainly is — let us start at a more fruitful point and consider it as a description of what educators mean when they say that we are facing a crisis in education.

In the previous decade the crisis in education was seen mainly in

---

[1] U. S. Office of Education, *Innovation and Experiment in Education*, A Progress Report of the Panel on Educational Research and Development to the U. S. Commissioner of Education (Washington, 1964).

terms of shortages: shortages of buildings, teachers, and by implication, of the tax money required to remedy these faults. Now we must recognize that this was a superficial commentary on the educational task. For with more buildings and more teachers, the problem remains the same. We have not reduced the "dropout" rate, nor reversed the declining level of the I.Q. All too many adolescents continue to leave school ill-prepared to lead satisfying and useful lives.

Within the schools we have evaded some of the most crucial problems by taking the "difficult" children out of the normal class environment and putting them in special classes or even schools to try to correct their "incorrigible" behavior. Now the schools are increasingly hard pressed for special classrooms and teachers to handle all the children who for various reasons need special attention. The educators and testers are finding that one in three of the young people in the public school systems of the twelve largest cities have such handicaps that they are unable to profit from programs of education or even to participate in them. What is worse, instead of being helped these children's weaknesses are often compounded by the schools.

It does not solve the problem to refer to these students as maladjusted, focusing on some particular quality in the individual student. Our increasing knowledge of the behavioral sciences reveals that departure or deviance from the generally accepted norms of the wider community can indeed represent an adjustment rather than a failure to adjust. If we are to solve the problems posed by these young people we must change our way of looking at them and not attribute to them aims and views that differ sharply from those they in fact hold. From such a new perspective, for instance, it becomes possible to see youngsters who violate the law as in many cases being conforming individuals — conforming to the mores of their particular group — rather than as nonconformists, which is how the law generally regards them.

If a third of the school population leaves school having been incapable of successfully engaging in the school culture then it is clearly important to develop another kind of collective context within the schools that would enable these young people to benefit from the purposes of education and to become a part of the community. It has been customary to consider these youngsters asocial, incapable of having effective relations with others; the others being ourselves. On closer examination we find that these youngsters are highly socialized and effective in relations with those of their own subculture. And often it is precisely because of these intense relationships within their own subculture that they are at odds with the general community. Disregarding these relationships or unaware of them, the community attempts to deal with these young people by methods which leave them unaffected, or worse, confirm their opposition to the established community.

One of our difficulties in confronting this problem is that the recent creation of subcultures in our cities is a reversal of the process that characterized America during the late nineteenth and early twentieth century. Then Americanization was a centripetal process, a drawing inward of those who came from different places. First there was the transitional stage of the hyphenated Americans, the German-Americans, Italian-Americans, Irish-Americans. Then, as they acquired the language and other necessary skills these people became simply Americans integrated into the mainstream of American life. Various institutions, such as the settlement house, operated as part of the effort to assist them in making the transition.

The current situation is radically different because of the explosion of population and the technological revolution that have taken place in the meantime. As a result of this and of the rapid development of automation, the new subcultural groups of our cities are becoming stagnant pockets of permanently indigent families with very limited opportunities for working their way out into the mainstream of the economic and social life of the larger city. The isolation of these people is intensified by racial barriers. The youngsters who grow up in this environment have been conditioned to exclusion and denial. And within this limited context they have developed an even more limited adolescent subculture which is as serious a threat to the primacy of the adult world as the threats of poverty and racial conflict.

Alienated from the general community, thrust into the subcultures of age, of poverty, and of race, many of these young people are becoming hostile, unregenerate, and desperate. These are the children who must be understood by an increasing number of teachers. The stakes are high because only these young people can take up the task of shaping a new and better society. It is our hope that this book will be a contribution to this end.

ORGANIZATION AND CONTENTS

The book is divided into five parts. Every part includes an introduction and three stories, each of which is followed by a set of questions and a commentary. Each part concludes with a number of digests from relevant social science readings.

The introductions provide the context for each part. The stories are built around situations and incidents that occur daily in classrooms, school corridors, and administrators' offices throughout the American school system. But the stories go beyond this, sketching in the home backgrounds and circumstances of the children involved in the various incidents described. They illustrate what most teachers know from experience; namely, that the child comes to school not as an empty vessel ready to be filled with knowledge but as a complicated human being often troubled by situations and events that have little to do with school but that influence his behavior while he is there. The questions at the end of each story are included to help the reader pinpoint the central elements of the problematic situation. The commentaries carry this a step further, suggesting different ways in which critical incidents might have been handled with a more positive outcome for all concerned. The readings set the problems back into the wider context of social science findings. By using the digest form we have been able to cover more ground and present a greater variety of viewpoints than would otherwise have been possible.

In what ways can these materials be useful to the teacher? Recent research has shown that in race relations specific attitudes frequently change after the situation itself has already changed. Studies of military desegregation and housing patterns, for example, have shown that attitudes toward living and working with Negroes become decidedly more positive after persons have actually lived and worked with them.[2]

How can this be applied to our school situation? It suggests that if a teacher can modify his behavior in the classroom *despite* any negative feelings he may have toward his students, then his own as well as his students' hostility toward the classroom situation will be diminished. This will in turn create an atmosphere within which more favorable attitudes can develop. The evidence that attitudes do not have to be changed prior to modification of behavior is important and encouraging, for outright changes in attitudes are hard to achieve.

At this point it might be useful to discuss the terminology used in this manual, and to make clear the assumptions that underlie its use. When the relatively recent discussions of cultural differences as a factor

---

[2] ". . . a view of race relations which centers upon the concept of individual attitudes is severely limited. While there are some situations in which the behavior of persons toward others can be explained individual *qua* individual, in terms of specific attitudes, in the major and significant areas of social life — namely, jobs, business, and the community — this conception is not adequate. Thus most situations of racial contact are defined by the collectively defined interests of the individuals concerned and do not merely manifest their private feelings toward other races, for example, Negroes." (Joseph D. Lohman and Dietrich C. Reitzes, "Note on Race Relations in Mass Society," *American Journal of Sociology*, LVIII, Nov. 1952, p. 241.)

in education began, the term "culturally deprived" was used to describe those students who did not come from the dominant middle class. Though it was intended as a factual, descriptive term, some people considered that it carried connotations of a negative judgment. Other terms came into use: culturally divergent, culturally disadvantaged, disadvantaged youth, educationally alienated, and so on. But no matter which term is used, there are those who find that all of them imply condescension. We have used various of these terms throughout the manual. In all cases they are used as descriptive terms referring to those students who come from subcultures differing from those of the predominantly white, Anglo-Saxon, middle-class society. Because the schools reflect the values and aims of the wider society, they have approached all students as if they came from similar socioeconomic backgrounds. By doing this they have failed to meet the needs of culturally different youth. It is in this sense that these students are "deprived" and "disadvantaged," and that they have become "alienated" or "marginal." In no way is the use of these terms meant to imply that these youngsters are "inferior." There have been some unfortunate consequences in singling out and characterizing the disadvantaged child because of his lack of middle-class values, not the least of which has been to attribute to him an absence of culture. On the contrary, he is a product of cultural processes. Thus young people who are referred to as "culturally deprived" are in fact problem-solving individuals. The residual piling-up of their problem-solving responses has produced the subcultures of the deprived groups.

To some the terms used above are synonymous with the word Negro, and because so much of the material in this book deals with Negroes it might seem that we share this view. This is not the case. The "culturally deprived" or "divergent" in our society include all races. But this book is primarily concerned with those groups who have in recent years migrated to the large cities in great numbers. It is in this context that the strongest clash between the "old" and "new" city cultures has taken place and that the educational process has been most markedly affected. The American Indians, the Mexican-American migrant workers, the migrating white Appalachian unemployed, and the Puerto Ricans can all be considered as "culturally deprived" groups. But most of them are not of major concern to the metropolitan area schools. In the large Northeastern, Midwestern, and West Coast cities it is the arrival of rural Southern Negroes in overwhelming numbers that has raised the problem to its present level of intensity.

Although all lower-class Americans are not Negroes – indeed more are Caucasian — a far greater proportion of the total Negro population is to be found in the lower socioeconomic group. The reasons for this are historical and have nothing to do with any innate racial differences as such.

Our concern in this book is with the youth trapped within the confines of the urban ghetto. These young people have found our schools unsympathetic and alien places. It is our hope and our aim that this tragic situation be changed.

CONTENTS

PREFACE

GENERAL INTRODUCTION

PART I - CULTURAL DIFFERENCES AND THE TEACHING OF VALUES

INTRODUCTION, 1

"HUMANITY", 8

    Questions for Writing and Discussion, 11
    Comments, 12

"CITIZENSHIP", 17

    Questions for Writing and Discussion, 20
    Comments, 21

"CASHEW AND JESUS", 26

    Questions for Writing and Discussion, 30
    Comments, 31

DIGESTS OF SOCIAL SCIENCE READINGS, 37

    "Lower Class Culture as a Generating Milieu of Gang Delinquency," by Walter B. Miller, 37

    "The Disadvantaged Child and the Learning Process: Some Social Psychological and Developmental Considerations," by Martin Deutsch, 40

    "The Culturally Deprived Child," by Frank Riessman, 41

"Social-Class Variations in the Teacher-Pupil Relationship," by Howard Becker, 44

"The Separate Culture of the School," by Willard Waller, 45

"The Vanishing Adolescent," by Edgar Z. Friedenberg, 46

PART II - SELF—IMAGE

INTRODUCTION, 47

"PREPARATION", 54

    Questions for Writing and Discussion, 57
    Comments, 58

"AUTHORITY", 61

    Questions for Writing and Discussion, 63
    Comments, 64

"EVALUATION", 67

    Questions for Writing and Discussion, 70
    Comments, 71

DIGESTS OF SOCIAL SCIENCE READINGS, 77

    "The Mark of Oppression," by Abram Kardiner and Lionel Ovesey, 77

    "Racial Identification and Preference in Negro Children," by Kenneth B. Clark and Mamie Clark, 79

    "Social Status and Intelligence: An Experimental Study of Certain Cultural Determinants of Measured Intelligence," by Ernest A Haggard, 80

    "Teacher Comments and Student Performance: Seventy-Four Classroom Experiments in School Motivation," by Ellis Batten Page, 81

CONTENTS

PART III - THE SCHOOL PROCESS

INTRODUCTION, 83

"A LESSON", 90

>Questions for Writing and Discussion, 93
>Comments, 94

"TIME", 98

>Questions for Writing and Discussion, 102
>Comments, 102

"EXCLUDED", 106

>Questions for Writing and Discussion, 110
>Comments, 110

DIGESTS OF SOCIAL SCIENCE READINGS, 114

>Max Weber on Bureaucracy, 114
>
>"Bureaucracy in Modern Society," by Peter M. Blau, 115
>
>"The Teacher in the Authority System of the Public School," by Howard S. Becker, 119
>
>"Programs for the Educationally Disadvantaged," U.S. Department of Health, Education, and Welfare, 121

PART IV - ADOLESCENTS AND ADULT AUTHORITY

INTRODUCTION, 129

"MISTAKE", 137

>Questions for Writing and Discussion, 141
>Comments, 141

"PSYCHOLOGY", 145

>Questions for Writing and Discussion, 148
>Comments, 149

"TOUGH GUYS", 155

    Questions for Writing and Discussion, 158
    Comments, 159

DIGESTS OF SOCIAL SCIENCE READINGS, 165

    "Identity vs. Identity Diffusion in Adolescence," by Erik H. Erikson, 165

    "Delinquents in Schools: A Test for the Legitimacy of Authority," by Carl Werthman, 167

PART V - THE SCHOOL AND ITS RELATION TO LIFE EXPERIENCE

THE SCHOOL AND THE WORLD OF WORK, 169

THE SCHOOL AND PREPARATION FOR COMMUNITY LIFE, 172

"EXPECTATIONS", 176

    Questions for Writing and Discussion, 179
    Comments, 180

"SKILL", 184

    Questions for Writing and Discussion, 187
    Comments, 188

"VARIETY", 193

    Questions for Writing and Discussion, 197
    Comments, 198

CONTENTS   xix

DIGESTS OF SOCIAL SCIENCE READINGS, 200

"Social Structure and Anomie," by Robert K. Merton, 200

"Goals, Norms, and Anomie," by Richard A. Cloward and Lloyd E. Ohlin, 202

"Growing Up in a Class System," by Albert K. Cohen, 203

"The Religious Beliefs and Practices of Delinquent Youth," by Carl Wertman, 206

ACKNOWLEDGMENTS, 209

PART I
CULTURAL DIFFERENCES AND THE TEACHING OF VALUES

INTRODUCTION

Those of us born and raised in the United States, whether in cities or rural areas, all share certain cultural characteristics within the American tradition. In addition we all have patterned ways of acting, perceiving, and relating to one another which we learn and share because we are members of a particular social group. The consistency of our values and our own conduct are the condition of our status within the group and comprise our badge of membership.

While most Americans are proud of their country's tradition of cultural diversity, of the different ethnic and racial backgrounds and customs of many of their compatriots (which we might call subcultures within the larger American culture), there is nevertheless a pressure toward conformity, and this has worked to diminish this diversity. Differences are frequently tolerated and respected only until they begin to intrude on the values of the mainstream of society, and then the pressures for conformity begin. These pressures frequently lead to unfortunate or even disastrous conflicts and rarely solve the basic problems posed by cultural differences. So completely are we submerged within our own values that we have difficulty in realizing that habits different from our own — particularly ones that are annoying to us — may nevertheless have a coherence and value of their own.

Social scientists tell us that most aspects of culture such as values or forms of expected behavior are related to other aspects of the culture. Thus by pressuring someone to eliminate or change certain of his traits we may endanger his place within the particular group to which he belongs because that group values these very traits. By changing himself, he will be cut off from his psychic and social reference group, and since he cannot easily move into another group or internalize the rewards adhering to membership and conformity in the new group, he may well find himself alienated from both groups.

The school contains a number of built-in value conflicts. First there is a conflict between teachers and students because of the difference in age and generation. Teachers share adult values; students share the values of their contemporaries who have usually formed subcultures with their own habits and norms.

However, the conflict with which we are most concerned is that which occurs because teachers carry the responsibility of transmitting our cultural heritage. Students represent the contemporary culture of their particular community, and if this community is a culturally diverse one, the natural conflict between teachers and students becomes the more complex. Because the school is representative of the mainstream of American values formed by the tradition of the "melting pot" most teachers naturally tend to enforce middle-class values and manners.

By "middle class" we mean the mass of American society that places a high value on a stable family life, regular employment, education, and social and professional achievement. We will speak of the "lower class" as that population group which is made up of semi-skilled or unskilled workers, if they are employed at all, and which frequently exhibits an unstable family life or commonly a mother-centered family with no stable male present. In such contexts importance is often attached to toughness, excitement, and the ability to "con" or outsmart others. Young people from lower-class groups are insulated from the middle-class values around them, even though these values are the overwhelmingly apparent ones of our total society. Their early years have shaped their interests and social contacts into a mold that is not easily broken.

The teaching group largely perpetuates itself. Teachers are chosen or tend to choose the teaching profession when they are students because they feel they wish to have a part in the transmission of knowledge, or because they have found the profession and the mode of life associated with it congruous with their own interests and tastes. Students who do not fit the expectations of the school, who are dissatisfied, or "troublemakers" seldom go into teaching. Thus, a rather stable and orderly middle-class tradition continues. Indeed, it is worth noting that possibly it is only through the values of order and intellectualism, with all of their implications, that the school has been able to continue functioning as productively and stably as it has.

It is to this conflict between the school with its relatively stable middle-class goals and the lower socioeconomic group that we now turn, realizing that it is a long and painful process to recognize and accept the idea that separate behavior reflects a separate subculture, particularly if certain subcultural forms of behavior cause daily problems in teaching.

Changing values by talking about them in the classroom confronts teachers with a difficult task. Value change comes about slowly and usually through complex incentives, including the emulation of models. In this respect the teacher is as important in building character as he is in teaching academic subjects. He is a model and can be a great inspiration to his students, especially those who have not had a stable model in their homes. Although the fruits of the teacher's labors may not be readily apparent at the time that he is dealing with a student he may be achieving more than he realizes and because of his efforts subtle changes may appear in the student, years afterward.

One approach would be to launch a program which would point out to groups of alienated students the specific middle-class values and skills that are necessary for their survival in the economic order, and to emphasize that their command of these will help them in the future without threatening or violating the primary values of their family and community. But how do we distinguish between values which preclude the development of survival skills, and subcultural values which harm no one but are particularly annoying or perhaps shocking to us?

Certain kinds of know-how and communication must be mastered by *all* young people in order for them to find a place in today's economic and social order. The first of these is reading. This presents perhaps the greatest frustration to teachers, because such a large number of students are years below their grade levels in reading. Another important skill is how to ask questions in an acceptable manner. Many students appear to ask questions in a belligerent or purposefully naive manner. Often the teacher reacts negatively and does not answer because he feels that the student is simply acting out or testing him, when in fact the student does want information but does not know how to communicate in a socially acceptable way.

Communication by word and gesture is complex for children who come from homes where such skills are not naturally transmitted in the course of daily life. For example, a study of slum families in New York revealed that in one-half of the families examined, the children do not eat with their parents, nor do they have opportunities to talk to them about anything other than elementary matters of physical necessity. The togetherness of the middle-class meal, aside from its emotional impact, gives children the opportunity to converse with their parents or to listen to conversation about abstract matters. In fact, much of the social, educational, and cultural tradition that a middle-class child learns is gained in conversation over the meal table. In this area teachers could try to supplement the verbal skills of lower-class students by instruction in socially acceptable forms of communication and gesture, pointing out, for example, that one should look directly at a teacher, potential employer, or whomever one addresses instead of avoiding his eyes. Niceties of speech are taken for granted by most of us, but many a job has been lost, or question or plea for aid refused because the applicant could not ask his question or present himself in an acceptable way.

How to fill out forms is also a survival need, even to get an unskilled job or sign up for unemployment insurance. Another habit lower-class youngsters often lack is that of promptness and an understanding that one must keep appointments in the business world. Many of these children come from families where there is no father and the family lives on welfare, or where the father is unemployed. In such cases there is frequently no regular schedule for rising in the morning and eating communal meals. The importance of living on a time schedule is not emphasized, and the children must be taught promptness and conscientiousness in meeting appointments by the school. This can be more effectively done by dealing with particular cases of tardiness as they occur, by reminders, than by delivering general lectures on promptness.

There are other habits that are annoying, but are not potentially hazardous to economic survival. These, school personnel might try to understand and accept, even though the habits are unpleasant or even shocking. Weird speech forms could be accepted if they are not actually obscene; bizarre hair styles and clothes could be tolerated if they do not go beyond the limits of legally defined indecent exposure.

Certain styles of dress and speech may be of great survival value to the young person in his own social world. His dress is his badge of status and membership in his peer group. His means of communication is the way he copes with his world, which is frequently a different world from that of many school people. Many of the students we call culturally disadvantaged have weak or even evil self-images and bolster their self-esteem in ways that are alien to the middle class. The more flamboyant their dress, the greater their sense of belonging. We must try to see that the behavior and trappings of their world are often not those of the dominant society because their meaning is completely different. To understand and to try to accept, even though we disapprove, is perhaps the most difficult, but the most potentially productive way to react to this type of habit.

In considering the conflict between the middle-class school and the lower-class student, we have discussed the methods by which change can be brought about in the student, the extent to which such change can be expected, and the kinds of lower-class behavior which the school might tolerate without a loss to the learning situation. There is another element in this relationship between differing classes and their ways of living. While it is necessary for the lower-class group to be exposed to middle-class values, to adapt to them and sometimes even adopt them in order to survive in the dominant society, it is also necessary for middle-class school personnel to be exposed to the values and ways of life of the lower socioeconomic group. It is the very insularity of the middle-class person, his ability to live his life almost totally among others like himself, which so often gives him the feeling that his way is *the* way, the *only* way, and that all others must be converted to it. Little real education can take place in a situation where there is no trust and no rapport between the teacher and the students. In this context the notion of "teacher" may be expanded to mean the school as an institution, and "student" to mean the community of the students' families. This trust and rapport cannot result if all interaction, or rather action, between these groups is in one direction.

While there seems to be general agreement that the adoption of certain values of the dominant middle-class culture is necessary for survival in this society, such adoption cannot be forced. Perhaps an effective injunction might be: *expose, don't impose!* If school personnel can open the doors to their students without attempting to push them through, if they can sincerely convey to these students that there are different values which may be of practical help to them without intimating that their present values are worthless, if the school can allow the student to take what he wants without insisting that he take everything, then the student may be able to accept some of the school's values.

The ability to adopt certain values and habits to achieve practical ends, while retaining roots in and identification with one's own subculture has been likened to the owning and wearing of different kinds of clothes. Just as one puts on a suit for certain occasions and sport clothes for another, so one may assume middle-class habits for other parts of one's life. To be able to do this one must accept elements of more than one set of values, and to help a student toward this the school personnel must itself show a similar ability to accept more than one set of values.

If a teacher received a teaching assignment in a foreign country she should thoroughly prepare herself by reading, meeting with people who had been there and, if possible, with natives of that country in order to learn as much as possible of the culture of the people. She would undoubtedly feel that one of the main values of her stay in this other country would be the experience at first hand, of another way of life. It is unlikely that she would imply to the inhabitants that their way of life was inferior to that of her own country, whenever it was different.

Working effectively with people of a subculture within one's own country requires much the same approach. To begin to know and understand others one must know their history and the forces that have shaped them. An exchange teacher would undoubtedly study the history of the country she visited, and yet most school personnel see no need to learn the history of minority groups in this country, though admittedly they would have to make a special effort to do so since it has been either ignored or distorted in our history books.

The middle-class teacher who becomes familiar with her students' subculture might be surprised to find many positive elements in it, some of which she might even desire to incorporate into her own values. But even if this is not the case the knowledge which she has gained will enable her to better understand her students and to develop ways of teaching which will complement their ways of operating.

It is the actual or implied criticism of his way of living, his home, his very being which so demoralizes the lower-class student, especially if he is from a minority group. One example which involves that essential element in education, communication, is the special language of the youth of the now most common urban subculture — partly Southern, partly Negro, partly lower class, and partly adolescent. It is a language far removed from that of the dominant middle class, and the common reaction to it in the schools is to despise it as ungrammatical and undesirable and to try and wipe it out if possible. To the student his language is an integral part of his culture, his very being, and an attack on it is much more than an attack on his conversation, it is an attack on his own worth. Small wonder he so often reacts with sullenness, resentment, and defiance.

Yet if the teacher really listens, she will hear that this language is soft, rhythmical, and pleasant to the ear, that it is extremely inventive and communicates in an effective and realistic fashion. On the other hand, it is not going to be acceptable on a job application form, or in an interview, or in any other situation where it will be necessary to deal with members of the dominant class in order to achieve some desired end. If the teacher can let the student know she appreciates the positive qualities in his language, he will be more disposed to see the need for using the dominant language pattern at times and more willing to learn it. Here again the analogy of the appropriate suit for the appropriate occasion holds.

There will be other differences which can be handled on this same basis of what is necessary for the student to know for his own benefit, and not because the school is attempting to displace his "inferior" way

CULTURAL DIFFERENCES AND VALUES

of life with its "superior" one. Langston Hughes' poem "Motto" succinctly summarizes this value of knowing more than one way of life:

> I play it cool and dig all jive.
> That's the reason I stay alive.
> My motto, As I live and learn,
> Is: Dig and Be Dug in Return.

This applies to students and to school personnel alike.

The following stories illustrate problems stemming from cultural differences and the failure to recognize and deal constructively with them.

The story "Humanity" shows what happens when a "liberal" teacher who teaches the importance of respecting cultural differences, is unable to do so herself within her own classroom.

"Citizenship" points up the severe alienation from the school felt by some Negro students. The lessons taught in school have little meaning for them because of their own experiences within our society.

"Cashew and Jesus" vividly depicts some of the problems encountered by a boy who comes from a subculture distinctly different from that which prevails at his school. His problems within the school stem from this difference and the teacher's inability to cope with the classroom situation.

"HUMANITY"

"Great Spirit, help me never to judge another until I have walked two weeks in his moccasins." The Sioux Indian prayer was inscribed in bright red chalk across the front blackboard, above the date. On the display table to the right were several miniature teepees fashioned of wrapping paper and sticks and painted with gay water colors. At the left, a feathered head-dress matched with a buckskin jacket that looked a little too perfect to have been made by hand, hung over the bulletin board. Along the wall, over the other blackboard, were several large colored portraits of Indian chiefs: Sitting Bull, Geronimo, Dull Knife, Tecumseh, Chief Joseph. Then an outsized, glossy photograph of Ishi.

Miss Pearly Allen inspected her classroom with pride. It was neat, attractive, interesting, and orderly. She liked her "bungalow," as it was called, more than the classroom she had had in Shady Acres before she came into the city to do her part in teaching everybody's children. Her bungalow was very private, very independent, all her own. She was glad she was teaching in an integrated school. She was proud of her little Negro pupils. They were so cute, she thought, not really different from the others, and if a little more mischievous, also rather better humored. They were all just kids, all one happy group, and they were learning well too. They liked her — her pretty face, her motherly ways, her kindness. Miss Allen thought the world of them. She turned with a smile as her fifth graders began trooping through the door.

"Mornin', Miss Allen!" "Mornin'!" "Good morning!" "Hello, today!" "Hi!" They came in by ones, twos, and threes. Dr. Pearson's daughter, Nancy, handed her a bunch of sweet peas. Pearson was an anthropologist at the University. Ned, looking the other way shamefacedly, slipped a bright red apple onto her desk. Henry and Tom plunged through the door wrestling and shoving. "Boys!" She cautioned a little sternly, "That will do!" They broke it off, apologized, and went quietly to their seats. Then Stevey came marching in, short, solid, determined, carrying a big bat in his right hand which he pounded down on the floor at every second step. He carried a softball in his left hand. Miss Allen laid her hand on his shoulder as he turned to go to his seat, and he looked up at her, smiling.

CULTURAL DIFFERENCES AND VALUES

"Leave them there in the corner, underneath the quiver," she said, "so they won't get in your way at your desk."

"Oh, no, Miss! They won't get in my way!" The Negro boy's round face filled with apprehension now. "Not gonna let no one steal my things. Uh, uh! I keeps them with me all the time!"

"No, Stevey, they'll bother you. Leave them here." She spoke firmly and reached for the bat. Now the students were watching expectantly.

"Ain't nobody takes my things. Don't touch 'em! My uncle say. . . ." Stevey planted himself firmly, feet wide apart, both hands clasped around the handle of the bat, which he held before him, leaning on it, anchored into the floor. He had shoved the softball into his shiny blue nylon jacket.

"Stevey, please!" Miss Allen was embarrassed. She had to be obeyed, but she did not want any kind of scene, certainly not with a Negro child. "Just for me, please! Stevey, I'll watch them for you." She grasped the bat.

"You watch yourself!" There was anger in his voice. "Don't mess with my bat! I don't want you to do nothin' for me! You leggo!" He jerked the bat out of her hand, his eyes sparkling fiercely and his jaw set very firm.

"Stevey, you know you are making a very poor example of your people. Don't you trust me? Don't you know I like you? You go on, then, take your things to your desk, this time. But don't bring them to school, ever, anymore!" Stevey turned away from her, tossing his head righteously, and marched to his seat.

"Children, let's go over what we have been learning about Indians. What were the main tribes we want to remember, where did they live, what was their source of livelihood, how did they make a living and what were some special things about the way they lived? We'll make a chart on the board, and you copy it into your workbooks. Like this." Miss Allen wrote the outline of the chart she wanted to develop on the blackboard with a large hand. But her handwriting was a little uneven. She was still nervous from the incident earlier in the morning.

Spikey's hand flew up. "Those Indians had a lot of kookey ways of doing things!"

"How do you mean?"

"Well, burying bodies wrapped up in skins and hung in trees. Painting buffalo hides to keep a record of their wars. Taking prisoners in war and then adopting them as their own children."

Hands flew up all over the room. "Nancy, what do you think about it?"

"I don't see anything kookey about their ways. People have many ways of doing things. My dad told me about other countries. They do things differently, and they think we're kookey. Dad says some tribes in the Philippines have several wives for each man. And they treat them well! They think our men are funny to have only one wife and sometimes mistreat her."

"Several wives!" some girl exclaimed indignantly.

"Well, back to the Indians," said Miss Allen, nervously. "Was their way of writing history bad or just different? Was it of any value to them? Jack?"

"Well, it wasn't much good, that's for sure. I've seen photographs of those hides, and I couldn't make heads or tails of them. Didn't look like history to me! Jeez, those bodies in trees would stink a mile."

"Barry, what do you thing about buffalo hide histories?"

"Well, we can't read them, but the Indians seemed to be able to read them well enough to remember what happened from them. Actually, they couldn't read our books 'til we. . . . "

"In other words, different people do different things, but what they do makes sense to them. Stevey! What do you think you're doing!"

Dead silence fell over the room, and everyone's head turned from Miss Allen back to Stevey, who had been keeping himself morosely aloof from everything since the earlier episode. Now Stevey had brightened considerably. He extended one leg out in front and the other to the side, covering the bat which lay beneath his desk. He was a figure of deliberate relaxation as he casually tapped a cigarette on his desk top. Nonchalantly he put it in his mouth and let it dangle from his lips, gangster style. He folded his arms in front of him and threw his head back scornfully.

Miss Allen strode to where he sat and snatched the cigarette from his mouth. She noted with regret that it was no fake, a real cigarette, and a pack was showing in his shirt pocket. She was angry now, but she controlled herself. She was going to have to do something pretty drastic. She would talk to Mr. Norman during the lunch hour, but she'd take the cigarettes now. What had gotten into Stevey? He had been good before.

"You don't take my cigarettes. You keep hands off me! Why you pick on me today?" Stevey knotted his fist, stuck out his lower jaw at Miss Allen, and then looked around at the others. He caught Spikey's eye, but Spikey seemed disapproving. Everyone was looking at him, but his friends seemed to have abandoned him. Some faces showed pity, some scorn, and some mockery. The children were with Miss Allen. He

CULTURAL DIFFERENCES AND VALUES   11

grabbed his desk top in both hands, held tight and put his head down on his crossed arms. Miss Allen went back to the front of the room. The class was with her, but Stevey was furious. She wanted all her students to love her. She was near tears.

"I am sorry for the interruption, boys and girls. I know Stevey doesn't mean to be this way. Let's help him by paying no attention to him anymore. Felice, would you tell us what you found out about the Hopi?"

(Stevey was burning with anger. The way Uncle Farnold had told it, it would be funny to smoke a cigarette in school. Uncle had done it when he was a boy and everyone had laughed and it had got the teacher's goat. Miss Allen had no business making that remark about his being a Negro. He had wanted to get her angry and to get the kids to laughing. But it hadn't worked like his Uncle had said it would when he gave him the cigarettes. Stevey paid no attention to the talk about Indians. He got a big piece of art paper and a black crayon from the table nearby.)

"Thanks a lot, Felice, for what you have told us. We've been talking today about how people have different ways to do things, but they are not necessarily worse ways. We have to learn to understand differences and respect other people. What we do looks as curious to others as what they do does to us. Underneath people really are all the same. . . ." Suddenly the class sensed something was wrong. Miss Allen's voice became uneven and her words faltered. Her face turned bright red as she stared at Stevey. She started toward him, shame and anger on her face, then she seemed about to cry and covered her face with her hands. The boys and girls turned to look at Stevey. He was holding up a large crayoned sketch of a naked female figure, with wild Medusa hair, large drooping breasts with bright red tips and darkly emphasized pubic hair. The sketch was labelled in awkward letters "THE REAL MISS ALLEN."

* * *

QUESTIONS FOR WRITING AND DISCUSSION

1. What was your first impression of Miss Allen? Did it change? If so, at what point, for what reason? What was your final impression of her — as a person, as a teacher?
2. What positive awareness of cultural differences does Miss Allen show? Do you see any ways in which she violates this awareness in thought or deed? If you see such violations, does this mean she is a hypocrite or sincere but unthinking? How would you explain the

discrepancies between her statements and some of her beliefs and actions?
3. How do you explain Stevey's behavior from the time he arrived at school until the end of the story?
4. Do you feel the situation between Stevey and Miss Allen is related to the "cultural values" theme, or is it more nearly an isolated incident of a problem in the context of a normally good relationship? Give reasons for your evaluation.
5. What personal characteristic of Miss Allen's (apart from her attitude on cultural differences) was demonstrated in her teaching in general and in the episodes with Stevey? How do you feel about a teacher's emotional involvement with her pupils? Where can it be helpful, where detrimental?
6. How would you have handled Stevey and the bat? Stevey and the cigarette? Stevey and the picture?

COMMENTS

Miss Allen appears very progressive in her approach toward the teaching of cultural differences. She obviously is very successful in her attempt to engage her young students' minds with ideas of cultural diversity. Her approach shows imagination and offers the youngsters an opportunity, usually not present until high school or college, to view institutions of various societies comparatively. If children learn early that foreign or odd customs have important functions for the people who practice them, they come to respect differences and to be less intolerant and racially prejudiced.

The Sioux adage, whose meaning Miss Allen is trying to inculcate, offers us a point of contrast for some of her own attitudes. She is a good teacher in many respects. She seems to have the ability to communicate with and to motivate the majority of her pupils. As the children enter, the two scuffling boys respond easily to her calm discipline. When she first put her hand on Stevey's shoulder he "looked up at her, smiling." If Stevey did not normally trust her, a more likely response would have been an immediate jerking away from her hand, the usual response of children like Stevey toward attempts at physical contact.

The class discussion shows she has created a class atmosphere in which the children feel free to bring out their ideas, and she accepts easily such language as "kookey" and "jeez" which might have become an immediate issue for a more authoritarian teacher. At the time of the cigarette episode, it became obvious that the class was with the teacher rather than Stevey, and it is indicated by the description of the class that many of the others were of the same background as Stevey.

Yet in dealing with Stevey her weaknesses become apparent; her values emerge as inflexibly middle class. She forgets to reserve judgments, as the Sioux adage advises, and to look into the cultural determinants of Stevey's behavior. She has not walked in Stevey's "moccasins." She has no awareness of what it means for him to be nonwhite, and not of the middle class. The saying among Negroes is that no white person can ever know what it feels like to be black in a culture where the yardstick is white. This may be true, but it does not mean that Miss Allen's attempt to teach respect for diverse cultures is doomed to failure. The failure in this case stems from her lack of awareness of Stevey's feelings about his property, and her lack of understanding of his background.

Stevey presents Miss Allen with several problems, First, her authority as a teacher has been diminished in the home, where the authority of the teacher is traditionally reinforced. Stevey, like other lower-class children, does not have the kind of home conditioning which breeds respect for such people as teachers and policemen, as exemplified in the cigarette episode inspired by Stevey's uncle. Secondly, due to the conditions under which he lives, Stevey's attitude toward possessions differs from that of most middle-class children. Thirdly, although this is not directly touched upon in this story, he undoubtedly has strong sensitivities about being a Negro as do so many people of his race. This matter of negative self-image will be discussed in detail in Part II of this manual.

If she had studied the varying values of the nation's children, Miss Allen might have avoided the disastrous remark about Stevey's nonexemplary behavior ("You know you are making a very poor example of your people"). To assign to a young child the responsibility of maintaining some vaguely ascribed "proper" behavior for the sake of all the members of his group is both unfair and foolish. Under other circumstances Miss Allen would certainly have defended the right of people to pursue their individuality regardless of attempts by outside forces to relegate them to particular caste or class positions. In trying to apply an added dimension of control she appeals to Stevey as if he were more obliged to behave than other children in order to safeguard the image of all Negroes. This differential standard is perceived by most Negroes, both children and adults, as unjust.

Stevey's unwillingness to relinquish his bat might have been better understood if Miss Allen knew that a lower-class child has a very tenuous relationship with property. He has few things which are all his own, and in some neighborhoods he must struggle to protect them. This might explain the forcefulness of Stevey's refusal to relinquish the bat.

Stevey's pugnacious behavior could possibly have been controlled or prevented if there had been an established rule about the placement of personal property in the classroom. Knowledge of a rule which applied to all students would either have stopped Stevey from bringing the bat to school in the first place or would have prepared him to relinquish it to a "safe" place. Lacking a prearranged deposit box, Miss Allen might have perceived Stevey's deep feeling earlier and allowed him to keep his bat "this time only."

Instead, Miss Allen unwittingly extended the conflict and in doing so manifested her own insecurity. All children need authority and discipline. By showing her fear and need to be accepted by her students so clearly Miss Allen reduced the children's respect for her authority, at least from Stevey's point of view: "Just for me, Stevey," "She wanted all her students to love her," "She did not want any trouble, especially with a Negro child." She is intimidated by Negroes and the explosive issues and problems which surround them. The objectivity and poise so necessary in dealing with Stevey are unfortunately lacking. Stevey, in a most vindictive mood, intends to make Miss Allen "lose her cool."

Even at this point familiarity with the motivations and common types of behavior of lower-class children would have aided Miss Allen. The nature of Stevey's final attempt to wound his teacher is not bizarre or rare. New teachers going into lower-class schools should be prepared for these things. Sex and profanity are handled more openly by lower-class children. It is unfortunate that Miss Allen's poise is completely destroyed by Stevey's drawing. With this, she has relinquished control of the classroom, even though temporarily, to him.

The situation in which Miss Allen finds herself can occur in many professional settings when emotional needs overcome the professional's objectivity. We should not criticize Miss Allen for deriving satisfaction from teaching "everybody's" children, yet we must criticize some of the attitudes toward herself and the children which appear to handicap her. From the outset we know that Miss Allen feels her teaching in this integrated school to be a magnanimous gesture. Moreover, she must have her "liberalness" affirmed by being totally accepted by her students. That a teacher be consistently popular and well liked by all of her students is almost an impossibility, nor should the teacher see this as an end in itself. When Stevey refuses to demonstrate his trust in her, Miss Allen becomes ruffled. Stevey's rejection of her well-intended suggestions are upsetting to her, especially because he is a Negro. Stevey shatters for her the gratifying image she holds of herself, that she loves and is loved by all of her children. Miss Allen's need of unanimous approval leaves her unable to handle a situation when she is not loved, when a child does not respond to her plea to do something "just for me, please." Her effectiveness as a teacher is hampered, and her relationship with a pupil damaged, because she has put her needs ahead of meeting, or even recognizing his needs.

This is not to say that a teacher must remain emotionally aloof from her students. Some of the best teachers, especially of the culturally divergent, feel and express real warmth toward their children, receive it in return from many of them, and establish exceptionally good parent relationships as well because the parents realize that this teacher really *cares.*

A teacher who chooses an integrated or heavily nonwhite school to satisfy her need for authority, her need to feel superior, or to appear "courageous" and "liberal" will harm her students. Another danger in the teacher who "loves" her children too much is her interference with the normal parent-child relationship. She may find real joy in feeling she is giving the child more than the mother, but the child may be further alienated from the parent and the parent will certainly sense what is happening and be alienated from the teacher and school. This is especially dangerous when the child comes from a "deprived" family and the teacher from the majority culture, as the teacher may pull the child away from his own subculture, but, in concern over her own needs rather than his, give him nothing to take its place.

The important thing is that the teacher recognize any such involvement and understand her own motives and needs as well as those of the children. A teacher's personal needs may complement but should never conflict with her role as a teacher. This is the distinction Miss Allen failed to perceive.

The teacher also needs to be aware of the extent to which she takes a student's behavior personally. A young person who has a negative relationship with a parent may react to all authority figures as though they were his father or mother. He would, therefore, be likely to treat even a kindly, patient teacher with the hostility originally meant for the parent. When such a child defies the teacher, the teacher will handle the situation in drastically different ways depending on whether she takes it as an unwarranted personal affront or recognizes that she simply represents the authority figure. If she takes it personally, her reaction will probably be more punitive, thus reinforcing the child's conviction that all authority figures are to be feared or hated, or both. If she understands the real meaning of the behavior, she can handle the child without her own emotions being involved.

Caucasian teachers face a similar situation with students from minority groups. The Negro child, and his parents, see a Caucasian teacher not as an individual but as a representative of the group which has treated them as inferior and discriminated against them. The teacher may not feel this is fair. She may be unprejudiced, blameless in her eyes for any racial difficulty, so why should she be disliked for what others of her group have done. Miss Allen undoubtedly would have reacted in this way. But if the teacher can understand the reasons, if she can react on a less personal basis, if she can accept the validity of the student's right to these feelings of hostility instead of becoming defensive, she can handle him and his problems much more effectively.

A teacher needs to be able to take hostility and rejection without returning them. She is the adult and can expect a little more of herself than of a still maturing student. She must learn to live with frustration and not let it keep her from continued effort. She cannot expect results too soon, either in her own increased awareness of our culturally divergent children or in their reaction to her. She can demand certain standards of behavior; she cannot demand that children trust her or believe in her when they have had too much experience to the contrary.

These are the insights Miss Allen lacked, for all her good and probably sincere intentions. A combination of her intentions and of greater understanding of her students and herself could make her the kind of teacher she wanted to be.

"CITIZENSHIP"

"Got work for the Man?" There was sarcasm and scorn in the question. Lazarus looked up into the morning sun toward his friends, Sharred and Elizabeth, lounging over the brass railing at the top of the school steps. Liz's eyes laughed at him, and Shar was grinning mockingly. "Done what Manny say?"

"Ain't done nothin'," grumbled Laz, "It don't make no sense."

"Don't you wanna be a good citizen?" chided Liz, tossing her head back and forth, grinning widely. Her teeth were regular and pearly white, her skin dark, her eyes brilliant with mischief. Laz' glance shifted to the arm she laid along Shar's. She was patting Shar's hand. Laz was embarrassed and jealous, and he felt very warm. He wanted a girl like Liz.

"Shoot, man, that Constitution don't mean nothin' to us. That's for the whites. Wasn't written for us slaves. Just words, words, words." Shar was swaying back and forth, pounding the brass railing with his big right fist, while he caught Liz's neck within the crook of his left arm, rubbing the back of his hand up over her face.

"Yeah," said Laz. He'd never let them know he'd have tried to do the work if he'd had any chance. He slouched up the steps to where the pair stood cuddling. Liz's light blue skirt flared in the morning breeze, and Laz admired the rich brown jacket Shar was wearing. He kicked the top stair and looked sadly at his worn moccasin. Beside them, Laz backed up to the cement wall and, spreading his arms wide, inhaled deeply. The wall was warm along his back and arms, and it felt good to stretch, to tighten his muscles, to tense his legs. "Like to go fishing below the pier," he thought, "or to Dan's and work on the truck."

Suddenly the harsh metal clatter of the tardy bell sounded. Easily, with cool grace the three swung around, through the door, and moved with long, swinging strides down the hallways to Room 17. The hall had thinned by now, but about a dozen youths were still straggling to class. Laz slipped inside No. 17 and walked self-consciously to the back of the room. The other two lingered outside for a moment. Laz was already seated and Jeckel was staring at him with anger when Liz tripped through the door mock embarrassment on her gay face. She took a front seat and sat up pertly in feigned attention. Shar stared at Jeckel, thrust his face forward challengingly, then turned and strode slowly and deliberately to a rear seat.

Mr. Jeckel was angry, but he controlled himself, figuratively counting to ten as he looked around the room, appraising his first-period American Government class. They were a mixed lot, all kinds, all abilities. Eight Negroes, a couple of Chinese-Americans, some Mexican-Americans, the rest of old Caucasian stock. Some had I.Q.'s around 85, there were lots of 90's, but five in the class had higher than 110. Made it hard to teach. If you pitched at the class average, way below 100, you wouldn't be fair to the bright ones. But if you worked for the bright ones, you'd lose the others and they'd raise hell. How much do you overlook? Where do you crack down? For their own good?

"Sorry I'm late, Mister Jeckel. My mother never got me up" chirped Liz. Mr. Jeckel started to respond sarcastically and thought better of it. Her friendly smile overcame him, and he decided to roll with this one.

"Students, we'll have to work a lot harder on tardiness. We have got to learn to get here on time. School is a preparation for life, for work, for your future. Your employer next year. . . . "

Shar snorted contemptuously and slid way down in his seat, thrusting his chin down on his chest and pretending to sleep. Several others were sitting up rigidly, turned toward Jeckel, but with blank looks on their faces. Laz' glance shifted from Jeckel to the others. He was relieved there would be no scene. He felt a little sorry for Jeckel, for Laz knew that most of the students were not hearing him at all. Laz wished he could have done the homework, but he'd never had a chance. He wished he were as strong and handsome as Shar. He wished he had a car and a girl. He wished he had a father, like Dan. He turned again to Liz, who was pretending to follow Jeckel's admonition intently, and then to Daisy. Daisy was short, chubby, vivacious. She seemed to be listening, too.

"The key word is punctuality. Punctuality. That's a good word. Let's add it to our vocabularies right now." Jeckel strode to the blackboard and wrote the word beneath "bicameral" and "unanimous," near the "Thought for the Week:"

> License they mean when they cry liberty,
> For who loves that must first be wise and good.

"Today, we are going to look more fully at the Fifth and Fourteenth Amendments. While I take roll, I want you to look them over again.

You had some homework on them. Be sure you are able to tell me in your own words what those Amendments mean and how they affect all of us."

Several students slyly took out sheets from their notebooks and began to write rapidly trying to finish the homework they had begun in class the day before. Others opened their books and began reading. Three put their arms down on their desks and cradled their heads for a little rest. Shar slouched motionless. Liz and Anice were whispering, heads together between the aisles. Harry's head was turned dreamily toward the window. Beyond the shabby machine shops, aging warehouses, and run-down tenements, three gulls were circling over the bay. Laz opened his text to the Amendments and began to read them to himself.

He wondered if the baby was all right. His sister Letha would see to it. He never knew there was so much pain. His mother had groaned often the evening before, crying aloud in agony many times before it came. Mrs. Johnson knew what to expect — she'd had everything organized. But it had been a disturbing, noisy, painful, yes, even bloody night. But he'd been ashamed. He'd talk to Uncle Dan some day.

He was supposed to have written an essay showing the relationship between the Fifth and Fourteenth Amendments. He wasn't sure about it, really, but he thought he knew.

He wondered if Dan would get the truck finished today. Sharp, with the bright red cabin and the white-trimmed bed and stakes. Powerful.

"All right," said Jeckel, "Let's talk about it." He cleared his throat. "First, let's read these Amendments. Tony, start with the Fourteenth, page 436, go ahead, aloud."

Tony had a round body and a very big round head, with big, brown, friendly eyes. His hair hung about his face like straw on a thatch-roofed cabin. His eyes were frightened at first, and he shivered. Then he turned to his text and read "All parsons barren or natural. . . ." His Mexican accent made the words a little strange, even ridiculous. Jeckel stopped him.

Jerry waved his hand wildly and was called on to read. He performed well. Under his breath, Shar muttered, "Kiss, kiss." Jerry droned on through the five paragraphs. "Fine!" said Jeckel.

"Now, just what part of this Amendment relates to the Fifth?" Silence. Laz looked around nervously. He thought he knew, but he would never volunteer to say. Several boys slid lower in their seats. Jerry's hand was waving, but Jeckel would not recognize him. Laz looked at Daisy, but Daisy was watching the gulls too now. Liz was still whispering. Shar seemed to be asleep.

Suddenly, the classroom door burst open and Mr. Cato stepped in, slight, nervous, dwarfed by two gigantic police officers in blue wearing big revolvers in shiny black leather holsters. "Excuse me, Mr. Jeckel, but we wanted to speak to. . . ."

"Sharred Samuels! Come on, come on you!" called one of the officers jerking his forefinger at Shar. The boy sat bolt upright in his seat and then slowly and deliberately rose and stood tall beside his desk.

"Fuzz, stinkin' fuzz!" someone muttered from the rear.

Shar looked at Mr. Jeckel, and then from face to face around the room. His eyes communicated something to Liz; then he turned and looked at the principal and the two officers. He walked slowly toward them, swinging his long legs easily and proudly, his face a mask of contempt.

A girl let out a tiny gasp; then the room was perfectly still. "Come with us!" the officer ordered.

"Look over your books a moment," Jeckel said in a shaky, hesitant voice. Then he and Cato, the officers, and Shar went down the hall together. Instantly someone closed the door and the classroom was filled with an uproar of shouts and excited chattering.

"What's he done?" someone shouted. Then others: "Shouldn't come right into the classroom." "They and their big guns." "Cato looked scared." "They're the law, it's their duty!" "Coming right into school!" "Dirty fuzz."

Liz slipped out of her seat and hurried to the back of the room. She crouched in the aisle beside Laz, holding herself steady with her tiny hands grasping the desk top. Her black eyes were proud and defiant, glistening with tears. Laz felt a tightness in his chest. His breathing quickened.

"Laz," Liz whispered, "don't tell nobody. We took a car last night. Big Chrysler convertible. We blasted. We done bomb this ole city! Shoulda seen the whites' eyes bug! We took one big night. . . ."

Over her shoulder Laz could see the white gulls wheeling.

* * *

QUESTIONS FOR WRITING AND DISCUSSION

1. At what point in the story do you notice any alienation between the students and the school? What do you consider the basis for this alienation?
2. How do you react to the composition of Mr. Jeckel's class? Can you see any positive ways of utilizing the differences described?

3. What do you think about Mr. Jeckel as a teacher: his understanding of his students; his handling of discipline; his method of teaching the subject matter? Offer definite suggestions of changes you might make, if any.
4. Why do you think Laz did not want his friends to know he was interested in doing the work? Why wouldn't he volunteer an answer he thought he knew?
5. Do you see any way a boy with Laz' amount of motivation could have been reached? Would it have helped if Mr. Jeckel had realized Laz' home situation or would it merely have added to his feeling that nothing could be done for his students? Could another member of the school personnel have been used constructively?
6. The students make their racial feelings obvious outside of the classroom. Do you suppose members of the school personnel are aware of these feelings? If so, how could the school administration have made these students feel more a part of the school? How could Mr. Jeckel have utilized his government class to include rather than to exclude his students further? If members of the school staff are not aware of the students' feeling of racial alienation, how can they most effectively be helped to become aware?
7. What is your reaction to the entry of the police into the classroom? How do you believe such a situation should be handled? How does the attitude of the students toward the police fit into the larger picture of their attitudes toward school and society as a whole? Do you see any place for the school in helping to improve these relationships?
8. Where do differing class values enter into this story? Are they stated or implied? To what extent are participants in the story aware that these differences are a factor in the situation? Could more awareness have led to different behavior? If so, how?

COMMENTS

The first few lines of the story give us insight into the background, history, attitudes and temperament of Shar, Liz, and Laz. "Got work for the Man?. . . Shoot man, that Constitution don't mean nothing to us. That's for the whites. Wasn't written for us slaves." These young people are Negro and they are aware of their status, past and present, in America. They feel that they are a group apart. The school and the teachers are for them representative of the Man, the white man.

This group of adolescents seems to have been able to isolate itself completely from the school. Shar has nothing but scorn for the school and his teachers. Laz is very insecure; he wants to participate in class but he feels inadequate. He comes from a poor home and is very conscious of his shabby dress. With some encouragement he probably could become a good student. One facet of the cultural difference between Negro and Caucasian pointed up by this story is that of speech. The conversation between Shar, Liz, and Laz reveals a use of ingroup language heavy with meaning that outsiders would barely catch. This spoken language is often grammatically incorrect but nevertheless expressive to those within the group. The reasons for this difference in language are many, one of the major ones obviously being group separation.

The practice which allows the police to come into the school and especially the classroom at will presents added problems. It tends to identify the police as representatives of white authority with whom the school personnel cooperate. Most teachers consider the practice of allowing police in the classroom an unfortunate one. The procedure, particularly when the school is located in a low socioeconomic community, also contributes to poor relations between the police and the community. The attitudes of different social groups toward the same social institutions often vary. Because of a history of discrimination and brutal treatment by the police in certain areas of the country, the Negro community tends to have attitudes and modes of behavior toward law and law enforcement which are markedly different from those of the majority group. These attitudes include hate, hostility, mistrust, and contempt.

How has the school's image as a representative of the white man been reinforced for these students? How, instead, might they be helped to feel that they too have a stake in the school? These are secondary school students. It is not likely that in all their years in school they have seen themselves reflected back in a positive way in their classes. Middle-class standards have been incorporated in every lesson. Readers, library books, textbooks in all subjects as well as bulletin board displays have been illustrated with pictures of Caucasians. History, as taught, has been white history, except when the Negro has been mentioned as a savage or a slave.

One of the first questions we ask a small child in attempting to establish a relationship is "What does your Daddy do?" forgetting all those like Laz who do not have a Daddy, or all those others whose Daddy doesn't "do" anything because he can't find work. Such seemingly small things build up until it is little wonder that the Shars and Lazes feel apart from the school.

Language differences have been mentioned. Here again the very small child finds that the language of his family and his community is considered incorrect. He is faced early with the choice of rejecting his own roots if he is to become acceptable to the school, or of retaining what he sees as his own identity and rejecting what the school has to offer.

Laz didn't want his friends to know that he wanted to do the homework; he wouldn't volunteer an answer when he knew it. He saw no way that he could do these school-oriented things and still remain part of his peer group. It is worth noting that school social workers have often observed that the lower socioeconomic class Negro children referred to them as school problems tend to be well-adjusted personalities within their peer group, family, and community, when compared to those children from the same background who are meeting the school's standards in their behavior and their scholastic achievement.

The school needs to find ways to enable these students to take what the school has to offer and still retain personal worth, regardless of whether they are Negro, whether they have a father, whether he works, or whether their home language patterns differ from those taught at school. Gradually texts are becoming available which show interracial and intercultural ways of living, and which recognize minority group contributions to history. But this is happening so slowly that supplemental methods that can be put into practice immediately need to be developed as well. These methods call for a greater awareness of cultural differences on the part of teachers so that they will automatically include recognition and respect for differences as part of their teaching.

Adolescents are in general interested in sex. The three characters of this story are very clearly in the process of growing from childhood into adulthood. Laz wishes he had Daisy for his girl; Shar has Liz. This interest, particularly when it is manifested through overt behavior, often presents problems to the school. These problems will be discussed in more detail in Part IV.

The culturally deprived child often has an unstable home life. Laz, like many other young people, has no father at home. "He wished he had a father like Dan." There are highly significant psychological and social implications for children reared in a family where there is no stable father figure to carry out the traditional functions of breadwinner and disciplinarian.

In many middle-class homes where the mother is the only parent present, she is able to provide an adequate income and emotional stability for her children. In the lower-income groups, more often than not, such a family is supported by welfare assistance, and various "fathers" may come and go. Such families lack a stable pattern of male authority and a vocational model to encourage professional aspirations among the children. The women who have held together the mother-centered households, so commonly found among Negroes since the period of slavery, have exhibited amazing strength and toughness. And while this has been crucial to the survival of the children it has been accompanied by negative side effects, especially on the male children.

Boys who are reared in a predominantly female-centered household have difficulty in internalizing the essential components of the male role. A variety of ambivalences concerning masculinity and femininity often plague them throughout their lifetimes. The female likewise acquires an ambivalence toward her role as a woman and a mother, and often develops a basic distrust of men. The one-sex peer group — most obviously exemplified by the male street corner gang — generally becomes the stable reference group for such boys. The norms and interests of this group largely dictate and control the behavior of its members.

Laz had experienced a very special event in his home the night before, the birth of a baby without benefit of doctor. The elemental biological features of life are a much more important aspect of life in lower socioeconomic groups than in middle-class groups. After such an event as childbirth, it is not surprising that Laz's mind should wander out of the classroom, or that he had not completed his homework.

Mr. Jeckel is not a creative teacher. He uses a formal approach to teaching when an informal one might work better with this class. He does not seem to know, nor does he appear to be interested in, the backgrounds and interests of the children in his class. He does not seem to like the students nor do they seem to like him. The social studies teacher has an unusually good opportunity to use varied kinds of materials and devices to promote learning and to motivate interest in many areas. Mr. Jeckel, however, appears unable to capture either the interest or the imagination of his students. His method is based on repetition and recall and does not encourage the development of critical thinking or the building of skills. In order to achieve these objectives, the teacher needs to consider ways of relating the everyday experiences of the students to history. He needs to make effective use of current events, keeping in mind how the negative practices of society influence the attitude of these students. He must take into account the reading level of his students when he selects the materials to be studied as well as the background and past experiences that the children bring to the learning situation. He should carefully consider what social science skills are *needed* by these young people now and in the future.

Jeckel appears to have no structure within which his class normally operates, no set rules which are automatically taken for granted. One feels that he hopes to get through the hour without having to make an issue of anything, but that he is constantly angry at himself and at the class over his inability to control the situation. He largely attributes difficulties in teaching to the fact that the class is composed of a "mixed lot," of all kinds and all abilities. The technique of grouping has raised many questions for teachers. Many favor homogeneous grouping; others favor heterogeneous grouping; still others prefer no grouping at all. Since the type of grouping used is also a factor in the next story, a more detailed discussion of grouping follows in the next commentary. One might guess, however, that someone like Jeckel would not feel comfortable with any type of grouping unless he were dealing with an exceptionally able group of students who could be responsible for structuring their own work and developing their own learning devices.

"CASHEW AND JESUS"

Mr. Cashew shifted his feet nervously and looked out at the wriggling mass of eighth graders. It was 8:35 A.M. The room was already filled with youngsters, but two more were coming through the door. His eye shifted from the ripped window shade in the back, over the scarred blackboard and the ragged tag board, on which a dirty photograph of Khrushchev hung crookedly, and then up and down the aisles over his students. Already Jack was hunched raptly over a lurid paperback. Jane was twisting her lips and patting her hair as she peered into a pocket mirror. Tony slouched in the aisle haranguing three other boys about what he had told Mr. Hansen who had stopped him for smoking on the way to school. Helene and Frisby were talking excitedly about boys. Helene's skirt was tight and short. Mr. Cashew distractedly reflected upon his hurried breakfast that morning, his wife's surliness, and her peremptory commands as he started the day.

Thirty-eight of them, Mr. Cashew thought to himself, and not more than three of them give a damn about Benedict Arnold, George Washington, the American Revolution, or the Constitution of the United States. At the faculty meeting the previous afternoon, they had talked about the need to raise standards. The principal had explained that there was no reason in the world why these students shouldn't be performing just as well academically as others in other schools "up on the hill." It was just a matter of motivating them, of engaging their interests, and of showing them how history and government were relevant to their lives. The main purpose of social studies is citizenship training. These children had to be developed into good citizens for their own welfare and for the safety of everyone.

A shout "Fuck him!" ended Mr. Cashew's thoughts abruptly. Tony was waving his arms now, threateningly. Mr. Cashew tensed himself ready to take drastic action. But it was a false alarm. Tony was just letting off steam about Mr. Hansen. Half the class were in their seats now, shouting, laughing, bobbing about. In the back of the room, Harry was beating drums on his desk top with ruler and pencil. The harsh rattle of the tardy bell sounded; a few more students slumped into their seats; and the classroom roar dropped off a little. Mr. Cashew tried to look firm and determined as his glance canvassed the room. Resignedly, his lips still moving but no sounds coming forth, Tony slipped into his seat, his legs asprawl and extended far out into the aisles on either side. The others reluctantly surrendered too, and now the members of the class were all seated though not quite silent. Some faces were turned toward Cashew, vacant faces, faintly unfriendly faces, one or two expectant faces, at least three hostile faces, and two slightly mocking faces. Two artificial sneezes rang out from the back of the room. These were a routine part of Mr. Cashew's day, they were the means by which some students showed their disrespect, a play on his name.

The door swung open suddenly and a lanky, disheveled, brown-skinned boy sprawled into the room, his black eyes darting about from students to teacher, the vitality of his glances contrasting with the languid motions of his limbs. He moved away from the door, leaving it agape, and sauntered toward the back of the room. To Mr. Cashew the very way he walked seemed a defiance, a provocation. As he moved slowly on, the boy kept his eyes toward the class and his back toward Cashew. His back was a studied insult.

Jesus Peor, and there is none worse, thought Mr. Cashew. When Jesus finally slid into a seat on the blackboard side of the room, he turned deliberately far around, so that only his back continued to meet the angry glance of the teacher. Jesus threw his arms over the back of his own seat and leaned far over the aisle toward Tony, muttering something which Cashew couldn't hear. Cashew caught Tony's eye and tried to transmit determination. Hostility flared and died in Tony's face. He looked down and away from Jesus. Momentarily Mr. Cashew hesitated. Should he act on Jesus' tardiness? Then, "You're late, you'll have to get clearance from the office!"

"Cabron!" Jesus mumbled. "I'm here now, go on." He made no move to get up, and he avoided looking at the teacher. Cashew could see that he was out of sorts this morning. A comb had been through his hair, but most of the black locks were untouched, tumbling in thick, oily clusters. His jacket was torn or cut along the right sleeve; he wore no belt; his jeans were soiled with grease. Bright yellow socks showed between his tight trousers and his run-down moccasins. He jerked his head around, looking from student to student for an ally, and scratched his right ear nervously. "Go on, go on," he muttered, flourishing his arms, "Always on *me!*" Then, under his breath, he grumbled something else in Spanish.

A little Negro girl in the front of the room tiptoed to the door and closed it. The room became absolutely silent. Cashew had moved down from his desk in front halfway toward the Mexican-American youth.

Jesus did not look at him at all, but kept mumbling. He glanced to his left and saw Elise. Her big, brown eyes met his with silent sympathy. Jesus melted inside. He felt warm as his glance shifted over her abundant sweater and her fleshy legs. He put his head down in his arms on his desk and paid absolutely no attention to Cashew.

Abruptly, Mr. Cashew stopped in the aisle and said in a firm voice, "Let's hand in our homework first. Joan, will you collect from the front of each row? Go ahead, pass your papers to the front." The tension subsided, the noisy, boisterous voices of the class broke forth again. Boys tickled the backs of girls' necks with papers as they were passed forward. About half the students passed papers in. Helene called out that she'd have hers in later, it wasn't finished yet. Barbara, a Negro girl at the front of the room near the window called out, without raising her hand, "Man, I worked all night on that stuff!" A boy shouted, "You'se a fool!" Mocking laughter erupted from all over the room; Tony guffawed. Cashew glanced quickly and challengingly toward Jesus, but Jesus was still cradling his head in his arms, dormant, motionless. Cashew moving back to the front of the room felt suddenly tired; he knew this would be a bad day. Put 'em to work, he thought.

"Take out your history books now," he ordered. "Turn to page 48 and begin reading. I'll give you some further instructions later. Quiet down and get to work. No talking! Elise! Neil! Turn around there, Tony, and begin reading! Now!"

The class gradually settled down. Most opened their books, but very few were reading. Some peeked surreptitiously at Cashew over the tops or around the sides of their books. Helene and Frisby continued chatting quietly in the front of the room. Tony sat with his book unopened, looking around challengingly, not speaking, but catching the attention of other students in a provoking way. Jesus raised his head and turned toward Tony. Jesus had no book in sight.

In a flash, almost unconsciously, Cashew counted his score and gauged the game — he was losing! He had overlooked the "fuck" that had begun the period. He had not carried through the challenge Jesus had offered when ordered to the office. The entire class was restless, expectant. Now Jesus was without a book, and looking for trouble. He had to take a stand. He had to make an example.

"Jesus, get your book out and get to work!" he shouted, and strode toward the boy whose eyes shifted quickly about the room, fixed for a moment on Elise, met Tony's, and finally turned directly on Cashew.

"Ain't got no fuckin' book."

He glared defiantly, his lips moving, his teeth tugging at the side of his mouth, his hands working spasmodically, fists clenching and unclenching.

"I've told you a hundred times a worker without his tools is not worth a cent. Your job is to come here prepared to work. You're no use to yourself nor to anyone else without your equipment. Book, pencil, notebook. Get out of here! Get to the office right now! Maybe Mrs. Forte can get something worthwhile out of you! You haven't shown me or this class that you deserve to be among us. Get! Get! Move, I say!" Cashew was red-faced now, his voice high and shrill.

Jesus jumped from his seat, his mouth working, his black eyes flashing, fists clenched, legs far apart and firmly planted. In a flash, as Cashew noticed his bloody shirt, his greasy trousers, his blood-shot eyes, Jesus shouted at him, livid with rage, "Chicken shit! Chicken shit! Chicken!"

Cashew hurled himself at the boy, dragged him down the aisle, and thrust him into the hall, then pinning him against the metal lockers, he knocked him back against them and shook him violently. Behind, in the classroom bedlam broke loose — shouts, mocking laughter, curses, cries. Suddenly Jesus went limp and broke into tears, sobbing uncontrollably. Mr. Cashew led him off one arm pinioned behind his back. As he thrust the boy into the Vice-Principal's Office, Cashew's arm was trembling.

When Jesus was wakened by his mother's sobbing, it was day. He pushed back the gray blanket from his face, got up from the rusty iron cot, and went to the toilet in the bathroom off the kitchen. The long combination kitchen, living room, and bedroom was furnished with a rickety, oil-cloth covered table, several unpainted wooden chairs, the metal cot, and two large mattresses and bedding on the floor. Jesus saw his mother at the gas range. Tears were running down her cheeks and had dampened the front of the soiled red nylon slip which was trying to hold in her familiar, round, bulging body. She was frying eggs in a deep pool of grease. As Jesus dressed, his younger sister Helena was studying at the table, across from her father. The latter grumbled as he devoured three eggs, a plate of refried beans, and a dozen tortillas. Three little brothers, 2, 4, and 5 years old, scurried about beneath Mama's feet while Papa wolfed his breakfast. As Jesus dragged on his clothes, Mama patted his head, dripping tears onto his shoulder. She crammed a tortilla into his mouth. Helena sat very still and small, reading her book across from her father. Before Papa, on the red oil-cloth covered table top stood a big bottle of red wine from which he took a big swallow after every few gulps of food. On the stubble of his beard were splotches of egg and chili sauce. He breathed heavily; his face was sullen and his eyes bloodshot. Momentarily his eyes softened a little as he looked toward Helena. Then he cursed Mama, and as she brought him another stack of tortillas, smacked her across the tear-stained cheek with his heavy palm. He growled at her to stop the weeping, "Callete, puta!" As he staggered up to go to the toilet, he met Jesus, who was finishing the last buttons on his shirt. Papa stumbled into him, cursed, turned, and struck him a hard blow across the face. The little brothers scampered away and Jesus turned aside to keep his raging father from seeing his tears. He staunched the blood from his nose with his sleeve. Mama's weeping became a wail of sorrows, a very song of affliction, as she halted a moment before a large crucifix on the wall. "Tiempo!" she cried, and pointed to the alarm clock on the window sill. 8:25. It was time for Jesus and Helena to run off to school. The latter caught up her books, as Jesus grabbed a handful of tortillas and stuck them in his pocket. As they hurried from the apartment, which opened on a busy truck arterial, they heard Papa's curses mingled with Mama's cries of anguish.

Helena wanted to run, but Jesus sauntered slowly, kicking the dusty sidewalk and watching the heavy trucks which rumbled along the street. Childishly, his sister chided him for not bringing his books. "How you going to read them if you don't bring them to school?" Jesus winced. He knew his sister realized that he could not read the textbooks the school had given him, a secret he had hoped to keep from everyone. But Helena knew. And he knew that Helena *could* read his textbooks, for he had caught her doing so. He clenched his fist in anger, but the flashing laughter in her eyes was like a spring breeze in his face. He turned away from her and trudged along in silence.

A lean black cat slunk out from a doorway and sidled up to the children as they walked by. Jesus caught the cat under the head with a quick, vicious kick and sent it sprawling and crying into the rubbish-cluttered gutter.

* * *

QUESTIONS FOR WRITING AND DISCUSSION

1. After reading only the first page, what did you expect of the type of class portrayed and the possible relationships within it? How closely were your predictions borne out?
2. If Jesus had not been present, how do you think the day would have gone between Cashew and his class? Why?

CULTURAL DIFFERENCES AND VALUES

3. Do you see ways, both long range and immediate, by which Cashew could have headed off trouble? With the class as a whole? With Jesus in particular?
4. How did both Jesus and Cashew bring their home problems to school? Do you see any reason for using the two situations as a basis for understanding, or do they preclude anything less than the conflict which resulted?
5. It is mentioned that Cashew has a large class of all slow children, whereas at least part of Jeckel's difficulty was attributed to his having a wide range of abilities in his class. Which do you think is more difficult? Is either a handicap in itself? Are there varying teaching techniques which can be adapted to either type of class?
6. Would you recommend specific changes in Cashew's handling of his subject matter? In his handling of discipline?
7. What do you see as some of Jesus' basic problems? What possible remedies do you see for them? Which, if any, come within the province of the school?
8. How do cultural differences play a part in this story?

COMMENTS

While the day seemed to be a particularly unfortunate one for both Mr. Cashew and Jesus, one gets the feeling that most of their days are unfortunate because of their home situations and modes of confronting the realities and problems they face. Cashew, as a professional and responsible adult, should be able to do better; the fate of Jesus and his fellows can, hopefully, be improved by the schools.

Cashew began the day with resentment of his wife and pessimism about teaching an uninterested social studies class. He apparently lacked the ability and motivation to organize his subject matter in such a way as to make it relevant and meaningful to his students. Teaching history and citizenship to this class struck him as being a burdensome and hopeless task, not as a challenge that could be met with the use of some imagination and ingenuity.

Certainly the objective situation is not an easy one. The make-up of Cashew's class was homogeneous and, for this reason, is seen by him as self-defeating. He knows he has 38 of the least able and least motivated students in the school and that none of them is able to handle the work in such a way as to set an example or help the others. Inclusion of some students who have middle-class aspirations for learning, and who are potentially easier to discipline could have been helpful in this classroom given the many students with outside problems who were more likely to be volatile and less interested in the traditional class routine. But just such a mixture is what Jeckel had in the last story, and he found that combination "hard to teach." There are many factors to be considered in grouping. Jeckel's objection to a wide range may be as valid as Cashew's to a homogeneous slow group. Some educators argue that children are motivated and challenged by having others with more ability in the same class; others that children are only frustrated by the competition of those with more ability. Some argue that the fast student is held back by the presence of slow children in his class; others insist that the individual needs of both the fast and slow student are best met by grouping within a classroom, with perhaps different group make-ups for different subjects. Some teachers argue that it is not fair to them to have to meet the needs of a group with widely varying abilities and that curriculum materials are set up for certain levels of ability. Other teachers prefer the challenge of a variety of students seeing benefits to be derived by all types of students in exposure to each other, and to the teacher in the more interesting context provided by a lack of homogeneity.

Basic in considering this question are the criteria used in grouping, usually I.Q. and achievement tests. Since I.Q. tests are largely tests of past achievement and cultural exposure rather than of actual ability, it is obviously pointless to employ them as a basis for ability grouping. If grouping is done, it should be based on actual performance, with provision made for immediate change upward or downward as performance warrants.

Teachers such as Cashew and Jeckel would be likely to find teaching difficult, regardless of the method of grouping used. If they traded classes, they would probably soon change their opinions of what kind of grouping constituted a "hard-to-teach" class. Jeckel is shown as lacking an interest in his students and as making no effort to understand. Moreover, he does not seem to have planned his lesson or prepared for it in any way. Much of the same is true of Cashew.

Cashew did not seem ready to face his class at all. He did not have a lesson in mind before he began the class hour. Nor had he previously established patterns in activities, lessons, or discipline that would have given some structure to the class period. For a large and difficult class such as this, an established pattern of movement within the room and established expectations of work to be accomplished are essential both to meet the needs of the students and to provide a control structure. Deviation from the pattern and expectations can then be treated more easily, for the student knows what he is expected to do, and he can accept his deviation from the pattern as justifiable cause for question and correction. When Cashew did put the class to work, he did so in an erratic, almost desperate way to hide his own inabilities to teach and give direction. He did not ask the class to comment on their homework, nor follow-up the implications of why only one-half handed in the assignment.

Cashew could have enlivened his curriculum by presenting history in a way more relevant and vivid to his students. He could have organized his materials around biographies or specific events, or he could have simplified the textual material if it was too difficult or dull for them or provided a readable and meaningful commentary. He could have better engaged the interests of children from particular subcultural or ethnic groups by devising special materials illustrating the contributions of those groups to American history, or by giving children a choice of assignments that would allow them to follow their particular interests. Class discussions, acting out situations, pantomime and audio-visual aids would also appeal to many children who are not motivated by traditional classroom methods.

Cashew could also have tried to cope with the lack of reading skill among his students by using remedial techniques, though unfortunately, junior high and senior high school teachers receive little training in this area. He could have consulted other teachers or educational materials for suggestions on activities which bring out the subject matter more clearly and at the same time develop reading skills. Students' reading comprehension can be developed by discussions of the material read and by individual attention from the teacher. For students who are unable or unwilling to read, activities such as drawing or coloring maps, preparing bulletin boards and other exhibit materials provide a means of learning subject matter and perhaps of eventually stimulating an interest in reading. They also brighten up the classroom. These activities should be seen as an integral part of the learning situation, even though they are not remedies for a student's fundamental inability, or lack of motivation, to meet the demands of the regular curriculum.

The discipline problems stemmed in great part from the failure of the students to engage in the task before them. Cashew's ignoring the language and behavior of Tony, Jesus, and other students did not make the situation disappear. He could have arranged to meet with either or both of the boys out of the classroom and tried to reach an understanding with them without the class as an immediate audience and pressure factor. In "fair, firm, and friendly" encounters marked by a consistent emotional tone, a teacher can offer his students a certain range of permissible behavior yet still provide firm but fair authority. With a volatile boy it is not likely that one heroic incident will settle the situation, but an accumulation of reasonable and fair assertions of authority in the course of peaceful coexistence may have a permanent effect in changing the student. Some teachers resort to physical encounters feeling that they can impress students inside or outside of class with their victories, but such extreme methods of control are often only a sad escape from more sophisticated, reasonable, and lasting methods of control.

The problem of methods of control, however, is complicated by varying class values. Middle-class parents tend to use verbal discipline, scolding, explanations, or such methods as restrictions, withdrawal of privileges, etc., and the middle-class school agrees that these should be effective methods. Many a well-meaning teacher is completely frustrated when she finds such methods totally ineffective in establishing discipline. The reason for their ineffectiveness becomes clear once we understand that in the lower-class home, both because of pressures on the parents and a much lesser degree of verbal communication in general, meaningful punishment tends to be physical. The children have learned that as long as mother just talks she isn't too upset, but that when she means business, not only is a spanking likely, but usually it is administered with the help of a belt, strap, or switch laid on hard and immediately. This does not mean the parent is brutal or does not love his child; it is simply a different method of control, perhaps developed out of a culture where it was necessary for a child to learn immediate, unquestioning obedience as a very matter of survival. When this child comes to school, he is therefore likely to completely tune out on the verbal reprimands and explanations of the teacher, and to naturally suppose out of his experience that if she really wanted him to behave in a different way she would whip him. Since this is either prohibited by law or strongly frowned upon, the teacher is left in a real quandary, which each individual has to solve in his own way.

Opinions may vary on how Cashew should have responded to the matter of Jesus' forgetting his book. Because Jesus' book was obviously a symbol of his shame about his inability to read and to meet the fundamental demand of school, Cashew could have been more sensitive toward this problem and either said nothing about his not having a book, or asked him to share another student's book during this particular class at the same time reminding him that he should not forget his book next time. Any of these actions might have precluded the explosion that followed. His inconsistency in first demanding that Jesus go to the office for a tardy slip, and then in letting the matter drop, reflected his general inconsistency in setting patterns of behavior and correction for his students.

The tenor of communication of the teacher to his students in customary address, classroom discourse, or in the confrontation of a discipline crisis presents a very complex field for analysis. Prescription is difficult. Different modes of address and their implied attitudes — courtesy, sympathy, empathy, sarcasm, talking down to the student, or speaking above his head — can have differential effects and ramifications. There is the danger that the teacher's treatment of his students can serve as a valve for his own problems, as it probably did for Cashew. He can vent his hostilities on his class with some freedom from fear of retaliation, or use his superior position over his students as a way of building himself up. The position of authority always carries danger of misuse, and the misuse of power is frequently subconscious. The chosen victim is often the problem student. The fact that a student who is already a problem is thus singled out will often be a factor in his retaliation against the teacher so that a cumulative cycle of problems is perpetuated.

The story vividly depicts a boy caught between two cultural worlds: his Mexican-American family life, complicated by a drunken father, and a middle-class school situation with expectations he can scarcely hope to meet. The description of the physical features of the home situation may present an unsavory picture for the comfortable middle-class teacher to contemplate. Yet, it should be noted that Jesus' family lived in high style compared to most lower-class Mexican citizens and many Mexican-Americans. His family may be considered as already moving upward. A flush toilet, chairs, and cots are signs of affluence to the majority of Latin-Americans. Indeed, his parents may well feel they have made a great improvement in their way of life and may try to impress the children with their pride in what they have accomplished. The children, however, are caught in a bind when the dominant society labels them as deprived and inferior. Thus, the issue of cultural relativity must be considered in the criticism of any immigrant group's way of life and customs.

There are two separate dimensions of Jesus' home situation that should be considered: his Mexican-American subculture and the presence of a drunken father with apparently little understanding of the problems of his children. His Mexican-American background and the use of Spanish by his family gave Jesus a home life alien to that of the school world. Uncomplicated by the father's drunkenness and violence this could have provided the family with a certain meaningful security. Many Mexican-American children exhibit gentleness and great courtesy. But for Jesus the erratic and violent male authority in his life compounded his marginal situation and gave him an additional cause for reacting against authority. A consistent and understanding relationship with a male teacher could perhaps have provided him with a model he could emulate.

Although a frequent feature of the Latin-American household may be a drinking and distant father, the mother's strength and love for her children usually provides stability, and the father generally does not rage and bully the children in the home. The importance and power of the mother in Latin-American culture may have as encompassing an effect on the children as that of the woman in the mother-centered Negro home where there is frequently no permanent male authority figure. The confusion in the expected characteristics of the sex roles and the ambivalence toward male authority is more pronounced in the Negro subculture than in the Latin-American.

The fact that Spanish was spoken in the home made it quite natural for Jesus to give spontaneous classroom retorts in Spanish. This may well have further alienated his teachers, and may also have intensified his reading problems. The reading or speaking of English may have been avoided or even actively discouraged by his parents. His shame about his reading inadequacy could have led him purposely or subconsciously to forget his books.

Jesus knew that his sister could read. Quite possibly Helena, as a girl, had a better chance for success in school. It has been noted that the Latin-American female is often more pliant and tradition-bound in meeting institutional expectations than the male. For example, attendance at Sunday Mass and religious instruction is more regular among women than among men. The position of the daughter growing up in the Latin-American home is more protected and secure than that of the male who frequently has authority problems and must forever prove himself as a man. Even Jesus' father in his drunkenness softened his expression when he looked at Helena.

Because Jesus' domestic situation offers us little hope of family flexibility in meeting middle-class expectations or in understanding the problems of their children at school, we must turn to the schools for understanding and supportive guidance of the marginal child, often seriously handicapped by his existence between two cultural worlds.

DIGESTS OF SOCIAL SCIENCE READINGS

"*Lower Class Culture as a Generating Milieu of Gang Delinquency*"[1]

Miller suggests that a lower-class subculture is characteristic of a substantial segment of American society. This distinctive cultural system has certain focal concerns that are conducive to law-violating behavior.

Walter B. Miller is an anthropologist who has worked extensively with street corner gangs in a large Eastern city. In this article he outlines the characteristics of a separate lower-class cultural system which he has observed in the course of his work.

Miller's thesis may be reduced to three main propositions: (1) The way of life of the lowest social level of our society embodies certain distinctive values. (2) These deviate in varying degrees from the middle-class values which undergird the legal code. (3) As a result, behavior which conforms to certain lower-class values may automatically result in violation of the law. In other words, important practices of the lower-class way of life carry a high potential for law violation, since they run counter to behavioral norms that prevail in other sectors of the society.[2]

The "focal concerns," values, or preoccupations which characterize the lower class and which predispose its members to law-violating behavior are defined by Miller as follows.

"*Trouble:* Concern over 'trouble' is a dominant feature of lower-class culture. 'Trouble' in one of its aspects represents a situation or a kind of behavior which results in unwelcome or complicating involvement with official authorities or agencies of middle-class society. For men, 'trouble' frequently involves fighting or sexual adventures while drinking; for women, sexual involvement with disadvantageous consequences. Expressed desire to avoid behavior which violates moral or legal norms is

---

[1] Walter B. Miller, "Lower Class Culture as a Generating Milieu of Gang Delinquency," in *Sociology of Crime and Delinquency*, ed. Marvin E. Wolfgang, et al. (New York, 1962), pp. 267–276. Excerpts reprinted by permission of the publisher, John Wiley & Sons, Inc.

[2] See Miller's remarks in W. C. Kvaraceus and W. B. Miller, *Delinquent Behavior: Culture and the Individual* (Washington, D. C.: National Education Association, 1959), pp. 68–69.

often based less on an explicit commitment to 'official' moral or legal standards than on a desire to avoid 'getting into trouble,' e.g., the complicating consequences of action.

"*Toughness:* The concept of 'toughness' in lower-class culture represents a compound combination of qualities or states. Among its most important components are physical prowess, evidenced both by demonstrated possession of strength and endurance and athletic skill; 'masculinity,' symbolized by a complex of acts and avoidance (bodily tattooing; absence of sentimentality; non-concern with 'art,' 'literature'; conceptualization of women as conquest objects, etc.); and bravery in the face of physical threat. The model for the 'tough guy' — hard, fearless, undemonstrative, skilled in physical combat — is represented by the movie gangster of the thirties, the 'private eye,' and the movie cowboy.

"*Smartness:* 'Smartness' involves the capacity to outsmart, outfox, outwit, dupe, 'take,' 'con' another or others, and the concomitant capacity to avoid being outwitted, 'taken,' or duped oneself. In its essence, smartness involves the capacity to achieve a valued entity — material goods, personal status — through a maximum use of mental agility and a minimum of physical effort.

"*Excitement:* For many lower-class individuals the rhythm of life fluctuates between periods of relatively routine or repetitive activity and sought situations of great emotional stimulation. Many of the most characteristic features of lower-class life are related to the search for excitement or 'thrill'. Involved here are the widespread use of gambling of all kinds. The quest for excitement finds its most vivid expression in the recurrent 'night on the town,' a patterned set of activities in which alcohol, music, and sexual adventure are major components.

"*Fate:* Related to the quest for excitement is the concern with fate, fortune, or luck. Here also a distinction is made between two states — being 'lucky' or 'in luck,' and being unlucky or jinxed. Many lower-class persons feel that their lives are subject to a set of forces over which they have relatively little control. These are not equated directly with the supernatural forces of formally organized religion, but relate more to a concept of 'destiny' or man as a pawn of magical powers. This often implicit world view is associated with a conception of the ultimate futility of directed effort toward a goal.

"*Autonomy:* The extent and nature of control over the behavior of the individual — an important concern in most cultures — has a special significance and is distinctively patterned in lower-class culture. On the overt level there is a strong and frequently expressed resentment of the authority. Actual patterns of behavior, however, reveal a marked discrepancy between expressed sentiment and what is covertly valued. Many lower-class people appear to seek out highly restrictive social environments wherein stringent external controls are maintained over their behavior. Lower-class patients in mental hospitals will exercise considerable ingenuity to insure continued commitment while voicing the desire to get out; delinquent boys will frequently 'run' from a correctional institution to activate efforts to return them; to be caught and returned means that one is cared for.

"Focal concerns of the male adolescent corner group are those of the general cultural milieu in which it functions. The relative weighting and importance of these concerns patterns somewhat differently for adolescents than for adults. The nature of this patterning centers around two additional 'concerns' of particular importance to this group — concern with 'belonging,' and with 'status' achieved via cited concern areas of Toughness, etc.

"Since the corner group fulfills essential functions for the individual, being a member in good standing of the group is of vital importance for its members. One achieves 'belonging' primarily by demonstrating knowledge of and a determination to adhere to the system of standards and valued qualities defined by the group. One maintains membership by acting in conformity with valued aspects of Toughness, Smartness, Autonomy, etc.

"Status is achieved and maintained by demonstrated possession of the valued qualities of lower-class culture. The concern with 'status' is manifested in a variety of ways. Intragroup status is a continued concern, by means of a set of status-ranking activities; the intragroup 'pecking order' is constantly at issue.

"The concern over status involves in particular the component of 'adultness,' the intense desire to be seen as 'grown up,' and a corresponding aversion to 'kid stuff.'

"Concern over status is also manifested in reference to other street corner groups. The term 'rep' used in this regard refers to the 'toughness' of the corner group as a whole relative to that of other groups."

Miller's injunction to us is: understand the distinctive set of values that characterizes the lower-class subculture. If we do, then our remedies for those youngsters who come to us will be more relevant and effective.

Background variables strongly influence the patterns of development of the child's perception, language, and cognition, and this affects his aca-

"The Disadvantaged Child and the Learning Process"[3]

> Deutsch contends that the lower-class child enters the school situation poorly prepared for the school's expectations, and that his failure is therefore almost inevitable. His school experience does nothing to counteract the influences of a slum or segregated neighborhood.

demic and psychological performance. Teachers often say that lower-class children are "cute," "affectionate," and "curious" at the first grade level, but that by the fifth and sixth grades they become "withdrawn," "angry," "passive," or "trouble-makers." The greatest similarity among children from different socioeconomic or racial groups is to be found in the first grade, but the gap increases through the years.

Some of the factors holding children back are a history of discrimination, the instability of the Negro family, and the frequent absence of a successful role model from the home. Substandard housing and little opportunity to see clean and pleasant surroundings put the child at a disadvantage. In the lower-class home there is a scarcity of such objects as books, puzzles, and toys which are prototypes of school accoutrements and which help prepare children for the school experience. In addition there is a lack of energetic parental guidance.

Children are deprived of a variety of stimuli required for learning, and this affects both the formal and conceptual aspects of cognition. The results are a lack of perceptual discrimination skills, of the abilities to sustain attention and to communicate with adults for information. Lower-class children characteristically show a poor performance on standardized intelligence tests.

Not only is there a scarcity of objects in the lower-class home to stimulate visual perception, but the home is not verbally oriented, that is, the child experiences little non-instructional conversation there. He gets little practice in auditory discrimination or correction of his language by adults. This is apparently highly related to poor reading skills.

There is little interaction with parents which would foster anticipation of rewards for tasks completed. Tasks given in lower-class homes are generally motoric in nature and deal with concrete matters, whereas tasks given in middle-class homes would more often involve language and conceptual processes.

---

[3] Martin Deutsch, "The Disadvantaged Child and the Learning Process: Some Social Psychological and Developmental Considerations," in *Education in Depressed Areas*, ed. A. H. Passow (New York, 1963), pp. 163–179. Digest used by permission of the publisher, Teachers College Press.

Little communication with parents is typical of the lower-class home life. Children are unused to using parents as sources of information. The lack of this sort of purposeful communication hinders language facility and fluency which are essential in concept formation, problem solving, and in relating to and interpreting one's environment.

All of these factors lead to the lower-class child's lack of achievement in the traditional school system. Frustration from cumulative failure works against the child's motivation whatever the aspirations of the parents might be. The negative attitudes toward schooling usually develop after the child is in school.

Deutsch concludes that flexible experimentation is called for in developing new methods of teaching and training of personnel in the educational philosophy and learning procedure that this problem requires. In addition systematic training is needed for children in the early grades to help to fill in the deprivations in their background that foster failure in the school. New evaluation techniques are needed which can more accurately test these children. He suggests that more study by social and behavioral scientists of the cultural implications, and the use of the resulting knowledge by educators would be especially valuable.

"The Culturally Deprived Child"[4]

> Riessman suggests some of the positive features of a type of family that is increasingly becoming part of our urban scene. Awareness of these positive features can aid the teacher in developing a better understanding of children coming from extended families.

"The negative side of the underprivileged family is easy to see: the family may be prematurely broken by divorce, desertion, and death; the home is overcrowded, the housing facilities inadequate; considerable economic insecurity prevails; both parents frequently work, and thus the children may be neglected; and typically the irritable, tired parents use physical punishment in order to maintain discipline.

"But there is another side of the family which should not be ignored. Two things stand out immediately: there are many children, and there are many parents or parent substitutes. The home typically includes aunts, uncles, and grandparents, all of whom may, to some degree, play

---

[4] Frank Riessman, *The Culturally Deprived Child* (New York, 1962), chap. 5. Excerpts reprinted by permission of the publisher, Harper & Row.

a parental role. This pattern is technically known as 'the extended family.' In the Negro family the grandmother often plays a most decisive role. . . .

"The key to much of the family life is security and protection. The large extended family provides a small world in which one is accepted and safe. If help is needed, the family is the court of first resort and will provide it, at least to some extent. Time and energy, rather than money, are the chief resources provided. Hand-me-down clothes may be passed on to needy members; the mother's sister may work a little extra to supplement the limited budget. But it is in the providing of the services of helping with children or in the household generally that major aid is provided.

" . . . The family is seen as a major source of strength in a difficult, unstable world.

"Many commentators have placed considerable importance on broken homes as the source of emotional instability, mental illness, juvenile delinquency, and the like. The broken home, however, may not among the deprived, imply family disorganization (nor does it necessarily have the same implications for a deprived child that it might in a middle-class home). To think of the underprivileged family as consisting of a father, mother, and children alone is to miss vital aspects of this family today.

"The home is a crowded, busy, active, noisy place where no one child is focused upon. There are too many children for this, and the parents have too little time. Consequently, the children spend much more time in each other's company and with the relatives. Individualism and self-concern on the part of the children is much less likely to emerge and is, in fact, discouraged in this more family-centered home.

"Intense parent-child relationships are infrequent, and while the danger of parental rejection is present, over-protection is out of the question.

"The atmosphere is much more communal and, to some extent, cooperative. . . .

"Sibling rivalry and fear of a new baby brother seem to develop somewhat less here. Perhaps this is because the children never have had that much attention in the first place, and have less to lose. Perhaps, also, the fact that the children depend so much on contact with each other, rather than being overly dependent upon the parents, plays a decisive role. Whatever the reason, there does appear to be far less jealousy and competitiveness.

"Since physical punishment is part of the everyday pattern among the disadvantaged, there is probably considerable adaptation to it and it is not perceived as a major threat to the ego; as physical punishment and aggression generally are expressed rather easily and directly, it is unlikely that they have the sadistic overtones that often produce the negative correlates of punishment.

. . . .

"A number of studies have noted that deprived individuals strongly, and more frequently, support the statement that 'the most important thing a child should learn is respect and obedience to his parents.'[5] Not only parents, but older people in general are to be obeyed and respected. After all, if neighbors and relatives, including grandparents, are to take part in child rearing, respect for older people is important.

. . . .

"Control of children is not exerted by the withholding of love but through punishment. A child is expected to do what he is told, not because he wants to demonstrate love for his parents; rather, he does it because it is expected, and if he does not do it he will be punished. He does not accrue love by doing, nor lose it by not doing."

The worst thing an unwed mother can do in the culture of the deprived, is to surrender her child to an adoption agency. Abortion is also looked upon with some disfavor. Keeping the illegitimate child and accepting the responsibility is usually the most favored solution to this problem. The deprived, just as the middle class, prefer legitimate marriages.

"When something goes wrong, and this apparently occurs in all classes according to the statistics, the deprived prefer to incorporate the child in the household and to accept the attendant responsibilities."

. . . .

" . . . there are subgroup differences among the deprived that have to be taken into account in understanding the sexual mores. For example, a large section of the Negro group has a matriarchal family structure where the mother and grandmother play powerful roles. The attitude toward sex is likely to be somewhat different in this setting than in the more typically patriarchal cultures."

---

[5] Frank Riessman, "Workers' Attitudes Toward Participation and Leadership," unpubl. Ph. D. diss. (Columbia Univ. 1955).

"Social-Class Variations in the Teacher-Pupil Relationship"[6]

> Becker found that Chicago teachers reacted in different manners to the social classes of the students they taught. Teachers generally reported special problems in teaching, discipline, and moral acceptance when dealing with lower-class children.

Howard Becker, a sociologist, carried out a study in the Chicago school system using intensive interviews with teachers. The teachers distinguished three social-class groups with which they came into contact: (1) A bottom stratum, probably equivalent to the lower-lower and parts of the upper-lower class; (2) an upper stratum, probably equivalent to the upper-middle class; and (3) a middle stratum, probably equivalent to the lower-middle and parts of the upper-lower class.

In dealing with the lowest stratum, teachers felt that they had problems in teaching children not generally geared through background or attitude to the common teaching techniques. The teachers frequently felt that they had failed because their work presentations were not reaching the students. The students were not motivated because the lessons and rewards were not relevant to their real life experiences. The problems became more aggravated in each grade as the gap between what the children were expected to know and what they did know increased. Reading was a major problem.

When it came to discipline slum children presented particular problems. The conflict inherent in the teacher-student relationship was much intensified in this population group. These children were given to unrestrained behavior and physical violence. The use of physical force was socially approved by their parents and peers, and children were expected to fight back when provoked. Finally, there was the problem of moral acceptance by the teacher. Often the slum child offended the teacher's moral sensibilities because of his family situation, his lack of cleanliness and mode of dress as well as his moral behavior. Often the teacher observed that she found the moral behavior simply incomprehensible. She could not believe that any normal human being would act in such a way.

In general it was found that teachers experienced problems when confronting students who failed to exhibit the qualities of the ideal image of students that teachers hold.

---

[6] Howard Becker, "Social Class Variations in the Teacher-Pupil Relationship," *Journal of Educational Sociology*, XXV (April 1952), 451–465. Digest used by permission.

"The Separate Culture of the School"[7]

Waller suggests that the world of the young which has its locus in the school comprises a separate culture having its own mores, folkways, and moral codes.

Waller contends that there are two fundamental conflicts built into the school. The first is that which exists between the established cultural order of the society, and that of the local community that the students represent. The second conflict is between the culture carried by the teachers as adults and by young people who represent the indigenous culture of the group of children.

Waller distinguished three cultures in the school. The first is that which comes almost completely from outside the school, and represents the Western European cultural tradition. The school exists chiefly for the purpose of transmitting this body of knowledge to the new generations. The second culture is that which is partially derived from the outside but is spawned among teachers in general and specifically among the teachers in one particular school. This culture regulates conduct between the teachers and between the teachers and the administration. The purest form of the school tradition is that indigenous to the school. Concerning the latter Waller notes:

Teachers have always known that it was not necessary for the students of strange customs to cross the seas to find material. Folklore and myth, tradition, taboo, magic rites, ceremonials of all sorts, collective representations, *participation mystique*, all abound in the front yard of every school, and occasionally they creep upstairs and are incorporated into the more formal portions of school life. . . . All these things make up a world that is different from the world of adults. It is this separate culture of the young, having its locus in the school, which we prefer to study.[8]

Important activities such as sports, clubs, and varied activities are ritualized in the schools. These are partly developed by students and by the faculty who regard them as means of control and outlets for spontaneous energies. Thus such activities are institutionalized in the school system as being functional for both students and faculty.

---

[7] Willard Waller, "The Separate Culture of the School," *Sociology of Teaching* (New York, 1932), pp. 103–112. Digest used by permission of the publisher, John Wiley & Sons, Inc.

[8] *Ibid.*, p. 103.

"The Vanishing Adolescent"[9]

> Friedenberg contends that the school has certain functions to perform for its students. Its present mode of performing these functions works against the natural maturation process and limits the student in his personal and cultural development.

Friedenberg analyzes the major functions of the school as he sees them. The most relevant of these for our interests is its function as a teacher of Americanism. The young person learns to be an American and the teachers are manipulators in this process. Tied to this is the school's function of transmitting the knowledge, intellectual skills, and attitudes on which the tradition of Western civilization depends. The school generally has contributed to the development of a middle class. It teaches a common culture and similar categories of thought. While it does establish categories of thought and unconscious predispositions, it does not work to clarify the meaning of experience as Friedenberg believes it should. The school acts as a melting pot, trying to make all students the same, instead of recognizing and legitimizing differences. Uniformity, success, and contentment are the major goals. There is more interest in integrating and adjusting the unique student than in letting him realize his potentials.

The chief clash is between the stable middle-class tradition of the school and the teachers and lower-class groups. Those who enter the teaching ranks tend to be a middle-class self-perpetuating group. They are largely persons who seek security in a civil service type arrangement, rather than in rebellion or creativity. Friedenberg feels many teachers are more preoccupied with acquiring and maintaining small increments of status for a small investment and without much risk than with disciplined self-expression through the medium of professional competence. Traditions of a civil service do not encourage courage, feeling, imagination, breadth of vision, or independence of action. In general the teacher who manifested these characteristics would be thought to need help in adapting himself to his work and the group situation. Thus the student who needs teachers with these qualities to help him realize himself has difficulty in finding those rare persons who have maintained their individuality.

---

[9] Edgar Z. Friedenberg, *The Vanishing Adolescent* (Boston, 1950), chaps. 3 and 4. Digest used by permission of the publisher, Beacon Press.

PART II
SELF–IMAGE

INTRODUCTION

"Every Negro child on the day he enters school carries a burden no white child can ever know, no matter what handicaps or disabilities he may suffer," John Fisher, the President of Teachers College, Columbia University, has observed.[1] In writing of the Conference of Negro-African Writers and Artists (France, 1956) James Baldwin reported "It became clear as the debate wore on, that there was something which all black men held in common, something which cut across opposing points of view, and placed in the same context their widely dissimilar experience. What they held in common was the necessity to remake the world in their own image, to impose this image on the world and no longer be controlled by the vision of the world, and of themselves, held by other people."[2]

The burden stems in part from the Negro's obviously inferior economic and social position in American society. As a result of prevailing economic discrimination and of their concentration in the poorest parts of the city, Negroes have come to accept the statements made by the mass media that they are a different, inferior, and fairly incompetent part of the American population. That small children feel their difference and accept it as denoting inferiority, is confirmed by the well-known experiment conducted by Kenneth Clark, a social psychologist who showed that Negro children begin placing a higher value on white dolls than on Negro dolls at a very early age. Mary Goodman[3] in her nursery school studies, has shown that even pre-schoolers of both races are aware of the formula white/brown (or white over brown with a line between). In areas of academic achievement, the Negro does not perceive himself to be as good as his white counterpart. This defeatist

---

[1] Charles E. Silberman, *Crisis in Black and White* (New York: Random House, 1964), p. 267.

[2] James Baldwin, *Nobody Knows My Name* (New York: Dell, 1961), pp. 28–29.

[3] Mary Goodman, *Racial Awareness in Young Children* (Reading, Mass.: Addison-Wesley, 1952).

mechanism is seldom reversed by the Negro's school experience, rather, it is in many ways compounded.

Part II of this book seeks to impress upon school personnel that to educate youth effectively this problem of negative self-image must be dealt with. For the schools the Negro student's low self-esteem raises many problems since it is reflected both in his behavior and in his lack of attainment in class. Nor is this surprising. There are experiments which suggest that stress can lead to intellectual impairment in such areas as recall of nonsense syllables, arithmetic, digit span, sentence formation, and in the performance of other relatively difficult tasks involving higher physiological centers of learning.

The child from a low socioeconomic background tends to "act out" with more aggression than children from middle-class backgrounds both in the classroom and on the playground. This may be related to various elements in their culture — the use of physical rather than verbal modes of expression, the difference in the type of discipline used at school and at home, and so on. But in many ways this is also a symptom of the child's negative self-image. If he sees himself as unable to achieve or to gain recognition in acceptable school ways, he may well resort to using negative means to gain this recognition, even though it may result in punishment or further trouble. At least he is seen; he has accomplished something, if it is only to "bug" the teacher.

Even extremely delinquent behavior may have this origin. Readers of *The Cool World*[4] will recall that although Duke's driving purpose seemed to be to obtain a gun, he was not actually a violent boy. Though tender and affectionate in many relationships, he saw the gun as his one way to be somebody, to be recognized: "There goes Duke," he daydreamed, "He's a cool killer." If he could have achieved such recognition within the structure of middle-class society, he would not have been driven to this extreme need. In our schools we have the chance to help students with such needs to find recognition in more socially accepted ways.

In the past the school has reflected the pattern of the dominant American society in neglecting to show Negro participation in the social structure, thus the Negro student sees no place for himself in the school structure. Until very recently the Negro never saw himself in a magazine, or in movies or TV, except as a slave or a buffoon; never in a way that would make him feel part of the world around him. The school has reinforced this pattern.

---

[4] Warren Miller, *The Cool World* (New York: Fawcett, 1965), p. 267.

SELF-IMAGE

Reading texts have typically centered around a two-parent, three-child, two-pet family, living in a toy-filled, single-family house with a large yard and a white picket fence. The father, dressed in a well-tailored suit, works in an office. The mother stays home and engages in ladylike pursuits. And the children, who are immaculately dressed and almost as immaculately cleansed in spirit, play and work happily, day in and day out, without friction. The world pictured in the reader is artificial by any standards, but to many children it is totally alien. Nowhere does the lower-class or the minority-group child see himself depicted. It is recognized that the experiences read about must be meaningful to the child, and yet this seems to be forgotten in teaching the nonwhite, lower-class child to read. He has no motivation to learn to read about these sterile characters. Yet, if he fails to learn to read his self-esteem drops even lower, and so usually, does his behavior.

Other texts, reference books, and illustrated classroom materials, almost without exception, show only Caucasian faces. The one exception is social studies; here the Negro face is finally seen, but either as a tribal savage or a happy plantation slave, neither image being calculated to raise low self-esteem. Nowhere, from kindergarten to high school, is there a true depiction of the important role Negroes have played in the history of this country and of the world. Again, the negative self-image is reinforced. If Negroes have never contributed anything worthwhile in the past, why should the student expect to do so in the future? Why should he even try?

The stories that follow illustrate as well the importance of the encounter between teacher and pupil in determining whether the child will feel encouraged or discouraged in his school work. Children are highly impressionable, and the teacher's opinion of a child as conveyed to him will be significant in determining the child's attitude toward himself. Negative and defeatist assumptions about his students expressed by the teacher do in fact affect the learning process.

There are numerous ways of alienating the child from the school, and many of them are subtle. Not giving value to the children in their own right, or ridiculing the things they value does not aid in bringing the child "into" the school. We must recognize what has value for the student, without implying that it is bad because its origin possibly lies in his culture. We do not want to perpetuate "bad notions" of his culture.

There are three main areas in which a Negro child's handicaps are intensified upon entering school. The first is the inclusion of only Anglo-Saxon models and mainly Western accomplishments in school texts. The second is the attitude of the teacher which often shows ignorance of

Negroes or disdain for them. The third is the ignoring or ridiculing of Negro cultural elements, which represents to the child a rejection not only of himself but of his people.

There are ways, however, in which the school has a unique opportunity to replace the negative self-image with which the Negro child enters school by a positive one, and slow steps are beginning to be made in this direction. The importance that the type of readers used plays in the beginning school achievement of disadvantaged children is now being recognized. Experimental readers and other texts which are interracial and intercultural are being developed.

Nevertheless it will take time until these texts are in general use, and in the meantime the creative teacher can develop substitutes and supplements for the current readers. Children can write their own stories based on their own experience and illustrate them. These can be reproduced and used as readers for the class. Children may find magazine pictures which are meaningful to them and compose their own stories from which reading booklets can be made. Sylvia Ashton-Warner,[5] working with Maori children in New Zealand — in some ways a comparable subcultural situation — teaches reading by having the children tell her a word which has meaning for them and which they wish to learn. She writes this word for them, they take it home and study it, and when they can read it to her, it becomes "their" word, and then they ask for another. As their words accumulate, they continually read them to her and use them to form sentences, and eventually stories. Any word they forget is taken away and is no longer "their" word until relearned. These beginning words may be quite complex and have three syllables, but she finds that the children retain them even though they have been unable to learn to read at a pre-primer level in traditional readers. This is because "their" words have real emotional content for them.

For such techniques, for class discussions, for language work, it is essential that all materials be interracial and intercultural: bulletin board displays, illustrations on experience charts, magazines available for cut out, library books, and the like.

The curriculum area in which the school can contribute the most to a positive self-image of disadvantaged children is in social studies. Information on Negro history is available in a large number of reference books. Some of these may differ in interpreting the facts, as do books about all historical events, but they will provide minority group chil-

---

[5] Sylvia Ashton-Warner, *Spinster* (New York: Simon and Schuster, 1959); *Teacher* (New York: Simon and Schuster, 1963).

dren with information about their heroes and give them pride in the contributions members of their race have made both to America and the world. It may well surprise some teachers to learn that certain African civilizations were already in the Metal Age forging iron and creating works of art in bronze while Europe was still in the Stone Age. Or to discover that parts of our basic legal code were derived from African civilizations. Students will be interested to learn that there were Negroes with and among the early American explorers, one, Little Stephen (Estéban) discovering the area which became Arizona and New Mexico. A Negro, Matthew Henson, was a member of Peary's expedition to the North Pole and planted the American flag there. Students familiar only with the Negro's role as a slave should learn that there were numbers of rebellions among the slaves, and numbers of free Negroes among the abolitionists. They should know that one Negro, Dr. Charles Drew, developed the use of blood plasma, and another, Dr. Daniel Hale Williams, performed the first successful heart operation in America. And how many teachers know that a Negro, Benjamin Banneker, helped to survey and lay out Washington, D. C.? These are only a handful of the facts which, if taught in our history courses, would give low-achieving Negroes an entirely different picture of themselves and help raise the level of their aspirations. Moreover the Caucasian students would also benefit from learning of the positive contributions made by Negroes to their way of life.

Negroes in the arts are better known but not normally mentioned in the curriculum. Poetry and music by Negro authors is appropriate from kindergarten through high school, and books by and about Negroes can be incorporated into English classes and into the extracurricular reading lists usually compiled by elementary teachers.

Many teachers and their superiors are reluctant to include the teaching of Negro history and contributions out of insecurity in dealing with a subject they know too little about themselves. In such cases they should avail themselves of the increasing number of bibliographies on materials for both teachers and students in this area. Some teachers will find this material on their own, others will need administrators to provide it for them. What teacher, educated outside of California, would turn down a 4th-grade assignment because she did not know California history and, therefore, couldn't teach it? When the "new math" was adopted in the schools, it was recognized that the teachers themselves would need courses before they could use this new approach, and such courses were then provided. There is no reason why the same cannot be done to prepare teachers to teach Negro history. A teacher can begin with such simple books as Langston Hughes', *First Book of Negroes*, and Arna Bontemps', *Story of the Negro*, or Jane Shackelford's, *A Child's History of the Negro*, extending her own reading as she finds more material. A knowledge of Negro history and an awareness of the need to teach it positively to her pupils would certainly have helped the teacher in "Preparation," the first story in this Part, to bolster her Negro students' self-image instead of damaging it further.

Some school personnel are reluctant to teach Negro history and culture for fear of objections from Caucasian parents. They resist the idea of "siding too much" with the Negro. Many Negro parents have eagerly and enthusiastically supported teachers in this area once the positive reasons for this addition to the curriculum have been explained to them. Today, vocal Negroes are not only accepting but are demanding such additions in the textbooks and school curriculum. If school personnel explained the importance of this change in approach to Caucasian parents as well they might find that their fears of provoking opposition have been groundless or at least exaggerated.

Part I of this manual discussed differences in cultural values and the need for the school personnel to understand the cultures from which students come, without viewing the varying cultures as superior or inferior, but simply as different. To the extent that a teacher can really come to understand (not necessarily accept or approve of) the student's subculture, he can come to respect the person from that culture, without necessarily approving of his behavior. Any respect he gains for the student will be transmitted to the student and will to some degree improve that student's self-image, his motivation, and his achievement, the one leading to the other.

Some teachers, of course, will never be able to understand a way of life other than their own, and here it becomes the responsibility of the school to see that such teachers' attitudes are not transmitted into actions which will further lower the self-esteem of the students. Mrs. Snedley the teacher in the second story in this Part, "Authority," is an example of this. Such a teacher might be helped by in-service training to gain an understanding of the changes that have taken place during her ten years' absence from the school. However, if she is clearly beyond enlarging her horizons, she would do less damage in a school made up of students from a background similar to her own. If she is left at the present school, she should be informed that overt expressions of prejudice will not be tolerated.

To summarize, the Negro child brings with him to school a negative self-image but one not yet hardened into his personality. In the past the

SELF-IMAGE

school has reinforced this negative image and lack of motivation and low achievement have been the result. There are now ever-increasing means by which the school can substitute a positive self-image, and any activity contributing to this end should be considered within the province of the school, since academic achievement is so directly connected with it.

The following stories present problem situations focusing on self-image.

In "Preparation" a Negro child is prepared by her mother to meet the racial rebuffs she is likely to receive in life. In her classroom she shares in her mother's previous hurt as she witnesses a Negro boy being isolated and held up as being different by the teacher.

"Authority" describes the situation of a boy who is basically interested in his school work, but is rejected and discouraged by a rigid and biased teacher who attaches a strong negative importance to the ring he is wearing.

In "Evaluation" a teacher who is very concerned about prejudice in the community is trapped by his own unconscious prejudice because of his heavy reliance upon I.Q. scores.

"PREPARATION"

"You can get the nigger out of the South, but not the South out of the nigger." The words were impersonal and unattached. They floated over the check stands at Harold's Supermarket. The speaker was anonymous among the crowds of shoppers. Alice Anderson felt her mother squeeze her tiny hand convulsively, then hold it very tightly. The young man began ringing up their groceries. Something was strange about Mommy now. Alice could feel it in the way Mommy grasped her hand. She could feel it in the tensely drawn muscle as she brushed against Mommy's leg. She could feel it in the tall way Mommy stood, with her head high and proud. Alice wondered about the tear in Mommy's eye. She felt sad and a little frightened. When the checker came to the yams and the ham, Mrs. Anderson turned away. Alice thought that her Mommy's arm was trembling.

"What's the matter, Mommy?" Alice whispered.

"Hush, child," Mrs. Anderson said gently. Taking up her bag of groceries she led her daughter out to their green Plymouth. As Alice got in beside her, her Mommy gave her a big hug, kissed her forehead and smiled. A few moments later they drove into the carport of their trim bungalow on the hill. They unloaded their groceries and in the kitchen Mommy helped Alice out of her bright red coat. Then she picked Alice up and squeezed her tightly. But Alice saw that Mommy's eyes were still glistening. There was a damp spot on her nose.

"What's the matter, Mommy? Why did you cry in the store?" Alice looked up into her mother's face with puzzlement and longing for reassurance. Mommy turned away, putting the milk, eggs, and ham in the refrigerator, and stuffing the vegetables into the cooler. She tried not to look at Alice, but she couldn't avoid her question. She could not escape.

"Honey, let me get you some milk. Then I'll tell you. Just a little bit." She tried to calm herself as she poured the milk and put two graham crackers on a saucer in front of the little girl. Then she sat down beside Alice at the blue table. She hesitated.

"Honey, how do you like the new school? Are the other children nice? Do you like your teacher?"

SELF-IMAGE

"Mommy! Mommy, I told you all about that last night. But tell me why were you sad at what that man said at the store?"

"It's all the same thing, Honey. That's why you go to school. Some people think that other people are as good as they are. Some people think *we* aren't as good as they are." Mrs. Anderson laid her hand over Alice's on the blue table top. "They call us things. You know the words. Darky. Nigger. Darling, that's why you go to school. You must learn that you are as good as anyone else. You must get ready for things like that. You must learn you can do as well as anyone else."

Alice looked up and saw that Mommy's eyes were damp. Alice set down her glass of milk and patted Mommy's hand, as it lay upon her own. "I know, Mommy," she whispered. "I know. It's all right, Mommy."

Suddenly Mommy smiled brightly, and the tears in her eyes made her smile more beautiful. Alice smiled, too, and they understood. As Mrs. Anderson cleared away the glass and saucer, Alice tripped to her room her wide yellow skirt flashing in the sunlight that beamed through the hall door.

As Miss Harrison opened her room Monday morning to her second graders a knot of boys came tumbling in pushing their way through the group ahead. Someone was shoving. A girl fell forward into the room, scratching her knee on the floor. Barney, a husky little brown-skinned boy, was wrestling with Sam. They continued to scuffle ineffectually as they moved toward the back of the room. Some of the girls greeted their teacher with a cheery "Good morning!" but already Miss Harrison felt troubled.

She took a quick look at Henrietta's knee (nothing to worry about), nodded to Betsy, who grinned at her, and laid a restraining hand on Tommy's shoulder as he started to shove Henry.

"Children! Into your seats right away! Let's see which group can get quiet first! Not a sound!"

Hastily the children turned their little chairs into three circles. But there was trouble at the left. Tommy's group was about to have a civil war. Barney and Sam were trying to set the group up further to the left by the window, while the others were moving toward the middle of the room around the big round table. The other two groups were already arranged and beginning to settle down. Miss Harrison moved over toward the rebels. "Hurry, you won't make it!" she urged.

"Nah, we won't make it. Come on over here!" Barney was tugging Jack's shirt sleeve, trying to drag him toward the window.

"Barney, that's not cooperating. Help make the circle with the others."

"Why don't they help make the circle with me?" Barney cocked his head sideways and peered up at Miss Harrison with a sly grin. Then he turned and ran back to grab Shirley's arm. Hate flashed in her blue eyes as she shook herself free from him.

"Barney! You must leave the others alone. Don't you touch another child!" Miss Harrison started moving chairs herself to make the circle complete around the table. Sam surrendered and helped her. But Barney, silent now, kept pulling chairs out of the circle. When the others quieted down, Barney with an air of resignation pulled one chair far to the window and sat down, looking out over the playground.

"Barney, you come where you belong! Now!" Miss Harrison turned to survey the rest of the class. The three groups were all quiet. Most of the children sat very straight and still, with their hands clasped before them in their laps. It will be best to ignore Barney for a while, Miss Harrison thought. With her order hanging over him, he'd probably settle down eventually.

Jerry's group was praised for being the quickest and the quietest. Then Henrietta led the pledge of allegiance. Apparently her fall hadn't hurt her. She was smiling with pride as she asked the class to rise. "I pledge. . . ."

Miss Harrison glanced at Barney and regretted it immediately. He was still seated, his head turned toward her, his chin on the back of his chair. His wide grin was a provocation. She glanced away for a moment, unsure. She was getting angry.

Henrietta motioned the students to sit down. Miss Harrison turned to them. She hoped her face didn't show her feelings. She tried to seem calm. But the students sensed something. They were sorry and a little afraid. In Jerry's group, Alice looked up at Miss Harrison with wide, brown eyes, her face tense and expectant. Then she glanced at Barney, who was looking out the window. He was tapping his left foot on the floor and his right fist on the window sill, in perfect synchronization. Now every eye, except Barney's, was on Miss Harrison. Silence fell.

"What shall we do with Barney?" Miss Harrison asked.

The second graders settled down a little lower in their chairs. They turned their faces a little further upward at an angle to peer at their teacher. No one said a word. Henry started to speak but quickly dropped the idea and sat rigidly, his hands clasped tightly together in his lap. Twenty-eight faces were riveted on her. Suddenly Miss Harrison felt very alone.

Barney kept on drumming, louder now. He turned to grin once at the paralyzed class and the motionless teacher.

"Shall we ignore him, boys and girls? Shall we just ignore him this morning? Is that the best thing to do with people like him?" Miss Harrison could smile a little. She was pragmatic. If this failed, something else would occur to her.

Little heads swivelled from teacher to child, from the giant female figure of anger and determination to the tiny, shabbily dressed boy, who was drumming in the sunlight by the window. Some faces were hesitant. Some were fearful. Some were full of expectation. Alice looked at Miss Harrison and then at Barney. Then she discovered that two children were looking at her. She was puzzled.

"Shall we just ignore him, boys and girls? We can get along better without that kind." Half the children nodded vigorously. Relief showed on many faces. Two or three sighed audibly. Two were watching Alice, almost in sympathy.

Quickly Miss Harrison got the three groups down to work studiously overlooking the mechanical drumming in the corner. One group read with her aloud. Another read to themselves silently. Those in Jerry's group, which included Alice, were copying words from the blackboard. Alice was uncomfortable and confused. She looked over at Barney who was still drumming on his desk and looking out of the window, but with less assurance now. She glanced at Miss Harrison, whose strong face was softened a little now with confidence. She looked at the two other children who had been watching her. They quickly looked away. Carefully she headed her paper, just as she had been taught the previous week. She turned to the blackboard to copy her words. But she couldn't see them very well. Her eyes were glistening with tears.

* * *

QUESTIONS FOR WRITING AND DISCUSSION

1. What is your reaction to Mrs. Anderson's behavior in the store? To her later conversation with Alice?
2. Do you feel Alice would have had an easier or more difficult time at school without her mother's preparation?
3. Do you feel that preparation for being snubbed is necessary for a Negro child? Why? If so, would you prefer a method other than that used by Alice's mother? What other method might be used?
4. Why do you think Mrs. Anderson found it so difficult to handle a racial discussion with her daughter and to transmit to her a stronger feeling of self-worth?
5. Alice must be about 7 years old. Is it likely that she had gone this long without being aware of her racial difference?

6. How do you feel about Miss Harrison's handling of Barney? Would you have acted differently? If so, how? How do you think Miss Harrison saw herself in relation to Barney?
7. What specific things in the classroom episode hurt Alice? Do you think her mother's preparation made the situation easier, more difficult, or made no difference?
8. Do you feel Miss Harrison was handling Barney as an obstreperous pupil or as a Negro? Illustrate. Do you think she was including Alice in her comments? Did she realize Alice felt included?
9. Alice's mother told her she went to school to learn she was as good as anyone else. What do you think she meant by this? Where do you see the school's role in helping children feel equal in worth? What could be done in a second-grade classroom to make children of varying backgrounds feel equally important?
10. What are some reasons for Miss Harrison's insecurity?

COMMENTS

"Preparation" illustrates among other things the racial sensitivities of minority children, subtle middle-class prejudice, and the possible conflicts these elements can cause in the classroom. Miss Harrison, with some miscalculations and some vague, careless language, alienates some children in her class. Her insecurity in handling one child leads to the emotional withdrawal of another and to a general insecurity in the classroom. What might have been a situation calling for the disciplining of one child mushroomed into something much bigger, because the teacher made Barney seem to be representative of a group and because Alice's mother had "prepared" her. Thus the clash with Barney acquired a significance all out of proportion to its actual import.

Several children entered the room scuffling. When Miss Harrison reprimanded the class in general and put her hand on Tommy's shoulder, everyone settled down except Barney and Sam. Barney ignored her command to join the rest of his group, but continued to try to impose his will on the others, physically pulling one of the girls. When Miss Harrison reprimanded him sharply, he withdrew from the group completely. There is some question as to how much Barney's being Negro is an important factor up to this point. Hate may have flashed across Shirley's blue eyes on a racial basis or it may have represented the momentary reaction of any small girl to rough physical contact. The fact that Barney was a Negro may have entered into Miss Harrison's reprimands or she might have directed the same reprimands toward any child who had continued to disobey her as Barney had.

SELF-IMAGE

From this point on, however, as Miss Harrison becomes more disturbed by Barney's refusal to join the group, her remarks become a little more pointedly racial as she refers to "people like him" and "that kind." Even here she could have been referring to the kind who behave like that and the same remarks could have been made by a teacher about a Caucasian child in an all-Caucasian classroom. The important thing, now, however, is the reaction of the children and the way her remarks may be interpreted by them regardless of her intention.

The social psychological experiments that have been conducted with young Negro children show that they become aware of racial differences between the ages of three and five. If this general kind of awareness held for Barney, then we might assume that for him, a second grader in an overwhelmingly white class, the awareness of his racial peculiarity was keen. If he thought the teacher was reacting to him as a Negro, then he might feel, though vaguely and irrationally, that prejudice was being expressed.

Given the society in which we live, where race is not simply a descriptive tool but very often an invidious distinction, one must be very careful about injecting this element into any kind of conflict. Whatever Miss Harrison's intention, her choice of words is careless and easily subject to interpretation as a racial slur.

Miss Harrison is not aware that her attempt to control or limit Barney's disruptive behavior reinforces a negative racial identification in both of her Negro pupils. But whatever she intended to convey with her "people like him," to Barney, Alice, and at least two other children she conveyed that it was Barney as a Negro who had to be contended with.

In this instance, the use of peer-group sanctions is ineffective and destructive. The method of mobilizing group disapproval to bring a renegade youngster back into line should not be altogether discredited. Many teachers have attested to the effectiveness of this technique for disciplining. One reason for the failure of the method in "Preparation," however, might be the fairly homogenous nature of the class. In this context the appeal to Barney's predominantly white peer group to support the teacher's disciplining of Barney may create the impression that he is being subjected to disapproval because of his race.

The teacher's language compounded with Shirley's rejection and the formation of an opposite group can all be interpreted as stemming from racial prejudice. To use the class as a weapon for subduing Barney is a mistake since he is resisting normal participation in the class perhaps in part because he cannot feel he is of the class. The technique might have worked well with a child who normally felt the acceptance of his classmates. What Barney seems to be feeling in the first place is the lack of general approval. The group that manifests further rejection of his behavior does not entice him to join it. Instead, it only gives impetus to his resistance.

The importance of a teacher's sensitivity toward the element of racial identification is emphasized by Alice's response to the situation. Usually the early awareness Negro children have of their racial distinctness carries a negative tone. One could presume Alice felt some sort of link with Barney. This kind of identification is reinforced by Miss Harrison's "people like him" and "we can do without that kind."

What overwhelms Alice, however, is her awareness that two of the other children are staring at her, apparently labeling her as part of "that kind." Before she noticed the two stares she may have felt tense and ashamed of Barney. But stares awaken her to the realization that in these children's minds she is linked to Barney and "that kind of people." Private shame can be contained, or endured, but public shame, when several eyes reaffirm guilt is a little harder to bear.

It is important also to notice how the mother counters a racial rebuff early in the story by crying, exactly as Alice does later in the story. Mrs. Anderson is very vulnerable and easily bruised by any kind of racial suggestions. Like many Negroes, she struggles internally to find dignity and worth for herself, despite the fact that many media define her as not quite equal. Mrs. Anderson is not completely successful in making her feelings of her own worth independent of outside opinion. She cringes slightly while she purchases the ham and yams, foods reputed to be Negro favorites; and she cries when she hears an impersonal epithet.

The statement by James Baldwin that black men hold in common the desire no longer to "be controlled by the vision of the world, and of themselves, held by other people" has relevance here. Mrs. Anderson is still controlled by the unfavorable vision of herself. The memory of her mother's hurt possibly brings Alice to school prepared to be hurt by unthinking disparagements of her race. Some Negro children come to school every day convinced that they are not able to do well, that there is no use in trying, that they come from a people without a part in our culture.

If school personnel are aware that feelings of racial inferiority are likely to be there, the techniques suggested in the introduction to this Part can be used to build racial pride and self-esteem into the school. If Miss Harrison would put such ideas into practice in her classroom, she would be able to reprimand an obstreperous Negro child without evoking doubts of racial worth among her pupils.

"AUTHORITY"

"Hey, man, you got your paper with ya? Come here, let's check answers." Lam and Jon ducked in behind one of the many bungalows and set about comparing problems. "This old dividing business sure is a pain." Jon, agreeing, said, "I got my big sister to help me last night. She was in a hurry to go to town an' all she said was, 'Boy, these are all wrong.' I coulda tole her that myself." They looked up to see their teacher striding purposefully toward their bungalow over by the far corner of the fence. The small, original building that was their school barely showed among the gray portable hulks, long since the classrooms for most of the 1,500 pupils. Lam hurriedly crammed his traffic hat on his head and headed out for the street. "If Miz Snedley's goin' in, it's time for me, too."

Mrs. Snedley was known as a "tough" teacher: she was prompt, efficient, and demanded that things go her way. She was the kind of teacher many parents hoped for and kids hated. Jon knew she would not be happy with him at arithmetic time, but maybe something would happen before then.

The tea in the cup was strong and hot. Mrs. Snedley savored it as she listened to what the principal was saying. "These scores are really indicative of what's going on in this school! You know, out of all our 6th graders, 120 of them, our average I.Q. is only 94.4. You've got to have lots of low ones to get that low."

Mrs. Snedley nodded, her salt and pepper hair glistening in the sunshine. Her next year would not be any better. She remembered years ago when she first started in this school. Her room had been right next to the office. The children seemed nicer somehow, there hadn't been any Mexicans or Negroes then. Just nice children, like her own two. The constant frown on her pretty face deepened as she thought of coming back after being out ten years. Well, he needn't think it was easy teaching these kids. They didn't have much to work with, but they all tried. The downtown office had wanted her to go to the new school, up in the affluent hill section, but she'd asked to be at Kroger again. She loved this school, but maybe it had been a mistake.

The dark adult face poked through the doorway to the classroom. "Lam, it's time for traffic."

"Ah's here, teacher." Receiving Mrs. Snedley's nod of permission, Lam hastily pulled himself out of his seat, bumping Jon affectionately with the large STOP sign as he passed by. Jon glanced at the clock and knew there would be a half hour more before lunch, just long enough to deal with long division.

"Now, take out your papers from yesterday." Mrs. Snedley's voice urged. "Get to work, you all have plenty to do." She removed her jacket and started determinedly up the aisles, stopping here and there.

Jon unfolded his long legs from under the bench. He was a good looking 6th grader with shiny hair cut as short as it could be cut. His plaid shirt and black pants were exact replicas of those worn by the guys who came to see his sister. His "seat buckle" shoes gleamed as he strode up to Mrs. Snedley.

"I can't do this problem, it doesn't come out right." As he held the paper up, the sun shone through a small, smudged hole centered in the middle of the problem.

Mrs. Snedley glanced at the paper. These children would never learn to divide. "Why, that's the same mistake you made yesterday — don't be so sloppy. Can't you ever learn to watch your number placement?"

Jon's hand shook as he handed the paper to her. The teacher's eyes shifted for a second.

"Where did you get that ring?"

All heads turned toward the two to seek out the cause of this new indictment. Jon, looking surprised, stared at the offending object, a large green plastic spheroid which circled his black finger. The silver snake curled up as if to snap his fangs at the real venom before him.

"Did you take it? Did someone give it to you?"

"No, ma'am," mumbled Jon, "Ah got it out of the machine."

"Well, it's just junk; give it to me right now."

She held the ring in her hand a second before slipping it into her pocket. "Anyone else who wears this kind of junk is going to give it to me, too!"

In the front seat, Mike hurriedly stripped his finger and stuffed a ring into his desk.

"Now let's see if you can't get the rest of those problems right, Jon, there's not much time before lunch."

Late that afternoon Lam and Jon were idly shooting baskets. The recreation leader had long since gone home. Their books and jackets lay

SELF-IMAGE   63

on the ground. The only kids around were two little boys from the child care center poking in trash cans over in the corner of the play lot. "Oh, come on, Jon, let's bug outa this crummy place. Let's go down to the bowling alley."

"OK. My mother's workin' tonight, so I don't have to be home any special time. Wonder what those kids are doing?"

As Jon and Lam walked by, a glint caught Jon's eye. There at the bottom next to a few cast-off paper and milk cartons lay Jon's snake ring.

"That's my ring that old Sned snatched today."

"Hey man, that's luck, you can have it back," replied Lam.

"Fuck her!" retorted Jon, ignoring Lam's suggestion. And then, seeming to reflect a moment, he threw his arithmetic paper into the collection. It was Friday, and the cans would not be emptied until early Monday morning. Perhaps he would retrieve both the paper and the ring before class Monday, he thought to himself. But then, maybe not. Anyway the weekend lay before him with no Mrs. Snedley to worry about.

* * *

QUESTIONS FOR WRITING AND DISCUSSION

1. Mrs. Snedley is described as the "kind of teacher many parents hoped for and kids hated." Do you agree or disagree? Why?
2. Why do you suppose Mrs. Snedley made so much of the ring? What preceding comments might have led you to expect such an episode to take place?
3. How might the administration do a better job in warding off such situations? Discuss teacher assignment and orientation, in-service training, and any other relevant techniques. Do you think Mrs. Snedley could have been helped to do a better job at this school? How? Do you think she could have been an effective teacher at the hill school? Why?
4. What episodes in the story show Jon's motivation toward learning? How important is this in the learning process? Do you think Jon could have been taught to divide?
5. What meaning do you suppose the ring episode had to Jon? To the rest of the class? What is implied in the manner and contents of Mrs. Snedley's comments to Jon?
6. How is self-image involved in this story? Do you feel Jon's opinion of himself is affected by the ring episode? His opinion of Mrs. Snedley? Explain.

7. How important do you feel one teacher of this sort can be to a child? How representative do you feel she is likely to be of this school? Do you feel parents should become involved if they hear of such episodes? If this incident were reported to the administration by a parent, what do you think the role of the administration would be? What do you think it should be?
8. Is an episode of this sort likely to be more damaging to a Negro child than to a white child? Explain why or why not.

COMMENTS

In "Authority" Mrs. Snedley emerges as a very strict, unfair, and rigid teacher manifesting her bias in categorical rejection of minority people. Today, pressures from without and within the schools are forcing prejudice to be camouflaged in more subtle terms. Mrs. Snedley as the true villain, the classic smug, biased individual, is perhaps stereotyped — most teachers do not fall into this extreme category. However, many have been conditioned in comfortable middle-class neighborhoods to feel that their particular style of life is far superior to that of the lower-class Negro children they confront in the classroom, and that these children for one reason or another lack the facility for handling academic materials.

The problem lies in the fact that this perception, the idea the teacher has of the child, is communicated to the child in overt and covert ways, and the child, being impressionable, sees himself as the teacher sees him.

In the short episode between Jon and Mrs. Snedley we can make a few predictions as to what Jon's future will be in school. The ground is certainly being prepared in Snedley's class to help Jon into the "dropout" pattern. Incident by incident we can see the relationship between low expectation and rejection on the part of the school and low self-esteem and poor academic performance on the part of the child. The components which give this main idea consistency are stereotyping, preconceived notions, labeling and conflicting values, each reinforcing Jon's feeling of inferiority.

Mrs. Snedley is not solely responsible for her notions and invidious words. The idea that "We don't have much to work with" is in part generated by the principal who assures her that "you have to have lots of low ones to get that low." That kind of categorical labeling allows Mrs. Snedley to say with resignation, "these children will never learn to divide." Here then is the first step: Mrs. Snedley and the principal have

SELF-IMAGE

prejudged the children as incapable of solving numerical problems as complex as long division.

In panels and interviews teachers in lower-class schools often say that once a child is motivated to learn, he can be taught many things. Mrs. Snedley is not having the problem with Jon that many teachers have in predominantly Negro schools. The youngster in "Authority" is interested in his homework assignment. He was concerned enough to ask for help at home, on the playground, and finally in the classroom. The unfortunate part is that Jon never does receive assistance with his problems as the teacher disparages him to keep him from asking for that particular teacher's trust again. Asking help of anyone, especially a teacher who is the focal point of the whole class, requires faith that the teacher will not scoff or betray one's needs or lacks to others.

This teacher assails everything about Jon: his neatness, his performance, his competence, taste, integrity ("Did you take it?"). Shame and anger must have dissolved Jon's willingness to learn long division. In this exchange the teacher's professional role is submerged as she becomes a suspicious moralist, attacking the corruption symbolized for her by a piece of vending-machine jewelry. At a critical point, when the teacher has the attention, interest, and willingness of her pupil to learn arithmetic, she directs herself to an irrelevant issue, provoking a swarm of hostilities from Jon and probably other students who are astute enough to perceive the implication of her insinuations.

A sensitive teacher attempts to address herself to problems and needs as they arise. For Mrs. Snedley dealing with a dime ring which evidently is not even a distractive element in the class takes precedence over aiding the learning process. Two teachers selected for interviews to discover what makes teachers effective with youngsters in "slum" schools said "My job is to teach kids to think, not to be the way I want them to be." and "I am not being paid to be a detective and I refuse to be one."

The story "Authority" illustrates, then, a kind of cumulative defeatist mechanism potentially operating within a school system. The principal's expectations are low, and incorrectly so because achievement and I.Q. tests alone are not a realistic basis upon which to judge the intelligence of lower-class, especially minority youngsters, as is demonstrated in the following story. Thus Mrs. Snedley feels defeated before entering the classroom (with "lots of low ones") on two counts: first, she sees Mexicans and Negroes, as not "nice like her own two," and secondly, her principal has already informed her that there is little potential in the whole grade. She unreservedly communicates the low expectation she holds for her pupils. Her lack of any kind of esteem for the children will inevitably have several consequences in the classroom: rejection of her as illustrated by Jon's obscenity; a general reluctance among the children to ask for help because they want to protect themselves from ridicule; and a lowering of Jon's self-esteem especially as regards his competence in arithmetic.

A teacher's inability to look beyond convenient labels to see the individual's needs finally draws her into irrelevant details associated with the labels. This not only damages the student's self-image but interferes with the primary concern for effective teaching.

"EVALUATION"

"The whites in this community are full of prejudice." Karl Missling's voice was a little high-pitched. He tossed his spoon gently in the air to punctuate his complaint. He was big and handsome, freckle-faced and red-haired, robust but delicate in some indefinable way. Toni Brown put down her coffee, set her jaw firmly and responded.

"Well, I don't blame them for being concerned. They pay their taxes and they want a good education for their children. They don't want them to be beaten up, or corrupted." Toni was a bit sarcastic.

"Oh, I know," Karl complained, "but they're so prejudiced. They just assume all the Negro children are inferior, and thugs to boot. Why, some of my best students are colored. These parents just aren't broad-minded. I judge my students on their merits, if they work up to their potential. I have students with some pretty high I.Q.'s in my group. Besides, you can tell a lot about their ability from what they say and how they say it. I give them grades they deserve. That's the only *fair way*." He tossed his head righteously and drew out the last words with a virtuous ring.

"Oh, I treat them fairly, too." affirmed Toni. "They get the grades they have coming. But there's too much tension around here recently. I don't see any reason for this race thinking. I don't care a damn whether a student is black or white, he just has to earn what he gets. We have to help people see that rewards come from work. If the kids do promising work, I give them promising grades."

"I don't know about that." responded Karl. "Part of our job is to help the kids learn about reality. No point in raising their hopes unless their I.Q. scores show they have promise. It's a good thing for them to experience failure if that is what life has in store for them later."

"Well, yes. . . . " Toni began hesitantly.

"Maybe it doesn't do any harm to give encouragement once in a while to some of them." Tom Macher suggested quietly. He was the first Negro faculty member, newly added, welcomed, but not yet fully at home.

"Say, Karl," said Toni, changing the subject, "how'd you come out downtown?" Her voice had softened, and there was concern in it, almost tenderness.

"Oh, God, I don't know, dear." said Karl. "There were pages and pages of tests. Then interviews, hours of them. Supposed to hear any day now."

"Good luck. Maybe you'll be my principle some day. I'll remember when. See you!" Toni smiled at the men and strode from the room with her big bundle of papers and report cards. Karl went back to recording grades. He set things down with a flourish of finality, then turned each card over on to the preceding one. His thoughts wandered. He saw himself walking into the office one morning, his office, and greeting the teachers, his teachers. He would be friendly to all of them, respected, kind, loved. By the students, too. He would be fair and broad-minded.

Tom sat opposite Karl at the little table in the teachers' room, silently transferring grades from the roll book to the report cards.

Ned and Dink were eating their bag lunches together, sitting on the steps in the sun, blinking into the bright sky. Dink was thin, his blue jeans a little ragged, his red hair uncut and uncombed, his freckled face unsure, sensitive, a little melancholy. Ned was a roundly built Negro youth with neat, brown corduroy trousers, close-cut black curls, sparkling eyes and a friendly smile. Behind the smile was brooding worry. They didn't talk much. It was good to sit together in the warm sun. Dink munched a peanut-butter sandwich; Ned was finishing some French bread and bologna. They were oblivious of the others running and yelling, laughing and tussling out on the field.

"I'm worried about history." said Ned. He was gnawing a thumbnail now and jabbing at his old shoes with a little sliver of steel he had found in the street.

"Missling? I can't figure him out. Grades with him are just chance, I hear. Didja talk to him?" Dink's face showed concern.

"He said I was doing well for me, not to worry. Said C was a good grade for me. But I got a C last time. I gotta worry. My Dad. . . ."

"I know. I *gotta* get B's. I have Miss Brown for history. She's tough, but she'll help you. I talked to her, we all did. She has conferences. She says I have ideas. I'm in for a B from her. English I dunno, but I'm hoping, I'm hoping, I'm hoping." He began drumming on his knees as he repeated himself. The words faded while the drumming continued. There was a loud cry in the field, and both boys turned to see what was going on.

"Now, boys and girls, just as soon as you quiet down, I'll pass out your cards!" Mr. Missling stood before his eighth graders in their homeroom after school. He was enjoying their excitement, the suspense, the

SELF-IMAGE

anxiety written on many faces. He smiled at several of the girls. He patted the shoulder of a bright Japanese-American boy in the front row and received in return a big, confident smile. The hubbub gradually subsided. Mr. Missling went into his sermon, which all expected and accepted in good humor. It never varied more than ten words from start to finish. Ned sat in misery in the back of the room, his hands clenched together. There were several anxious faces, others filled with mischief and humor, some showing unconcern and boredom. Several of the larger girls listened to Missling with devotion. One big blonde was writing over and over again on her notebook cover, "Karl, Karl, Karl."

"You people know I want every one of you to do his very *best*." Missling drew out the word in his quaint way, his voice rising. "I'll do my part and you do yours. These grades are very good this time. Most of you are doing your best. I know! However, if you get a C or even a D in subject matter even though you are doing your best, don't worry! You can still get a good grade in citizenship. You can show your parents that an A in citizenship is worth as much or more than a C or D in scholarship. Everyone isn't a genius, thank God!" Some girls gasped in pleasant shock. "But everyone can be a good citizen, and most of you are. Okay, folks, get your mother's signature, and bring the cards back tomorrow. I'm proud of all of you."

Quickly Mr. Missling slipped up and down the aisles, swinging on the turns, adding a flourish as he passed out the cards, and complimenting several students for particularly good marks. Ned's anxiety was now so great he was unaware of the cards on his desk until Missling had passed by and reached the front again. B in English, B in P. E., B— in mathematics, B— in science, but C— in history, Missling's class. But he'd done the work! He knew the subjects! He'd worked so hard! Ned was unconscious of the gasps, the giggles, the cheers, and groans around him. He sat on in lonely silence while the room emptied. A handful of girls lingered awhile, chatting and teasing Missling. Finally, only the two were left. Ned fought to repress his tears.

When Karl saw the boy sitting back there, forlorn and silent, he knew what the matter was. Ned didn't have very much. Not a bit over 90. Oh, he tried hard. Regular in all his homework. Read up to grade expectations. Polite, reliable, quiet. Fine citizen. He got an A in that. Tried to recite, too, but his language was weak and his thoughts were all tangled up. His work was good, given his ability. Good example of a promising Negro student. But he was just low average. You couldn't give a boy with 90 I. Q. more than a C. Better help him understand his limitations right away.

When Karl Missling moved back to Ned's desk, the boy's eyes were glistening. He jerked his head to one side mutely. Karl was not offended. He knew Ned was not angry with him, only ashamed. He'd try to explain that he had done very well, really, considering. He'd help the boy to get a good sense of reality.

A block from the school grounds Ned stumbled along with his head down, kicking the dusty, unpaved sidewalk. Dink was waiting for him, sitting on a telephone pole in a vacant lot. Dink sensed what was up and said nothing as he got up to join his chum. They ambled off in silence through the tall damp grass, one in dejection, the other too kind to mention that his grades had turned out to be all B's. Miss Brown had graded him carefully and fairly, just as she had said she would in the little talk they had had. As they turned down H street, Dink saw the dirty streak under Ned's eyes and knew his friend had been crying.

At 3:45 Karl Missling finally got to the school office to check out. As he entered, Toni Brown and Tom Macher were signing the book. Karl checked his box and saw the letter from the board. His heart skipped a beat. He didn't want to open it now in front of his friends, but Toni had already seen him and her quick eyes caught the look on his face and the familiar imprint on the envelope.

"See how it went." she said kindly. Tom, who had turned to leave, hesitated too. Wordlessly Karl opened the envelope and his eyes spun over the typed lines. Toni touched his shoulder, and her hand was very cold through his coat. Karl felt suddenly tired and old. Toni read the news from the expression on his face. Tom looked up questioningly, his brown eyes soft with sympathy.

"They must have some secret way of judging." said Karl, his voice a mixture of assumed gaiety, anger, and pain. "They don't want me, fancy that. You have to be a genius to be a principal or some nonsense like that. Well, it's their loss," he joked. But his face was not pretty to see.

• • •

QUESTIONS FOR WRITING AND DISCUSSION

1. What does the term "evaluation" mean to you? Does your interpretation differ from that of Karl? Toni? Tom? How?
2. Are "evaluation" and giving grades one and the same process? Explain.
3. As far as you can see, what are the objectives in giving grades: motivation, prediction of future achievement, a report to parents, a form

of discipline, other? To what extent are they compatible with each other?
4. To what degree is the meaning of grades likely to be the same for the teacher and the student? To what degree different? Illustrate from this story.
5. What does an I.Q. score actually tell about a student? How can it best be utilized?
6. What types of "prejudice" are demonstrated in this story?
7. What kind of student does Ned appear to be? What picture do you get of his family? What predictions might you make for him? Karl describes him as follows: "tried hard, regular in all his homework, read up to grade expectations, polite, reliable, quiet, fine citizen." In view of this what effect is the C— grade likely to have on him?
8. How is self-image involved in this story? How do you think Ned sees himself? How do you think he believes Karl sees him after he gets his grade? Is his idea of Karl's opinion of him likely to affect his own opinion? How will his self-image affect his school achievement?
9. How is Karl's self-image involved in the sequence? Compare his evaluation by the administration and his reaction to it (expressed and otherwise) with Ned's reaction to Karl's evaluation.

COMMENTS

"The whites in this town are full of prejudice." says Karl Missling with some disgust. This statement, when aligned with others he makes in the course of the story, lets us know that Karl is only sensitive to one kind of prejudice. The kind of prejudice in judgment he himself exhibits is dangerous and pernicious. The story hinges on the issue of I.Q. Is I.Q. an adequate basis upon which to judge one's total capacity, or is it only a partial indicator of one's ability to fulfill assignments? Karl's reliance on I.Q. bespeaks a kind of prejudice — a judgment based on insufficient knowledge of his students' situations and of what I.Q. tests actually measure.

I.Q. and reading tests do not adequately reflect the reasoning ability and achievement potential of children from culturally different backgrounds. We have no way of knowing whether Ned can learn quickly and whether he can improve his skill in history. At any rate, Mr. Missling's rigid dependence on I.Q. scores leads him to lower Ned's expectation of himself. The notion of self-image is, of course, tied in with the limitation of aspiration. One who is taught to expect little of himself will deliver little of himself. This mechanism, mentioned later in the Comments on "Expectation" is known as the "self-fulfilling prophecy."

As it operates in this story, the commentary on Ned's grades ("a C is good for you, I'm proud of all of you") will be accepted by Ned as true and he is therefore unlikely to try to do more than fulfill requirements for a C grade.

The giving of grades by "chance" as Dink puts it, awarding grades according to what number one hit on an I.Q test, is a risky business if it means the discouragement of a student. Had Karl known the subtleties of meaning in I.Q. scores his grades might have been more fair. It seems appropriate here to point out some of the meaning of I.Q. scoring that Karl missed.

Tests used in a school setting generally fall into two categories: intelligence (I.Q. tests) and aptitude tests (in reading, arithmetic, etc.). Both kinds of tests can be given either individually or in groups. Group I.Q. tests rely on the reading of printed instructions, hence they are related to achievement in reading and can no longer be considered true intelligence tests. Yet, they are widely used and routinely given on the average of every second school year. Individual I.Q. tests, given only for a special purpose (placement in a mentally retarded class, in an accelerated class, or because of some other special concern) would appear to be free from this bias, as the test is given orally in a one-to-one situation. But here subtle factors seem to enter in to penalize the culturally deprived child: his lack of vocabulary, his lack of experience in expressing complex ideas verbally, and his anxiety in close contact with a stranger (often a stranger of a different race and social class). At any rate, much of the common sense and creativity evident in casual encounters with culturally different students seems lost in the testing situation.

For the time being, and for the foreseeable future, tests are here to stay, and in large quantities. Efforts to design culture-free tests have not been markedly successful. *Not* to test a large segment of the school population when the rest continue to be tested seems to carry implicit dangers as well.

The alternative, rather, seems to lie in having teachers become more sophisticated in their *use* of test results. After all, laboratory tests ordered by a physician become the basis of action only after they have been analyzed by the physician in the light of what is known about human physiology in general and the particular patient's make up in particular.

Similarly, intelligence and aptitude tests should become the basis of professional action by teachers only after the test has been looked at in detail (all tests have sub-tests measuring specific aspects of the thinking process) and in terms of the teaching needs of the particular class *and* its individual members. Hence, it is totally erroneous to decide as Karl did that a youngster with a 90 I.Q. can only aspire to a C grade or that a group with an average I.Q. of 94 cannot be thought much of as implied in "Authority." Scores have to be looked at in terms of strengths and weaknesses — strengths to be built upon, weaknesses to be overcome. Such scores can be discussed with the class in relation to individual goals. This tends to break down the magic that a score assumes in our statistics-minded era.

To illustrate, let us take the example of the reading test given at the beginning of first grade. Its results are expressed as a prognosis for the learning of reading, i.e., excellent, good, fair, poor. And here we have our typical dilemma when we see a score: if the prognosis is "poor," do we assume that the child is "not ready," i.e., not prepared physically and mentally to learn to read? Hence, that no action is best, for maturation will be our greatest ally and pressure our greatest block to future growth? No doubt, there are such cases. But what about the many cases where slow physical maturation is complicated by emotional or educational deprivation, or both? Do we wait or do we attempt to counter the deprivation with measures of compensation (conversation, vocabulary building, personal attention, enriched life experiences, and stimulation of the child's imagination)? Clearly, a test can only be the beginning, the data from which hypotheses spring and experimentation starts. And since tests are so inevitable, why not teach the youngsters something about the goal-setting potential of tests and thus develop in them an interest and a skill in coping with the testing situation?

One prime use of the I.Q. test is worth special discussion since it affects so specifically the nonwhite, lower-class child. This is the program for the mentally retarded, a program now mandatory in California for "educable" retarded and permissible, with increasing use, for "trainable" retarded. The latter are considered to be those children with an I.Q. below 50, the former between 50 and 75. In recognition that the score may vary from reality somewhat, children with tested I.Q.s up to 80 are often accepted in the educable M.R. program. As a safeguard against the placement of children in these classes at the whim of school personnel, state law requires testing by a credentialed psychologist. This "safeguard" assumes, however, that the I.Q. tests given by such psychologists will result in valid scores of a child's mental ability. For all the reasons already discussed here, we know this is not so, and as a result a supposedly M.R. class may be almost filled with culturally divergent children, usually aggressive Negro boys.

It is highly likely that large numbers of children in regular classes would test as low as or lower than many children in the M.R. classes, but since it is impossible to give individual tests to everyone, the children who are tested tend to be those who are causing trouble in the regular class. It is significant that the majority of children in these special classes have scores in the 70's, many in the high 70's, and it is easy to see that these scores reflect their impoverished educational experience, cultural divergency, lack of test "know-how," and lack of motivation, rather than true mental retardation. Though this is not always the case, the truly retarded child, even in the educable category, tends to be slow, quiet, conforming and eager to please. The majority of children in M.R. classes, however, are volatile, eager when interested, alert, show real ingenuity in meaningful situations, and tend to be aggressive and difficult to discipline when handled as retarded.

Also included in these classes may be some emotionally disturbed children, on whom it may be impossible to get a valid test score.

Although many school personnel are aware that the special classes are not actually made up of retarded children, they defend the special class placement, on an I.Q. score basis, as providing children with special needs a smaller class with less pressure and more attention. These benefits might exist if the realities of the program were faced. But emotionally disturbed, mentally retarded, and culturally disadvantaged are three distinct categories requiring three methods of handling, and so long as the teachers are trained in working with retarded children, curriculum is developed in relation to retarded children, and meetings are in terms of retarded children, the unretarded children are not benefiting from the program. Retarded children need a quiet, calm, extremely routine, undemanding environment. Disturbed children also need the calmness and routine but flexibility within limits in line with their disturbance, and an intellectually stimulating environment. Culturally divergent children need a constantly challenging environment, conversations, trips, new experiences of all kinds, a wide range of materials, and a flexible curriculum which can accept them as they are and let them move ahead at their own speed. With the proper needs met for each, the retarded child will learn comfortably up to a limited capacity, but the "low I.Q." culturally divergent child will progress eventually to normal achievement, perhaps gradually, perhaps by leaps and bounds.

With the different needs not met, however, with the low I.Q. culturally divergent child labeled as retarded, he is unlikely to achieve his actual ability level. He takes note of the fact that he is in a "dumb" class, and his already low self-image drops even lower. There is usually an upper ceiling of a C grade placed on special class children, so already

SELF-IMAGE

low motivation drops lower as he realizes that although he learns to read and perhaps climbs through two grade levels in all academic subjects in one year, doing almost perfectly all work assigned, he still cannot receive above a C until he reaches grade level work. All of the problems of the culturally disadvantaged child discussed throughout this manual are multiplied by placement in a retarded class.

How then might Karl use test results to better advantage? It has become very obvious during the past few years that teachers' styles vary widely and that there are many good practices. The highly experienced, intuitive teacher is apt to want to meet his pupils first and to look at records later, as a check on his own judgment and to discover meaningful discrepancies so that he can refine his approach to individual students. Other teachers, perhaps more analytically inclined, carefully read records for background information before they meet their new class. Both approaches seem to work *when their goal is to broaden the alternatives open to a teacher rather than to narrow them.*

Last, but not least, because of the bewildering number of tests now routinely given and recorded on record cards, some expressed in age-scores, some expressed in grade-level scores, some in percentages, it might be wise for faculties to secure some help from the school department's testing bureau in clarifying the meaning of all these scores so that the available data can become an effective basis for educational decision-making.

Along with the discussion of I.Q. meaning and its relation to grading might be included some questions about grading itself. Dr. Harry Rivlin, Dean of Teacher Education in the New York City Colleges, has questioned whether numerical or alphabetical grading has any use whatsoever as it is open to such varying interpretations and has so many purposes. He feels each purpose would require a different method of grading, for instance, using *actual achievement* as the criterion if the goal is to find the point of departure for programming and future planning, and *effort* as the criterion if the goal is motivation. Educators often say the purpose of recorded grades is to predict future success, but Rivlin has given statistics showing the very low correlation between test scores and later achievement, with many unpredictables entering into what an individual actually does. The schools try to combine all of their goals and methods into one grading system which usually ends up serving no valid purpose whatsoever, and grades become merely a whip held over a child, a form of "tattling to parents."[6]

---

[6] From a talk given at a Conference on Disadvantaged Youth, U.C.L.A., November 9, 1963.

While many teachers who have sweated over reducing a child to a grade will agree with Dr. Rivlin, there are other educators who will disagree on the basis that grades are one of the ways of preparing a child for adult life where he will be evaluated constantly by various methods. In the concern over the best way to grade, school systems range from strict ABCDF grades beginning in 1st grade, through ESN (excellent, satisfactory, needs improvement), to check lists on varying behavioral and academic traits throughout six grades. Despite careful mandates from administration, grades continue to be highly subjective evaluations by an individual teacher and a parent is rarely in complete contact with her child's school life if she relies on grades alone.

Elementary schools have developed the use of the parent conference as a substitute for, or in combination with, report cards. But the value of this method depends on the individual teacher's skill with it, and frequently it is least effective in the culturally disadvantaged areas where parents may be unable or reluctant to come to school. Home conferences or group meetings with a teacher can be especially helpful in these cases if a teacher is aware of the parents' feelings and able to establish rapport with them.

The entire question of evaluation will continue to be a knotty one and will require a great deal of further study. But some way must be found to protect children from the whims of teachers as shown in this story.

Perhaps Karl's evaluation of Ned, or rather his misevaluation of Ned, gives us an indication of why the downtown office does not make a more favorable "evaluation" of Karl's credentials for principal.

DIGESTS OF SOCIAL SCIENCE READINGS

"The Mark of Oppression"[7]

The discrimination Negroes must live with results in psychological damage to them. This makes them less effective in dealing with personal problems and less likely to make social contributions than whites.

Psychoanalytic studies demonstrate that the special conditions under which the Negro lives give the Negro personality a distinctive configuration. The Negro must adapt to the same culture and accept the same social goals as the white, but without the ability to achieve them.

The self-esteem of the Negro suffers because he is constantly receiving an unpleasant image of himself from the behavior of others toward him. This is the subjective impact of social discrimination. A person who is discriminated against tends to react with aggression. But to survive in the world the Negro finds he must replace aggressive activity with more acceptable behavior, such as ingratiation and passivity. He is constantly ill at ease, mistrustful, and lacking in confidence. At the same time there is a tendency for the Negro to take the white as his "ideal." The "ideal" answers the question: "Whom do I want to be like?" Accepting the white as ideal is a recipe for perpetual self-hatred, frustration, and for tying one's life to unattainable goals. Self-hatred generally requires some form of projection outward in an attempt to stay its damaging effects. The simplest form it takes in the Negro is to hate other Negroes, and to attempt some personal restitution by laying claim to some attribute of the whites. Identification with the white oppressor means a loss of group solidarity.

Lower-class Negroes, who constitute the great majority of the Negro population, have the strongest need to set up compensatory activities to deal with discrimination. Among the activities for bolstering self-esteem are flashy and flamboyant dressing, especially in the male. Narcotizing the individual against traumatic influences is effected largely through

---

[7] Abram Kardiner and Lionel Ovesey, *The Mark of Oppression* (Cleveland, 1951). Digest used by permission of the publisher, The World Publishing Company.

alcohol and drugs. Gambling is used as a magical aid to self-esteem. Here everyone has a chance at beating fate, if only for a day. This is exploited by both white and Negro racketeers, at a great cost to the Negro community. For many Negroes there is the general tendency to live from day to day; thus explosive spending when they have money is frequent. An occasional illusion of plenty and luxury can thus be created. The imitation of whiteness or white attributes (e.g., doing away with kinky hair) costs the Negro population a vast fortune annually. Religion does not answer the needs of most Negroes, hence they are constant prey to new religious adventures.

Upper- and middle-class Negroes are not subject to all the disastrous effects on personality that strike the lower classes, but their lives are embittered by a constant preoccupation with attaining status and self-esteem. These Negroes strive hardest to live and feel like the whites. They are more conventional, have more rigid sex mores, and set more store by "respectability" than do lower-class Negroes. They tend to drive themselves harder, make greater demands on themselves for accomplishment, and are obligated to refuse the compensatory activities open to lower-class Negroes. This greatly augments their internal self-hatred and makes it more difficult to accept Negro status. There is pressure against any form of passivity or subordination, especially to other Negroes. The upper- and middle-class Negroes fear success even while striving for it. They feel guilty about being successful. Yet many of them take advantage of the handicaps and miseries of the lower classes.

The inadequate adaptations Negroes make to life's problems are not of racial origin, but owe their existence entirely to the arduous emotional conditions under which the Negro in America is obliged to live. To sum up, the Negro, in contrast to the white, is a more unhappy person. He has a harder environment to live in, and his internal stress is greater. There is not one personality trait of the Negro whose source cannot be traced to his difficult living conditions. The final result is a wretched internal life. The Negro must be more careful and vigilant, and must exercise controls of which the white man is free. The necessity to exercise control diminishes the total social effectiveness of the personality, and in this regard the society as a whole suffers from the internal stresses under which the Negro lives.

"Racial Identification and Preference in Negro Children"[8]

> By means of the "Dolls Test" the authors studied the development of race awareness, identification, and preference in Negro children. They found that children as young as four and five are aware of racial differences and are already forming racial attitudes. Children know that brown skin is evaluated negatively by the larger society. They take on society's accepted racial values and show an identification with and preference for light skin. With increasing age they learn to place themselves correctly in the Negro group.

The subjects were two hundred fifty-three Negro children, some from segregated nursery and public schools in the South and others from racially mixed nursery and public schools in the North. They ranged in age from three to seven. The children were shown four dolls, identical except for skin color. Two dolls were brown with black hair and two were white with yellow hair. The children were asked to respond to the following requests by choosing *one* of the dolls:

1. Give me the doll that you like to play with — (a) Like best.
2. Give me the doll that is a nice doll.
3. Give me the doll that looks bad.
4. Give me the doll that is a nice color.
5. Give me the doll that looks like a white child.
6. Give me the doll that looks like a colored child.
7. Give me the doll that looks like a Negro child.
8. Give me the doll that looks like you.

At each age the majority of children preferred the *white* doll and rejected the colored doll. Most of the children said it was the colored doll that "looks bad." Only a third of the children thought the brown doll was a "nice color."

Most young children know the difference between "white" and "colored" in reference to skin color. This knowledge develops more definitely from year to year. Fewer children know the meaning of "Negro" but their knowledge increases from age five on. When children were asked to pick the doll that "looks like you," their selection was largely determined by their own skin color. Dark Negro children chose the colored doll more often than Negro children of lighter color.

---

[8] Kenneth B. Clark and Mamie Clark, "Racial Identification and Preference in Negro Children," in *Readings in Social Psychology*, ed. Theodore Newcomb and Eugene L. Hartley (New York, 1947), pp. 602–611. Digest used by permission of the publisher, Holt, Rinehart & Winston, Inc.

In general, Northern and Southern children shared their preference for the white doll. However, Northern children were somewhat more favorable to the white doll than Southern children, while Southern children were less likely to reject the brown doll than the Northern children.

"Social Status and Intelligence"[9]

Because current intelligence tests ignore the influence of cultural background and motivation, they do not give true estimates of the mental ability of underprivileged children in our society. Haggard's experiment suggests that revising intelligence tests to remove the middle-class bias in them helps lower-class children to get higher scores, but that even more investigation is needed before truly adequate mental tests can be created.

Haggard's experiment was designed to investigate some culturally determined factors which influence the performance of children on intelligence tests. These included social status, practice, motivation, form of the test items, and manner of presentation of the test items. The subjects were 671 children matched on social status, age, school grade, and I.Q.

In the experiment a standard intelligence test was administered to the children. It was found that the test, being highly saturated with middle-class experiences and language forms, penalized lower-class children. As a result, the scores of lower-class children were considerably lower than those of upper- and middle-class children.

An important result of the experiment was that when the effects of various experimental conditions were worked out, there was no significant difference between high- and low-status children in their ability to learn to solve intelligence test problems. But mere revision of the test items alone was not sufficient to reduce the difference in performance between high- and low-status children. The marked discrepancy between the two groups was only decreased when the conditions of motivation and practice in doing tests were also present.

Results of the study suggest that lower-class children can perform better than they usually do, even on standard "intelligence tests," if they are sufficiently motivated to do well. Factors such as test motivation and practice are largely a function of the individual's cultural training,

---

[9] Ernest A. Haggard, "Social Status and Intelligence: An Experimental Study of Certain Cultural Determinants of Measured Intelligence," *Genetic Psychology Monographs*, XLIX (May, 1954), 141–186. Digest used by permission.

socialization, and attitude. These factors differ sharply among high- and low-status groups, and so cannot be expected to reflect only differences in native mental ability.

Adequate measures of mental ability cannot be obtained by merely revising current intelligence tests to remove their middle-class bias. Before adequate mental tests can be developed, information is needed on lower-class and ethnic children's values, attitudes, motivational systems, the nature of their daily experiences, and the modes of thinking they use in solving the problems of life.

"Teacher Comments and Student Performance"[10]

> This study suggests that when the average secondary teacher takes the time and trouble to write "encouraging" comments on student papers, these comments have a measurable and potent effect upon student effort, attitude, or whatever it is that causes learning to improve.

Seventy-four randomly selected secondary teachers (of grades seven through twelve), administered to 2,139 students in their daily classes whatever objective test would occur in the usual course of instruction. This was done without indicating that the testing was also experimental. After scoring and grading the test papers in their customary way, and matching the students by performance, the teachers randomly assigned the papers to one of three groups. The *No Comment* group received only grades; the *Free Comment* group received in addition whatever comment the teachers felt was appropriate for the particular student and test concerned; and the *Specified Comment* group received certain uniform comments designated to be generally "encouraging." These were:

    A. Excellent! Keep it up.
    B. Good work. Keep at it.
    C. Perhaps try to do still better?
    D. Let's bring this up.
    F. Let's raise this grade!

Teachers returned tests to students in a routine way without any discussion. Then teachers reported scores achieved on the next objective test given, and these scores became the criteria of comment effect.

---

[10] Ellis Batten Page, "Teacher Comments and Student Performance: Seventy-Four Classroom Experiments in School Motivation," *Journal of Educational Psychology*, XLI (August, 1958), 173–181. Digest used by permission.

Results showed that *Free Comment* students achieved higher scores than *Specified Comment* students, and *Specified Comment* students did better than the *No Comment* group. When samplings from twelve different schools were compared, there were no significant differences in comment effect among them. When the class-groups from grades seven to twelve were compared, no conclusive differences of comment effect appeared among the grades, but if anything, senior high classes were even more responsive to comments than junior high classes. Although teachers believed that their better students were also much more responsive to teacher comments than their poorer students, this belief was not supported by the findings.

PART III
THE SCHOOL PROCESS

INTRODUCTION

Some of the discussion of the school process that follows may seem unduly negative and judgmental toward the school system. Our aim, however, is not to condemn but to describe and understand conditions that frustrate and thwart many of the school personnel at all levels of the system. We fully recognize that numerous characteristics of this system are also evident in other institutions of our society, and that many are inevitable unless changes are made outside of the school system. The last section of this introduction will deal more fully with these implications, but it would be helpful to keep them in mind as the first section is read.

The major portion of in-service training programs is directed toward the teacher on the logical premise that she has the individual contact with the pupil so that her attitudes can most effect the child. Yet over and over teachers complain that they cannot carry out their creative plan because their principals or supervisors will not approve them. These superiors, in turn, report that they cannot initiate policies within their school but must follow policies set by the central office staff. In the central office, each administrator is responsible to the superintendent, who usually feels responsible for carrying out the policies of the board and the community and sees innovations within the school system as controversial and likely to put his job in jeopardy.

The whole school process thus tends to be self-perpetuating and extremely slow to change. It tends toward the retaining of conventional, conforming personnel who see eye to eye with their superiors or are willing to forego expressing or trying to implement their own ideas. Some, aware that the system is not functioning to its potential and that they are not getting the teaching results they desire, find themselves unable to challenge authority and turn their frustration inward. Others all too often direct it toward the student, his parents, or his culture — seeing changes there as the only way to achieve the efficient school program they envision.

Others still, do try to change policies, or "go underground," experimenting in their own classrooms without securing permission or seeking approval. Some leave the teaching profession altogether. Those who try to change policies openly, by disagreeing with the status quo in faculty room discussions, by asking the principal for permission to try something new, or by making enthusiastic suggestions to central office personnel, all too often get the reputation of being "rabble-rousers" and "trouble makers" and may be considered too unstable for promotion to a level where their ideas could affect policy.

The teacher who "goes underground" may accomplish a great deal with her own class with strong parental cooperation. She runs the risk of difficulty with her superiors if her methods are discovered but has to be willing to take this chance. Sometimes this kind of teacher, by getting good results, by earning the obvious respect of the children and community, by having few discipline problems, and by securing noticeable scholastic improvements among her pupils, can succeed in having her ideas approved and perhaps even recognized as worth using by others. But this requires the taking of a risk by the teacher which no outsider dare really ask.

When creative teachers leave the profession, the schools may be driving out some of the people they really need most.

The risks and alternatives described for the teacher exist to some degree all through the higher echelons of the school system, with no administrator at any level being completely free to initiate possibly controversial or "different" policies and programs. Many creative administrators resort to the same modes of operation as frustrated teachers, including "going underground," but with increasing difficulty as they reach higher levels in the school system.

What, specifically, are *some* of the integral parts of the school system (to which there are always exceptions) which encourage the conventional and discourage the creative school personnel, which perpetuate the same methods and hamper experimentation with new techniques?

One of these integral factors is the cyclical nature of the system itself where everyone is responsible to someone else so that no on has authority to make changes without consulting someone else. There are situations where the bureaucratic red tape of the system hinders change even when educators themselves desire it. Changes thus occur only when some individual takes a chance, or when a fundamental shock to the society at large — such as the launching of Russia's Sputnik or the Negro Revolution — sparks a major reassessment of the whole society. The school system thus shares problems inherent in most large institutions.

A second fact is the dependence upon the community's voting power for necessary funds. This can hamper progress for a number of reasons. On the one hand, fear of unfavorable public reaction may hold back changes that educators consider necessary. On the other hand, the power of non-educators to direct policies which school personnel may feel are educationally unsound tends to make educators reluctant to accept any suggestions from outsiders even if they might accept the same suggestions from professionals within the system.

Thirdly, policies are usually made to fit a general situation without the flexibility to meet the needs of a particular child or situation. As a result, requests to meet individual situations are usually turned down because "making exceptions" might set a precedent. As a practical solution the individual child is thus placed in the general category he seems to fit most and is treated in the same way as that group rather than according to his own characteristics and needs.

Policies are also set by the people in the school power structure who are the most removed from the child. The teacher who sees him most often, knows him best, and is therefore best suited to make recommendations benefiting him is often left out of the real decision-making. The only way to solve this is to ensure cooperation between teachers and administrators in the making of policy.

Another factor is the tendency for career educators to be conforming individuals who have successfully identified with the middle-class values of the school, have achieved scholastically, and have not been behavior problems. They often have had little contact with cultures and behavior other than their own and tend to fit readily into a school pattern in which conforming to the norm is the only acceptable manner of behavior, both for faculty and students. Those who come from a lower-class group are even more likely, in trying to succeed, to reject the values of their past and to cling to middle-class values.

And lastly there is the time lag between the general acceptance of new information about various aspects of education and the application of this knowledge. For example, from research and experience, professionals concerned with education are generally agreed on the following facts:

1) *I.Q.s are invalid as a measurement of the ability of any one child, especially the nonwhite, lower-class child.* But schools continue to administer I.Q. tests and to use them as criteria in the placement and judgment of children.

2) *De facto segregation — often called racial imbalance or some other term — exists. But this problem is rarely acknowledged, let alone dealt with.*
3) *Children learn academic skills at different rates just as they learn to walk and talk at different ages, and boys are behind girls in this development during early elementary years.* But children are still admitted to school on the basis of age rather than readiness, are expected to cover certain material in certain grades, with the result, among others, that boys often become the "behavior problems" and "low achievers."
4) *The early years are the most important, because at this stage attitudes are fixed and feelings of success or failure set patterns for achievement in later years.* But schools continue to use corrective methods later rather than preventive methods early.
5) *Small classes offer greater potential for the success of students and teachers.* But only recently has a movement in the direction of smaller classes begun.

The stories in this Part point up situations where the school process takes over everyone involved: school personnel as well as students. In "Lesson," a bright boy becomes a school dropout because his grades are low enough to warrant demotion and because "he could do better if he tried." John, the individual with a history of physical illness, constant changes of home and school, no parental help because of the parents' own problems, is lost. John treated as an individual, could probably have been saved, but categorized as a boy who just wasn't trying, wasn't working up to capacity, he could not be.

In "Time," the much used procedure of sending all discipline problems to the office not only kept several boys out of class for long periods unnecessarily, but kept the vice-principal from contributing efficiently to the school. If each boy had been seen as an individual, or if there had been a method whereby the teacher was responsible for handling certain situations, less frustration would have been felt by all.

"Excluded" points up the unfortunate result of labeling students. Here a boy is punished for an act which he actually did not commit. Because of the emotional involvement of the teacher and the principal's automatic response to "a chronic trouble maker" rather than to Dirly himself, a boy is caught up in an incident in which no one took time to look at the actual facts or to try to understand them.

These aspects of the school process affect all children. The effects are greatly multiplied, however, when applied to the culturally divergent child. Even an all-Negro school is still a "culturally divergent" school in the sense that, as an institution, it represents the majority values of the Caucasian, middle-class total community rather than those of the neighborhood in which it is placed. It is the culturally divergent children who learn least from traditional methods, who most need the stimulating teacher and the administrator who is willing to throw out set forms and encourage new techniques.

How can the traditional school structure be changed to become more flexible, more responsive to the individual personalities of its personnel as well as its students? At what point in the cycle of responsibility — from parent and pupil through teacher, various levels of administrators, to the school board, the community and back to parents and pupil — can we fasten the beginning of change?

First we need to recognize that the school is one of the main components of our total society and reflects the general values of society. Every criticism leveled at the school process may justifiably be aimed at all of our society. It is society as a whole which has been slow to recognize changing conditions and to adapt to them; which has been unwilling to spend money to prevent social problems and has therefore had to spend much more to correct them; which has categorized people and then reacted to the category instead of to the individual; which has assumed that only the values of the majority are right and that any departure from these is wrong.

It is perhaps natural to criticize the school when things go wrong since the school reaches more people and at an earlier age than any other agency in our society. But in expecting the school system to change from within, we face the larger question of whether the school is right in merely reflecting society or whether it should assume the responsibility of leadership. Schools share with other large institutions the problem of bureaucratic inertia, but administrators likewise face common dilemmas when attempting to make changes.

In fact, our schools have been making changes rapidly in recent years in response to legislative mandate. "New" math, foreign languages in elementary schools, history and geography instead of social studies, the dropping of so-called "life adjustment" courses in favor of more academic preparation have all been forced on the schools. Some of these changes have had good results, but others, as was recognized by school personnel at the time, have been especially detrimental to the children with whom we are here concerned. For example, the mandatory teaching of a foreign language to all children in elementary school is of questionable value for children who are still having difficulty mastering

English, itself a second language to children with a strong regional and cultural dialect. The educators themselves have been instrumental in having this law made more flexible.

Then, as teachers were still absorbed in taking courses to learn new approaches to subject matter and experimenting with new techniques such as team teaching; as elementary teachers were trying to cope with handling more than a dozen different subjects efficiently; as the school was trying to satisfy community pressure for academic achievement above all else, especially in science and math (to catch up with Russia in space), the snowballing Negro Revolution began to demand other changes in school patterns. Although the fairly recent concern with the "culturally divergent" child does not apply only to the Negro, it seems obvious that it was precipitated by increasingly vocal insistence by Negroes that their children had not been receiving an equal education and demands that the *de facto* segregated schools of the North be integrated.

The changes advocated are the ones emphasized throughout this manual and so will not be discussed in more detail at this point, but it is obvious that they are often diametrically opposed to the other recent demands of the public upon the school. This helps to explain the defensiveness of school personnel toward "outside" recommendations and puts into a somewhat different perspective the difficulties of bringing about changes in the inherently conventional school system when this system is being besieged by public demands for contradictory changes, and at the same time is facing difficulty raising necessary funds from this same public.

One other recent controversy concerning the educational system, instigated by noneducators, also affects the concerns of this manual. There has been loud and bitter debate over the function of the teacher-training institutions. One side believes future teachers should concentrate on thoroughly mastering the subject matter they will be teaching. The other alternative is seen as learning methods of teaching this subject matter to the student. But where, on either side of this controversy, is allowance made for the things with which we are here concerned: that school personnel learn more about the children themselves, especially those children whose values and ways of life vary from that of our society's mainstream; that they recognize that differences do not always imply rightness and wrongness; that they come to understand that these differences affect learning under the present educational system and that a more flexible system needs to be developed to encompass *all* students within its structure? Is all of this to come from in-service training, or does not the function of the teacher-training institution enter in here?

Noneducators have much to do with fostering of the existing system of education. If this self-perpetuating school process — which seems currently to be frustrating so many students, parents, those in other fields concerned with human behavior, the general public, creative school personnel, and, underlying their defensiveness, most other educators as well — is to be changed, it must be challenged on many fronts.

Educators cannot be asked to experiment and to innovate in the face of constant public criticism and lack of financial support. If a student is to learn, he must be given the chance to make mistakes without being made to feel that he is a failure. If creative teachers are to develop, they must be given support by their administration even when experiments fail. If a creative, flexible school system is to develop, the society it serves must allow it to make mistakes, to begin over, to fail at times. If our society wants a progressive school system, one ready to try new ideas, one in which children are seen and treated as individuals, it must let the schools know this, must demand that they move in this direction, and then support the educators as they attempt to implement the necessary policies to achieve this. If our society does not really want these changes, the present conventionalism is likely to continue.

Much is now being asked of educators, not because they are to "blame" for society's ills, but because they happen to be in the position to accomplish the most in correcting these ills. Educators are not likely to develop their full potential to help improve our society as a reaction to criticism. They may well do so if the creative opportunity which lies to such a great degree within their power is recognized.

"A LESSON"

"There's not much to discuss." Tom Stobb, the school counselor, sighed with regret. He handed the manila folder to Miss Birden, the vice-principal, who placed it carefully on the desk before her and leaned her head backward to get a long, somewhat sidewise look at the records inside. She flipped through them quickly. Tom knew she would get a clear picture of John Keats's case in a very few moments. She had a reputation for insight and determination.

"I've talked to him a dozen times," murmured Tom, "but I really don't think it does any good."

"Talked to the parents?" asked Miss Birden.

"Not the easiest thing to do. Father's an alcoholic. Doesn't seem to care about anything but his own entertainment. I talked to him once, a year ago. Good-natured, happy-go-lucky, not a bit hostile. The world is just one big joke to him."

"How about the mother?" asked the vice-principal.

"Haven't seen her, but understand she's a partial invalid. Maybe mentally disturbed. At least she's a hypochondriac. John loves her, that's clear, and I suppose she loves him, too. She's about the only thing in his life. But from what I can gather, she's a pretty pathetic thing, ready for an asylum. I don't think her husband spends any more time around her than he has to. Wouldn't be surprised if he had some other irons in the fire." Tom threw his hands forward, palms upward, in a gesture of resignation.

Miss Birden tapped thoughtfully on her glass-topped desk with a long lead pencil, a very deliberate rhythmic pattern. "It's really up to John, I think. He's old enough to decide things for himself. He's bright enough to know what he wants. His parents cannot and will not help him. He has a chance to do something with himself. He has some of our best teachers. It's his choice."

"I don't think we have any choice at all," said the counselor with a sigh of resignation, "it's up to him. He knows it. And he just isn't cutting it."

The records were unequivocal and complete. John's father was an immigrant from London. He worked as a ship's painter when he worked. John's mother, born in Ireland, had been a waitress for a year or two. Mostly she had just kept house, when she was not too ailing even for that. Her problems ranged from nervousness to ulcers, and she had had bouts of pleurisy and pneumonia. She was a semi-invalid and probably in need of psychiatric attention.

John's father, a big, rugged man with a smiling red face and a rolling walk, had no handicaps other than liquor and women. There were no other children.

When John had started school, he had great difficulty in learning to talk. He had been assigned to a special speech class in the first and second grades. He had always been sickly, thin, frail and withdrawn. After chicken pox and mumps, he had been so weak that he had to have home instruction for a year. From those contacts, the school had learned a good deal about his family life. John lived in shabby, tiny apartments, where the father seemed no more than a visitor.

In the third grade, John had contracted polio, which had led to a slight weakening of his legs. He had to be excused from all physical activities at school for several years. He had suffered a series of difficulties with glands, with nosebleeds and restlessness. Records showed him to have been a daydreamer. At the end of elementary school he had a severe attack of pneumonia. During his first seven years in school John had been moved seven times, as his father shifted from one resort to another, working on boats and enjoying himself — Lake Tahoe, Clear Lake, San Diego, Long Beach, Oceanside, Los Angeles, Oakland.

John had a quick, keen mind. When he entered junior high school, he was far ahead of his peers in reading and number skills but he had no friends and little interest in much of anything the school had to offer. He was skinny, withdrawn, and somewhat hostile to teachers and fellow students. He talked about girls, but no girl would look at him. He usually had a book from the public library which he read all through class, ignoring everything else. He mangled his junior high school questionnaire with preposterous answers. He filled in many extravagant references to his interest in girls. He listed dating as his favorite pastime. If teachers tried to coerce him into doing his school work, he became unruly. He was truant several times in junior high school. He would not bring his textbooks to class. His self-selected reading ranged from *Mad* and college humor magazines to *The Galilean* and *Peyton Place*. He had twice been issued a citation for misconduct in the halls. He scorned the student monitors and was surly to the sponsor of the student welfare program.

When John entered senior high school, he was a tall, lanky, and very awkward young man. His face was haggard and his cheeks sunken, but his eyes were full of fire. His voice was changing. He was ashamed of the funny sounds that came out. He avoided others as much as he could, tried to keep out of teachers' way, never had much to say. He had one friend, the nurse. She was a good-hearted, middle-aged woman who had a gay smile. She could be patient when he talked, but she couldn't understand why he kept coming to see her. His dirty and unkempt appearance made her uncomfortable. She had recommended he should see a psychiatrist.

In senior high school his cumulative records showed a wide range of I.Q. scores: 109, 122, 125, 132. He had never been given an individual test. He had exceeded the top level of every reading test he took after sixth grade.

On his senior high questionnaire he stated that his favorite subjects were history, gym, auto shop, English, and crafts. He wrote that he wanted to graduate from college, get a job in a big orchestra as a musician and get married to a nice girl. He listed his greatest interests as his church, his music, automobiles, and working on boats. He claimed membership in the "Dukes," a gang prominent in the neighborhood. But nothing in his school behavior indicated that he really belonged to anything.

He claimed he worked 28 hours a week, evenings and Saturdays, cleaning up for a boat company. He also said his recreation included seeing about 12 movies a month.

John was 16 now, in the tenth grade, and it was April. He had been dropped from the band as truant and unruly in October. Though he said that history was his favorite subject, he had been reported four times by his world history teacher for being disrespectful, disorderly, and inattentive, and for not bringing his books to class and not doing homework. His English teacher had sent him to the office once for failing to do his work and again for refusing to do his work. He was incorrigible. His physical education teacher reported that he was a weakling, unable to participate. Only his science teacher had a good word to say for him. He felt John was entirely too dirty and careless of his appearance, but he had a keen mind. Unfortunately, he did not do his homework. John had little interest in science. He liked auto shop, but the shop teacher reported that he was a "screwball."

Now, at the end of the fifth report card period, John stood to receive 3 F's and 3 D's.

"Do you think we ought to recommend a demotion?" Miss Birden's question was flat and expressionless.

"I don't see how he can go on to the eleventh grade next year unless he brings his grades up, and I don't think he will. But he could, that's clear enough. He's bright. He can read and write way above the average. Fact is, the last time Mr. Errol threw him out for not having his world history textbook, he was reading some heavy historical novel. He just won't conform. He is worth saving, but we have to jolt him, prove to him we mean business! We've got to get tough for his own sake. Let's face it — he could be earning A's and B's in every subject. Maybe we ought to make him do the tenth grade over again." Tom sounded firm, but his face was worried and unsure.

"Let's talk to him," said Miss Birden, "and make clear that he must clean up his person, change his attitudes, and get to work. Otherwise, we'll recommend he repeat the tenth grade next September!"

"He won't change," said Tom, "We'll have to demote him."

The following September, after things had settled down a little, Miss Birden checked with Tom about the program that had been arranged for John Keats. She wanted to know how he was doing and what his attitude seemed to be as he started to repeat the tenth grade.

"He never showed up." said Tom, a little wistfully. "He never showed up. One of the kids says he's working down at the yacht harbor."

* * *

QUESTIONS FOR WRITING AND DISCUSSION

1. In what sense do you feel John is typical of our dropout problem? In what ways atypical? What were his special problems?
2. What additional services might have been provided for John before the point at which this story begins was reached?
3. Given the situation as it exists at the beginning of the story, do you see any actions open to the school other than demotion? Do you feel it is realistic for the school personnel to say, "It's really up to John. It's his choice. It's up to him," given the accumulation of difficulties John had to cope with?
4. Given his obvious intelligence, what do you see as the reason for John's extremely poor grades? What role did his failure to conform play in his getting poor grades and in the decision to demote rather than to provide active help for him?

5. How does the existence of "school process" as such enter into this story? Was an individual such as John foredoomed in relation to it, or were there methods within accepted school practice by which he could have been treated differently?
6. To what extent do you think it is necessary that the school have procedures for treating students alike, making the same demands of all of them? To what extent do you think it could become more flexible and adapt to individual needs?
7. Is it likely that the school personnel initiated further contact with John after he failed to return in the fall? Should they have? Is John likely to resume his education later on his own initiative?
8. What comments or possible solutions, do you have to offer on the dropout problem in general, apart from John's case?

COMMENTS

The high school dropout presents a problem about which the entire nation should be concerned. At the present time about 30 percent of our high school students do not receive diplomas. Those who withdraw prematurely range from those having low intelligence to geniuses, from high socioeconomic status to extreme poverty, from suburban white to rural Negro. They represent all kinds and all abilities.

Many factors influence students to leave school. Some have economic reasons: to help support the family; to earn their own money; to buy clothes and a car. Some leave because of a lack of interest in school; others lack motivation. Some leave because of failure in achievement; others want to get married.

In spite of the wide range of students who drop out, social status is an important variable. The social environment of the child — the family, school, church, neighborhood, gang, or group — all contribute to his ability or inability to adapt and function in society. The nature of the characteristics within the family are especially influential in determining a child's commitment to or premature withdrawal from school.

The family and home life of John, the boy in our story, are unusually bad. With an invalid and mentally disturbed mother and an alcoholic and dissolute father, John was left without any guidance or direction. No one at home was interested in his schooling, and no one there gave him any encouragement. It is possible that the impact of immigration and adjustment to a different society plus their low socioeconomic status may have contributed to the demoralization of both parents. Clearly, their difficult and unhappy situation had grave consequences for their young son.

The child from a family where morale is low often develops many problems which he brings to school and with which the school must deal. For one thing, children from low-status families often hold their families and thus themselves in low esteem. This seems to be true of John; he daydreams, he withdraws, he is hostile to teachers and fellow students, he refuses to bring textbooks and materials to class, he misbehaves, and he is careless of his appearance.

There seems to be a positive association between student achievement and emotionally supportive home situations. Aside from frequently insuring practical help with homework assignments, high family morale often encourages high standards of achievement among children. It encourages positive attitudes toward school and teachers. John shows a marked lack of motivation and incentive. In spite of the fact that he is a high ability student, he is failing. He lives in a dream world. "On his senior high questionnaire he claimed his favorite subjects were history, gym, auto shop, English, and crafts. He wrote that he wanted to graduate from college, get a job in a big orchestra. . . ." However, problems associated with his personality development prevent him from doing well. He refuses to apply himself to his work and to make the necessary preparations to accomplish his goals. Therefore, he is dropped from the band. He is inattentive in his history class. He refuses to do his English assignments. He is unable to participate in physical education. In every way he fails in his subjects and in the goal that he has set for himself. It is not surprising that he drops out of school.

John obviously needed some adult models to whom he could relate. If any of his teachers or the counselor could have taken the initiative in pursuing his interest through personal conferences and pointed up to him the fact that his keen mind, his reading abilities, and his definite interest areas could carry him to good future potentials with further education, he might have stayed in school and improved his level of school achievement. The personal relationship with interested adults called for here also seems very important to a boy who has had no strong adults in his family to whom he could relate or with whom he could identify. John, of course, represents an unusually complex case. It was stated that the nurse had recommended he should see a psychiatrist, but there was no follow-up on this proposal. At the least, the special counseling services division of the schools should have been alerted to his case.

Certainly the causes and effects of the high school dropout are many; but once a clear understanding is reached as to what they are in general and in each specific case, the next step should be to reexamine and plan our school programs in order to salvage the potential dropout. Our story points out the role that the counselor can play in dealing with these children. However, the professional function of the counselor in the schools needs to be more clearly defined. What is his role? Is he a general guidance worker with responsibility for school programs, curriculum development, grouping, imposing discipline, and devising teaching procedures? Is he or should he be a therapeutically oriented specialist with responsibility for helping individual students with home, school, and personal problems? Or should he be the benevolent do-gooder? Whatever the role is or becomes, the counselor himself has to be sincere, self-confident, and well prepared.

Tom Stobb had investigated the case fully and could present a clear picture of the situation to Miss Birden, the able vice-principal. Yet, he could have displayed more determination in attempting to deal with John himself. Throwing up one's hands in a gesture of resignation is hardly constructive.

It seems significant that no attempt was made to contact John's parents beyond one superficial interview, even though the unusually unstable nature of his homelife was on record. The whole area of school-parent relations is a complex one. Just how far the school should go in aggressively seeking out teacher-parent contacts is an issue about which administrators and teachers disagree. Probably all of them would agree that stimulating parental interests in children's school experiences would improve performance. Yet, there are discouraging aspects about approaching parents. Many parents are interested in their children's education but do not know how to communicate with school personnel. This is frequently due to their own sad experiences with schools, with the continual failure of their children to achieve in school, or because of continual notification that their children are behavior problems. Many parents do not respond to notes. Many have no telephones, and their work schedules make visits to the school difficult. Teachers do not like to spend extra hours outside of school in making home visits, or in calling parents. Released time during school hours for such purposes is in most cases an unrealistic dream. Some school administrators actually forbid home visiting by teachers, while others encourage it.

Many teachers contend that parents will respond positively if they are approached in a manner which suggests that the teacher is asking *their* help in how to solve their children's problems or is suggesting to them how they can help their children outside of school. Obviously this is more likely to be effective than if the teacher deluges them with a direct attack on the children or complains about the children's misdeeds and offers patronizing directives on how to discipline the children. Large numbers of teachers feel that when approached in a constructive manner parents will react well to home visits or will come to school for parent-teacher meetings, outside of the formalized PTA structure. The positive reaction of parents frequently diminishes the teacher's feeling that he is having to put out extra time to no avail, or that his personal free hours are being intruded upon by work obligations.

Those teachers and administrators who encourage home visits consider that the visit is also an educational experience for the teacher who frequently lives far from the community which his school serves and knows little of the actual living conditions of his pupils. Moreover, it is reassuring to parents for teachers to come to them instead of the opposite. It has to be remembered that to many of these parents the school is a threatening institution alienated from and hostile to their community.

Other programs that the schools can adopt for potential dropouts are work experience programs, vocational guidance, and increased preventive work. The work experience program can help the child who does not intend to go to college to bridge the gap between work and school. Since sons are often likely to follow their father's occupation, it is possible that the vocational guidance program can help to improve the occupational mobility of these children. Once a potential dropout has been spotted, the school should take a positive approach by encouraging the good qualities and interests of the youth.

For the youth who does drop out of school after all preventive efforts have failed, yet another avenue should be kept open. The role of continuation education should be increased and improved. The case of John Keats is an unusual one, but many children come to school with some of the same problems. The question is what can be done by the schools to help such a child plan and work for a better future for himself?

"TIME"

"All right, no talking here! You wait your turn and be quiet about it!" Mr. Farbold strode into his dingy little office and surveyed his guests with distaste. It was 9:30 A.M. He had just had his morning coffee with the principal, Mr. Pierce. Now he found his office filled with the discipline cases which had accumulated so far this morning. Seven shabbily dressed boys sat before him on worn oak armchairs crowded between file cabinets and stacks of old records and unclaimed lost clothing. He shifted his eyes from the youngsters to his untidy desk, a chaos of disorderly paper, and back to the boys, who watched him nervously, exchanging quick glances with each other.

"We'll just take you right around the circle there. You're wasting time here, wasting *your* time, your *teachers'* time, *my* time. It costs money to run schools for you people, lots of money, and you don't get an education cooling your heels in my office. Time is money! Now, what are *you* doing here?" He shouted at the first lad on the end, a slender, disheveled eighth-grader, who was fidgeting with a half-healed cut on his left palm.

"My sister burn up my sentences. . . ." the boy hesitated.

"What sentences? Why are you here? Why aren't you in class where you belong?"

"Mr. Simon sent me. He want my sentences. I wrote 'em. Wrote all hundred of 'em. Had 'em home last night and my sister throw 'em in the fire. Simon won't accept it. Wants me do 'em again. Simon. . . ."

"You mean, 'Mr. Simon'." Mr. Farbold thundered.

"Uh huh."

"You mean, 'Yes, sir'!" Mr. Farbold pursued.

"Yes, sir. I don't have no sentences now. Can you excuse me to Simon? I did the sentences once."

"What were you supposed to write?"

" 'I won't talk no more in metal shop.' "

"You won't talk *any* more in metal shop! Now, if I do excuse you to Mr. Simon, will you keep out of trouble, keep out of my office, do your work, try to do what's expected of you and get your education here without bothering your teachers or other students? Think you can do that?"

"Yes, sir! Yes, Mr. Farbold. You excuse me, I won't bother you no more at all." The boy was pleading now.

"All right, Peter," said Mr. Farbold, laying a kindly hand on the boy's shoulder, "You get along with you and give this slip to Mr. Simon. Now, you, what's *your* problem?"

A chubby Negro boy with an expressionless mouth but fearful eyes shoved a piece of paper into Mr. Farbold's hand and stood rigidly beside the vice-principal's desk. "Miss Jameson, she sent me."

"Why did she send you?" Mr. Farbold's voice was very stern.

"She just give me that piece. . . ." He wiped the side of his mouth with his sleeve.

"It says here," declaimed Mr. Farbold, "'Henry was eating in class and got frosting on my California. . . .' Now, just what does that mean? Were you really eating in your first-period class? Don't you have any control over yourself at all?"

"I eatin', eatin', I, I. . . ." Henry began stuttering uncontrollably, then caught himself with a severe effort. "I eatin' my cinnamon snail. I eatin' my cinnamon snail for breakfast."

"What about California?" Puzzled, Mr. Farbold was less fierce now. His jaw was still very hard, but his eyes were softening.

"I didn't hurt California. Jameson, she sent me, sent me to the map. I just got a little teeny bit of frostin' on Yuba City, but I wipe it off. I wipe off the frostin'."

"Now, Henry, we're not going to permit you to eat your breakfast in class. You are going to have to eat breakfast before school or wait until lunch time. You can't eat in class. And I don't want to see you in my office again. Do you understand that?"

"I won't eat the other cinnamon snail 'til lunch, hones' I won't. I won't. I won't come back here, at all. I, I, I. . . ."

"All right, you take this to Miss Jameson, and you get back to class, pronto. Git!"

"Yes, sir." Henry's round body hurtled out the door and down the hall.

"You! Why are *you* here *again*?" Mr. Farbold seemed to have noticed for the first time a stringy, ragged, tousled blond who wore faded jeans and torn tennis shoes. The boy jumped to his feet, then slouched awkwardly before Mr. Farbold.

"Late."

"Late? What do you mean, you were late?" Mr. Farbold was already becoming angry. "I thought we got through with you yesterday. Why were you late? What are you doing here? You are going to have to learn to be on time, in class, punctual. Why didn't you get cleared and go back to class?"

"Only two minutes late. Supposed to come to the office and get cleared."

"But it's nearly ten o'clock! What have you been doing all this time? Why didn't you get cleared by the clerk?"

"She didn't pay me no mind. Supposed to see you."

"Sylvester," very sternly, "were you in that office all this time, from 8:50 'til I came in? Why didn't the clerk take care of you?"

"I was under the clock. Maybe she didn't see me. Anyway, I always see you."

Mr. Farbold rose from his chair. His tall form towered over the youngster. His face was flushed and his anger was very plain. "Sylvester, I'm sending you home, and I do not want to see you again without your father."

"Want to see my mother, like yesterday?"

"No, I do *not* want to see your mother, like yesterday. I want to see your father!"

"You won't see him right away."

"Sylvester, I am telling you," Mr. Farbold was shouting now, "I am telling you, you are going home right now and bring back your father with you."

"Not today. When he finishes the truck." Sylvester was polite, matter-of-fact, casual.

"I don't care anything about any truck. He's got to come see me about you!"

"He won't come without the truck. He won't come with the truck 'til Friday, at least. Sure you don't want to see my mother?"

"I don't want to see your mother! I want your father! Before Friday!"

"He gotta come in the truck. Only way he got to come. Ain't no motor in it now. Got to put the motor in it before it will run. Truck won't run at all without the motor."

"I am telling you, Sylvester, you bring your father here Friday, if you want to get back into school!" Mr. Farbold's voice thundered through the thin partitions. The other waiting students glanced at each other with apprehension.

"That's if the truck runs, after he puts the motor back. Sometimes when he works on them, they don't run afterwards, least right away."

"You take this note! You tell him! You get out of here! And you go home! Now!

"See ya." Sylvester sauntered casually by the other boys, who glanced fearfully from him to Mr. Farbold, whose face was a mask of fury. Sylvester seemed unconcerned. As he turned beyond the doorway to stride down the hall, a thin smile broke his lean cheek.

Just then a slender, grey-haired lady peered into the office, her eyes twinkling as they surveyed the scene. "Do you have a little time right now to discuss that dance for next Monday?" she asked sweetly. Mr. Farbold looked embarrassed, tried to calm himself, smiled weakly, and replied to his partner, the girls' vice-principal, "Not right now, Miss Perry. Not right now. Lot of boys here wasting their time in my office. See you at noon. Okay?"

"Just fine." smiled Miss Perry, turning away, her eye catching the knowing grin of one of the boys.

Mr. Farbold seated himself again, leaned back in his chair to catch his breath, and glanced around the four walls of his office. There were no windows, no access to the sunlight and the sky, in this grubby, crammed, shabby interior room. On the chair which Henry had vacated three fat, grey flies swarmed over a smear on the arm. With resignation, Mr. Farbold addressed himself to the next youth, a slender, handsome Negro boy.

"Who are you? What are you here for?"

"Randy Thomas, sir. Miss Paix sent me. She sent me see you account I was in the teachers' parking lot, after tardy bell rang. She sees me."

"Why were you playing around the teachers' parking lot after school had begun?"

"I been to first-period class. Then I see it, and went outside to fix it. She caught me."

"What did you see? What were you going to fix?"

"Well," Randy hesitated, "I see the light on in the car, and I was fixing to turn them off. My uncle has a car like that and I wanted to turn off the lights, save the battery."

"Well, did you explain that to Miss Paix?" Mr. Farbold was calm now, a little impatient, tired, but almost friendly.

"She didn't want to hear about that. Accused me of messing around with teachers' cars. Said for me to tell you my story."

"You sure you've told the story straight, Randy?"

"Hones' to God, Mr. Farbold, I was just fixing to turn off the lights in Mr. Pierce's car. That's all, hones'!"

"Well, Randy, I believe you this time. Don't you ever cause me to doubt you by getting sent back to this office. Take this slip and go back to class. Thanks for turning off the lights; I'll tell Mr. Pierce and I am sure he'll appreciate it."

"Oh," hesitated Randy, "I didn't turn off the lights. They still on, I guess, leastwise they was. The car was locked."

Now Mr. Farbold became heated again. "If you didn't turn off the lights, why didn't you tell me a long time ago? You've been sitting in this office for more than an hour and a half, wasting your time, your teacher's time, my time, and wearing out the battery in Mr. Pierce's car!"

"I sorry, Mr. Farbold. I real sorry. When you come in, you tell us no talking, keep quiet, wait your turn."

* * *

QUESTIONS FOR WRITING AND DISCUSSION

1. How is the scene in the vice-principal's office representative of the school process as you know it?
2. Could you suggest an efficient school procedure which would eliminate the expenditure of the vice-principal's and students' time in this manner?
3. Give at least one reason why each of these boys had been sent to the office. Give at least one reason why each should not have been sent.
4. Do you feel Mr. Farbold has any clear cut plan of discipline or is each decision made on the spur-of-the-moment? Give instances. If you do not feel he is acting with reason and understanding, what valid reasons might he have for not doing so?
5. What does Mr. Farbold's office tell you about the school?
6. In the case of Peter, Henry, and Sylvester there are indications that at least part of the difficulty is caused by a lack of understanding of the student's way of life by the school personnel. What are these indications?
7. How is the problem of self-image involved in Randy's case? How is it involved in the general relationship shown between the school personnel and students?

COMMENTS

The short story "Time" raises clearly the issues and problems that surround authority and discipline within the school. Mr. Farbold suffers from the overwhelming burden of having to deal with trivial problems of discipline which could probably be handled by the teacher. The sheer volume of offenses Mr. Farbold must deal with could easily have set him in the mechanical rut in which he appears to be. Even a highly motivated, imaginative vice-principal can be "eroded" by this system.

Although he is supposed to represent a figure of great authority for the students, they don't really respect him, for they reappear time and again for the same "offenses." They ask forgiveness which he frequently gives in order to get them out of his office but they are really "jiving" him when they say "I promise I won't ever do it again." His office is the dumping ground for the miscellaneous nuisances which teachers would prefer to pass on to someone else.

If we look at the exchanges between the vice-principal and the boys to be disciplined, we can see that the relationships of these youths to the school is an unfortunate one. "And get your education here without bothering your teachers or other students." Mr. Farbold seems more concerned about Peter's bothering the teachers or students than how Peter's behavior interferes with his education. Implicit in Mr. Farbold's handling of the situation is the notion that keeping out of trouble is the key to success, regardless of whether the boy learns anything in school. In his moralizing manner Mr. Farbold gives Peter the magic note which will for the time being permit his reentry into the class and restore his apparently tenuous relationship with his teacher.

"Sylvester, I'm sending you home and I don't want to see you again without your father. I don't want to see your mother! I want your father!"

Mr. Farbold reveals a very middle-class attitude in making assumptions about the authority structure of Sylvester's family. He does not want to deal with Sylvester's mother, perhaps because he has had little success with her previously, but one suspects also that he wants to speak with the "head of the family," the primary authority figure, which he presumes to be the father.

The problem of authority is twofold here, touching on the respective responsibilities of both the school and the parents for disciplining the children. Sylvester cannot come back to school unless his father appears with him, which means he may not come back at all.

Perhaps this latter possibility would help Mr. Farbold more than if the boy did indeed return with his father. For while Mr. Farbold probably bears no malice toward these youths and shows no outward signs of prejudice, his concept of the role of the educational system with respect to "problem" students reflects his system of values and conditions his methods of coping with discipline problems.

"It costs money to run schools for you people, lots of money. Time is money."

This rather crude statement is calculated to instill feelings of guilt in the students, to make them feel that they are not truly entitled to an education but that the school has magnanimously condescended to allow them to sit before its teachers and maps. A Negro child reacts to this type of attitude in a series of very familiar ways. The child devises methods of dealing with the "Man's" system. Other minority groups who do not fit the expected patterns of the traditional school system react similarly. Such expressions as "you people" are recognized by the student as discriminatory. He knows that he is little more than "you people" to many of the school personnel, that he is not really expected to achieve on a high level but is merely expected to be quiet and stay out of trouble until the system can legitimately get rid of him. Such a student may at times exaggerate the situation, but he is naturally sensitive to the prevailing tenor of the school and its attitudes towards him.

With Randy, Mr. Farbold is himself uncertain as to the correct method of handling the problem. His reaction reflects a vindictiveness which in the final analysis will most likely serve to confuse the boy. He congratulates him for turning off the lights, and then when he finds that Randy was not successful in turning them off, he reprimands him for "wasting time." This is a flagrant contradiction from a simple logical point of view. The issue is not whether the lights are on or off but whether or not he should have left the classroom, and here Mr. Farbold seems to think that it would have been reasonable only if the final results of the trip to the parking lot had been successful.

Mr. Farbold is clearly not a villain. But his attitudes toward the students reveal his indifference to their individual value as human beings who can be educated and should receive the maximum of attention and insightful counseling. Mr. Farbold's approach is sterile and unimaginative. He is vacillating in his judgment of situations and seemingly ignorant of the underlying reasons for the behavior and attitudes of the students and their families.

Mr. Farbold himself may be seen as the victim of his general school administration. It may be that frustration with his office and with the system that puts him in this position contributes to his ineffectualness in dealing with the students. A description of his office shows what low value is placed on this school. If the vice-principal's office is windowless, crowded with worn furniture, stacks of papers, and records, and lost clothing, one wonders about the rest of the school. Are the students spending their day in a physical environment which makes them feel that no one really cares to make an effort for them? Children in one school, when asked to be frank in airing any complaints they had about the school, put at the top of the list the fact that it usually needed painting and that when it was painted it was always repainted brown. Please, they asked, let us have a pretty school. Mr. Farbold might well thrive in more pleasant surroundings.

The major lack, and one usually decided at the vice-principal level, is that there seemed to be absolutely no procedure in the school for dealing with problems except to "send them to the office." The writing of assigned sentences and eating in class would certainly seem to be matters with which a teacher might be expected to deal directly. In some systems, tardiness is handled totally by a teacher (making up double time after school, for instance), but in others a tardy student must receive office clearance. If the latter is the case, the office secretary should certainly be able to handle this as a matter of routine, leaving it up to the teacher to decide whatever follow-through is necessary. In Randy's case as well, how much simpler if the teacher had listened to him and sent word to Mr. Pierce that his car lights were on. Perhaps teachers, too, are operating without clear policies and areas of responsibility for discipline and need help from the higher echelons.

"EXCLUDED"

"That does it! Come along with me to Mr. Merrill's office!" Hal Barlow, history teacher, jerked his head to the left as he turned to the big Negro student. His face had become hard with determination, for there had been many exasperating incidents with this particular youth. Dirly bent down to retrieve his "stingy-brim" hat from the floor. The hall was noisy and densely packed with lines of nervous and quick moving junior high school youths. Someone bumped Dirly as he bent over and he tumbled forward before he could reach his hat. Then a large, round girl stepped on it. He stumbled, snatched up the hat, then worked his mouth with anguish when he examined it. His prize was crushed out of shape. A large white smear marred the left brim. Dirly turned and plunged after the teacher who was marching smartly down the hall. He mumbled angrily, clenching the hat in his right hand. He swung his legs widely as he walked, rolling his shoulders, brushing aside other smaller students. He twisted his lips over his white teeth and pounded the soiled hat against his left forearm.

By the time they reached the vice-principal's office, Dirly was beside Barlow. He was trying to conquer his rage, but he was utterly unwilling to show any deference or remorse. Barlow escorted him through the door and signed for him to take a chair in the outer office. He peered into Mr. Merrill's inner room, then went in and shut the door.

"Got Dirly out there. You know him, Dirly Linkum! Think he went over the edge this time." Hal appeared calm, deliberately keeping himself under control. He clenched his left fist to suppress a slight tremor. He faced Mr. Merrill, who remained seated, nervously fumbling with the pen in his red marble desk set.

"Now what's he done?" asked Mr. Merrill, a hint of boredom in his voice.

"Struck me!" The words seem to explode from the teacher's lips, then he added, "Wearing one of those silly hats they fancy, sauntering down the hall like he owns the school. I've told him a dozen times this month not to wear a hat in the halls. Even wore it in my room last week. I tried to use class pressure to get him to conform. Asked him if he was born in a barn. Didn't make any difference. I had to *order* him to remove it."

"Well, what's happened now?" asked Mr. Merrill.

"He was barging through the halls, his crazy hat perched high, just testing me. When he passed, I just tipped it a little, nudging it, and said, 'You're not at home, you're at school. Take it off! Well, actually it fell off. But he turned when I touched it and struck me across my arm and chest. I didn't do a thing, didn't strike back. He didn't really *hurt* me, but I brought him right here immediately. This is about the limit, Mr. Merrill, as far as I'm concerned." Hal's tone had the ring of outraged patience and resignation. He stood expectantly, his arms at his sides. It was all right, he told himself. He hadn't lost his temper. The whole thing had been neat and clean. Dirly Linkum had to be taught a lesson for he was the only boy who had given Hal any real trouble for a long time.

"Send him in." said Mr. Merrill. Hal opened the door a little, motioning to Dirly, who sat with his long legs spread wide apart, his dark head low down nearly between his knees, his precious "stingy-brim" held gently in both hands beneath his face. He was almost in tears, but he rose and stood straight before Barlow, brushed his left forearm across his eyes and mouth, and walked slowly across in front of Barlow through the door into the office.

"Stand there!" Merrill ordered the student. Mr. Barlow closed the door and sat down at Mr. Merrill's right, before the big, glass-top desk. Dirly stood before them, his legs far apart, his hat in his hands, his face turned toward Merrill.

"Did you strike this teacher?" asked Mr. Merrill, evenly, without emotion or emphasis.

"He knock my hat into the floor. He smash my hat in the hall. He hit it from behind. I never see him. I just turn, kinda brush him, kinda natural thing. Didn't even look. Just bounce a little one off his arm. He smash my hat!" Dirly would not look at Barlow. His eyes were pleading with Merrill to understand. But the vice-principal took little notice of Dirly's faltering explanation. Mr. Merrill was more concerned with the act itself, a teacher had been hit.

"You might as well go back to class." said Mr. Merrill to Hal. "He admits it. I'll carry through." Hal stood up and glanced again at Dirly, triumph in his eyes, but Dirly still avoided his glance. Hal went out the hall door, closing it gently behind him.

There was not much that could be brought to Dirly's defense, Mr. Merrill mused. His record was almost entirely negative. He was bright enough, came out of elementary school with a head start in reading, good marks in arithmetic, and a recorded I.Q. of 110. But ever since his entry into junior high school, he had been a hostile, violent, and rebellious boy. The record indicated that his father had disappeared when Dirly was five. His mother had four other young children. She worked at a laundry and had neither the time nor the interest to do much with them. Once Mr. Merrill had managed to get her down to the school, the time Dirly had knocked out several teeth of another boy at lunchtime by smashing his head down onto the drinking fountain. But the mother had been as bad as Dirly. Seemed to hate whites and to despise school people. Seemed intelligent, but had a very strong identification with the Negro civil rights movement. Saw the school as an enemy. Probably was encouraging Dirly's negative attitudes, probably added to them.

He was a ninth-grader now. He had six suspensions of a week or more in the last two years. Cursing in metal shop. Fighting in physical education. Throwing scissors into the bulletin board in art. Defiant and threatening to a music teacher. Chronic cutting from social studies. Truant several times already this year. Reported by the counselor as head of a gang of troublemakers. Mr. Barlow had reported him a month before as the center of difficulty in his geography class. Kept the others from learning, turning them against the teacher.

And Hal was a good teacher. One of the best in the system. Intelligent. Had an excellent background in history. Was sympathetic to students. A very skillful and resourceful fellow. Even a bit of a reformer. Wanted to do a good job for this kind. . . .

Merrill knew that the kid had potential if only this could be brought out somehow. Dirly had to adopt a more positive attitude toward his teachers and school in general. It simply wasn't fair to the other children in class when the teacher had to walk on eggs to keep Dirly from "exploding." And what if a teacher like Hal couldn't cope with him any longer?

The school was fairly steady right now, but there had been a few clashes lately. Perhaps it would be best all around if the youth was suspended. Maybe this act would bring him to his senses. Nothing else seemed to have any effect. And besides, the teacher had to be backed up. Striking a teacher was way beyond the limit, regardless of the conditions.

"Do you really have anything to say for yourself, Dirly?" Merrill asked. "After so many times of being brought to the office? And now you've struck Mr. Barlow."

Dirly looked at Merrill a long moment, expressionless, looked away at the conference table and the bookshelf, then out the window where in the shrubbery two birds were duelling. He turned back to Merrill. He squeezed his eyes shut, flailed his left hand, wide open, helplessly,

THE SCHOOL PROCESS 109

against his trousers, worked his mouth. He held out toward Merrill in his right palm the hat, remolded now and most of the white smear worked out.

"My new hat. Bought it las' week. He knocked it into the dirt. I never mean to hit him. I just swing around. My hat all smashed."

"I'm sorry, Dirly. I'll have to send you home." "Went too far this time. You'll likely be home a long time, I'm afraid. Better get your things from your locker. Turn your books in to Miss Leer. Be back here in my office in fifteen minutes."

Hal spent his conference period trying to put together a quiz in geography. He had a little trouble concentrating. He was relieved, he told himself, to be rid of Dirly, at least for a while. He thought he was winning most of the rest of the class, gradually getting them interested in geography. There was a way to do it, he thought, but you had to make allowances. Cut out some of the theoretical stuff, get down to their experiences. Show them how people did things differently in different places. But just when he thought things were going well, he got some kind of challenge. Had had a nightmare about the class the other day. The most troublesome student was Dirly. It wasn't the hat, or the "kinked" hair, or the profanity. Not even the shouting. It was the look on his face, a kind of scorn and defiance. Without saying a word, everything Dirly did seemed to mock teachers, books, the school.

Hal wanted to reach these students. He was convinced many of them had potential. They deserved to learn. They needed to find their rightful place in our society. But it seemed that you just had to weed out the troublemakers first, the ones that not only wouldn't conform, but insisted on striking out.

The worst of it was, in his own way, Dirly was the brightest student in the class. But he was too proud, too scornful of authority. Maybe he'd come back a bit chastened. It would be good for him, good for the others. Nothing wrong about making one an example, when he *was* an example, Hal told himself.

As Hal inserted the key into his door to open for fifth period, he felt a hand on his shoulder. He turned to let Mr. Merrill enter before him.

"Thought I'd let you know how things came out. Sent Dirly home." Mr. Merrill smiled reassuringly.

"Well, sorry to see it happen, but two weeks will probably do him and his mother, too, some good. Help the morale of the others. We have to draw the line." Hal's voice was not as sure as his words. He was trying to convince himself.

"It'll be more than two weeks, I think. He's probably gone for good. Downtown has taken a special notice of this case because of the seriousness of the charge."

Hal's face was a mixture of relief, sorrow, and shame. He glanced quickly at Mr. Merrill and then turned to the pile of papers on his desk.

* * *

QUESTIONS FOR WRITING AND DISCUSSION

1. School procedures usually all but demand suspension, at the least, for a student who strikes a teacher. Do you agree with this policy or should the individual circumstances be taken into consideration? Even if such a policy is, and should be, in effect, should Dirly's action be included within it?
2. What were the things about Dirly — aside from his overt actions — that Hal and the school found difficult to accept? How were these things part of the general picture of cultural and racial divergence?
3. What things about Dirly, as shown by his actual behavior in the story, contradict the picture built up by his "record"? What kind of boy does the record show? What kind of boy does this episode show?
4. What things about Hal contradict the picture of him given by his record? Do you think he and the school are aware of any contradiction?
5. What did the hat represent to Dirly? What to the school personnel?
6. Leaving the justification for it aside, how do you feel about the use of suspension as an effective form of punishment?
7. What more productive role might Mr. Merrill have played in this entire episode?
8. What reasons do you see for Dirly's general behavior? What do you see as his future? Do you see any effective procedure the school could have used to salvage Dirly since he had shown that he was intelligent and had aptitude for learning?

COMMENTS

"Excluded" points up the inhumanity that can develop in an American school where there are no attempts to encourage an understanding of student behavior, where the cardinal principle for dealing with aggressive pupils is to brand them troublemakers, and where insults and recourse to suspension are the only means used to solve the school's human problems. A system that advocates and practices these principles can only deteriorate and alienate its pupils.

The school seems to feel that "There was not much that could be brought to Dirly's defense. His record was almost entirely negative." He was a hostile, violent, and rebellious boy. No father. A poor home life. An indifferent mother. He has thus been branded as a chronic troublemaker.

Whether human beings are endowed with a measure of control over their lives, and hence of responsibility for them, is a question that has plagued man throughout history. The answers that have been provided vary from the extreme position that the fate of each depends exclusively on circumstances beyond his control, to the other extreme that each is personally responsible for whatever happens to him. Most teachers would probably take a position somewhere between these two extremes. They would endow the individual with a measure of free will and hence applaud his character to the extent that he is able to exercise his will. There is a wide difference of opinion, among teachers as among the rest of mankind, concerning the kind of environment that is most conducive to the development of will power. However, there seems to be general agreement that both extremely harsh and extremely soft environments are debilitating. Dirly's environment has clearly not been "soft."

Dirly appears to be a reluctant learner. With reluctant learners the standard school punishments are ineffective. Seeing the principal, or the chief of police for that matter, is actually rewarding to a child who takes pride in his misbehavior. To be expelled or suspended from school is no hardship; indeed it is a relief to the child who hates school anyway and finds no satisfaction in it. Hence, threats of these so-called punishments are empty and had far better not be made. Unless the child values education, the withholding of it and of further opportunities for it will please rather than displease him.

Dirly's extreme reaction to Hal's knocking off his hat should have been considered in another light. The hat very probably was to him a symbol of his identity with his peer group — his most important and meaningful reference group. Dirly felt that both his personal and group identity had been attacked by the blow at his "stingy-brim." Adults frequently do not understand the significance of distinctive adolescent modes of dress, language, and life styles. Often those young people who have been most deprived in their home and general social life cling more strongly to external symbols such as dress and gait, because they need these as reassuring signs of their personal identity and worth.

Further, such symbols serve to integrate young people into their own peer subculture, thereby providing visible signs of group solidarity. In this way, Dirly's "stingy-brim" constitutes a "sacred" symbol of his reference group just as saying the Pledge of Allegiance or saluting the flag provides a mechanism of group identity for members of the dominant Anglo-Saxon society in America. Trampling his hat underfoot may in this sense be compared to stamping on the flag.

While Hal is "one of the best teachers in the system," he nevertheless fails to understand the socio-cultural factors which influence both Dirly's attitude to, and behavior in, school. Hal appears to be puzzled as to how to deal with Dirly. While being aware of his educational potential, he does not understand the youth's hostile behavior. He in turn reacts hostilely toward the boy, has nightmares about him, and feels Dirly to be a threat to his control of the classroom. Therefore, during the incident in the hall, in a moment of exasperation, Hal seizes the opportunity to have Dirly removed. After reporting Dirly, Hal convinces himself that his judgment had been just; that Dirly's removal would benefit his classroom and the school by averting trouble for the teachers who would have had to cope with the youth later on. A more fruitful course for Hal would have been to avoid making such a big issue over Dirly's attachment to his hat and to concentrate on awakening the boy's interest in classroom activities.

A goodly portion of the teacher's art consists of making learning desirable. Some teachers seem intuitively able to do this. But many teachers have to be willing to spend a lot of time devising varied means to awaken the multifarious interests and abilities of their students.

Hal's blindness to himself renders him wholly ineffective in working with Dirly. This is probably confusing to him. He is perhaps misled by believing that his liberal social views will suffice to make peace with Dirly and students like him. He does not consider that Dirly, the boy with his special needs, may be in special need of a positive relationship with a male authority. Indeed, Hal to Dirly must appear hypocritical, if not phony.

The teacher's self-understanding and awareness are basic to a successful pupil-teacher relationship. This is particularly necessary where the teacher has communication problems with his students. A teacher should assess and accept his attitude toward a particular pupil. He should ask himself, seriously and continuously such questions as: How do I feel about this person? Do I like him? Do I dislike him? Why does he threaten me? Can I accept my feeling about him? How does he see me? Only if he does this can the teacher hope to move in the direction of understanding and responding to his pupils and their learning problems.

Teachers also need conferences or group sessions with colleagues focusing on understanding the motives and behavior of their pupils. In these seminars they should feel free to share and accept their feelings about their pupils and work toward constructive solutions with the support of the group members. At times necessary expert help might be sought, because in informal exchange negative impressions and advice are often generously given. Moreover, such exchange sometimes makes constructive solutions all the more difficult, if not impossible.

In addition, school principals have an opportunity to play a constructive role in pupil-teacher relationships. In "Excluded," the principal was not personally involved with Dirly and so was in a position to listen to both parties and to discover that actually Dirly had not "struck a teacher," at least intentionally. Rather, Dirly had over-reacted in turning quickly to retrieve his hat. Instead, the principal at no point attempted to evaluate this specific incident but handled it on the basis of his general opinion of Dirly in terms of the disruption of the school routine and the threat to a teacher's morale. Although the principal may have felt that the school's authority was vindicated by Dirly's expulsion, an opportunity was nevertheless lost to strengthen both the teacher's handling of a difficult student, and the student's feeling that he would receive fair treatment from the school.

DIGESTS OF SOCIAL SCIENCE READINGS

Max Weber on Bureaucracy[1]

Max Weber reminds us of the comparative efficiency of bureacracy in the historical sense over other types of organization. However, when large numbers of people have to make common use of facilities and institutions, the service they provide is geared to the needs of the average person rather than to those of particular individuals. It is difficult to have a one-to-one relationship with clients in a bureaucracy. The structure acts as a levelling influence. This takes us to the core of the problem bureaucracy poses.

"The decisive reason for the advance of bureaucratic organization has always been its purely technical superiority over any form of organization. The fully developed bureaucratic mechanism compares with other organizations exactly as does the machine with the nonmechanical modes of production.

. . . .

"Bureaucratization offers above all the optimum possibility for carrying through the principle of specializing administrative functions according to purely objective considerations. Individual performances are allocated to functionaries who have specialized training and who by constant practice learn more and more. The 'objective' discharge of business primarily means a discharge of business according to *calculable rules* and 'without regard for persons.'

. . . .

"Its specific nature develops the more perfectly the more the bureaucracy is 'dehumanized', the more completely it succeeds in eliminating from official business love, hatred, and all purely personal, irrational, and emotional elements which escape calculation. This is the specific nature of bureaucracy and it is appraised as its special virtue.

---

[1] H. H. Gerth and C. Wright Mills, ed., *From Max Weber: Essays in Sociology* (New York, 1946), pp. 214–216. Excerpts reprinted by permission of the publisher, Oxford University Press.

"The more complicated and specialized modern culture becomes, the more its external supporting apparatus demands the personally detached and strictly 'objective' expert. . . . Bureaucracy offers the attitudes demanded by the external apparatus of modern culture in the most favorable combination."

"Bureaucracy in Modern Society"[2]

Blau deals directly with the reaction of the client to bureaucracy. He describes how informal groups tend to spring up in large-scale organizations which can serve to make its operation more humane.

"Think of the last time you accused some officials of being so entangled in red tape that they could not work effectively. Was it after you had made a careful investigation and obtained evidence that given operating methods were disadvantageous *for the bureaucracy?* More likely, it was when *you* felt disadvantaged by a bureaucratic decision, and you gave vent to your powerless anger by levelling the accusation without knowing whether inefficiency was involved or not. We all do this — it makes us feel better.

"The individual client stands helpless before the powerful bureaucracy, awaiting decisions that often vitally affect his interests. Greatly concerned with his case, he sees in it a number of exceptional circumstances that deserve special consideration, but the impersonal bureaucratic machinery disregards these and handles the case simply as one of a general category. Raging against adverse decisions or interminable delays is worse than futile, since it does not sway the impersonal organization and merely emphasizes one's impotence. Frustrated clients can relieve their pent-up aggression, however, in discussions of bureaucratic stupidity and red tape. Whereas the organization's ruthlessness, not its inefficiency, is the source of their antagonism, by expressing it in the form of an apparently disinterested criticism of performance, clients derive a feeling of superiority over the 'blundering bureaucrats' that serves as a psychological compensation for being under their power. To be sure, we are incapable of direct retaliation when the actions of powerful bureaucracies hurt our interests, but we retaliate indirectly by

---

[2] Peter M. Blau, *Bureaucracy in Modern Society* (New York, 1956), chaps. 3 and 6. Excerpts and digest used by permission of the publisher, Random House.

contributing through our opinion and ridicule to the public esteem of bureaucrats in our society.

"Findings of a survey on attitudes toward bureaucratic red tape support this interpretation. [Merton, *Reader in Bureaucracy*, 1952, pp. 410-418]. People who placed a high value on social equality were found to be more critical of red tape than those who did not. If this criticism were based entirely on factual observation, such a difference would probably not exist, since persons without an egalitarian orientation are as likely to have encountered bureaucratic inefficiency as those with one. If severe censure of red tape, on the other hand, is motivated by resentment against bureaucratic power, the reason for the difference becomes apparent: the more a person values equality, the more objectionable is the experience of being subjected to the controlling power of officials. The same principle can account for the finding that criticism of red tape was most pronounced among individuals who were particularly sensitive about their powerless position."[3]

By definition, bureaucracy is designed to induce an impersonal and rational orientation toward tasks which is conducive to efficient administration. According to the technologists, efficiency suffers when emotions or personal considerations influence administrative decisions. Furthermore, if the operations of hundreds of employees are to be coordinated, each individual employee must conform to prescribed standards, even in situations where a different course of action might appear to be more rational.

But, does the behavior of the individual members of the bureaucratic organization correspond precisely to the organizational blueprint? Can employees become human cogs in a large inhuman machine? Peter Blau, one of the topmost authorities in this area, would tend to disagree. According to Blau, bureaucracy in operation works quite differently from its abstract physical portrayal in the formal structure.[4] Personal contacts and interactions develop within the formal organization which result in an informal organization serving to protect the integrity and autonomy of the individual. "When we examine sufficiently small segments of bureaucracies to observe their operations in detail, we discover patterns of activities and interactions that cannot be accounted for by the official structure.[5] The work group is characterized by a network of informal

---

[3] *Ibid.*, pp. 102–103.
[4] Peter M. Blau, *The Dynamics of Bureaucracy*, (Chicago: The University of Chicago Press, 1963), chap. 1.
[5] Blau, *Bureaucracy in Modern Society*, p. 53.

relations and a set of unofficial practices which have been called its "informational organization."

Blau suggests that these observable deviations from the formal blueprint are not accidents but are instead socially organized patterns of interaction between the employees which constitute new elements of the organization. Patterned expectations and orientations among the employees arise in the course of social interaction within the work group which tend to structure it. In other words, deviations from the formal structure of the organization represent standards which have emerged from the work group itself and which are shared by all its members. Such standards will govern the behavior of the workers and will also constitute the most precise measure of the network of interpersonal relationships, which can be interpreted in terms of the self-image each agent has of his role in the work group and the attitudes of the other group members toward him.

The fact that the members of a work group become interested in each other as individuals as distinct from their organizational roles is a necessary condition for social cohesion in the work group. These social ties within the group are not planned for in the formal structure of the organization but result from common interests and the satisfaction group members derive from their social interactions. Once these cohesive groups exist in the bureaucratic organization they develop their own standards of conduct and enforce them by threat of ostracism.

Using direct observation, Blau studied the behavior of officials in two governmental agencies, one a state employment agency and the other a federal law enforcement agency. Blau analyzed these organizations on the basis of their daily operations and the interpersonal relationships among the government officials. He discovered that an individual's full acceptance by his colleagues into the work group was furthered by the extent of his personal relationships and by his professional competence. Although, stemming from these two means of membership in the group, Blau found extensive interpersonal relationships within these bureaucratic organizations, there was a distinct difference between these relationships and the intimate personal relationships usually found among friends. In the former, mutual obligations are confined to those agreed upon in advance; the social obligations that officials assumed in their interpersonal relations on the job were clearly circumscribed and had significance only within the limited context of the work group. Thus, an agent had no obligation to his clients, his supervisor, or even his co-workers, except those specified by existing norms. Members within the work group treated each other as social types rather than as individuals, and if "friendships" did exist between officials, they usually involved members of different departments. The virtual absence of intra-departmental friendships was not accidental. "The special character of *intra*-departmental relationships — personal interest in particular individuals, linked with clearly delimited social obligations — made them integrative and simultaneously assured that they did not interfere with bureaucratic operations in an unpredictable manner, as intimate friendships well might."[6]

Although the relationships were not close, the social cohesion which did exist contributed to effective operations by reducing anxiety and thus improving the quality of the decisions made. Social cohesion made most agents secure in their departmental group by removing disruptive tensions and enabling them to remain detached in negotiations, even when clients became excited. The agent who was not sufficiently integrated so that he could recuperate within the departmental group from the strains in the field had the strongest inducement to adopt an authoritarian approach both with his associates and his clients.

Blau observed in his study of the two governmental agencies that the "fearful overconformity" often presumed an innate danger of bureaucracy was not, in fact, one of its intrinsic values. On the contrary, he found that bureaucratic conditions engender favorable attitudes toward change. The ritualistic adherence to the rules and regulations was not so much a reflection of overidentification with the objectives of the bureaucracy or of a strong commitment to established procedures as it was an expression of insecurity due to inadequate social relationships within the work group, made acute by anxious concern with the attitudes and opinions of superiors. Also, the less the official's knowledge of the rules, procedure and regulations, the greater was his resistance to changes in them. Therefore, if insecurity pervades the work situation, risks will be avoided and rules and regulations will always be selected in preference to novel means of coping with a problem even though such means might be the most efficient path to the given goals.

Bureaucracies are thus not such inflexible and inhuman structures as has been thought. Conditions change and in the course of dealing with them the members of the organization develop new procedures and often transform their social relationships, thereby modifying the picture. Patterns which have not yet been officially institutionalized reveal bureaucracy in the process of change. Blau's findings, in both the agencies he studied, support his conclusion that congenial informal relations be-

---

[6] Blau, *The Dynamics of Bureaucracy*, p. 176.

tween co-workers — not completely impersonal — do exist and are a prerequisite for efficient bureaucratic operations. "Administrative efficiency cannot be preserved by ignoring the fact that performance of individuals is affected by their relations with colleagues, but only by taking cognizance of this fact and attempting to create those conditions in the organization that lead to unofficial practices which further rather than hinder the achievement of its objectives."[7]

The overriding conclusion that emerges from the analyses of Max Weber and Peter Blau is that bureaucracies are an essential feature of modern society — they are here to stay. All of us must function within bureaucratic structures. These collectivities set limits on what we can do but at the same time provide us with resources for addressing the problems of delinquent youth which would not be available if we were operating alone in a one-to-one relationship. One solution to the problem of a large caseload has been to formalize, standardize, and professionalize the display of warmth, sympathy, and understanding. Little attempt has been made to document the reactions of delinquent youth to this approach. The volume of traffic in a bureaucracy does put pressure on us, but it is possible to relate to clients in a constructive and humane way. As yet, however, attempts to find this "way" have not proved particularly successful.

"The Teacher in the Authority System of the Public School"[8]

Becker suggests that the school is a tight system of authority and social controls, with relations between teachers, and between teachers and principal working toward maintaining the status quo and preventing outside interference from parents or the community.

Becker, from his work with Chicago teachers, states that teachers feel that by virtue of their specialized professional training, they have the legitimate authority in the classroom and that the parent should not

---

[7] Blau, *Bureaucracy in Modern Society*, p. 59.
[8] Howard S. Becker, "The Teacher in the Authority System of the Public School," *Journal of Educational Sociology*, XXVII (November, 1953), 128–141.

interfere with this. The teacher is careful to confer about children with parents who will not challenge her authority, nor blame her for the children's problems. Similarly there is a fear of any charge of incompetence in teaching. The teacher prefers that the parent not get involved in the school's operation any more than is necessary. When the teacher must confront a parent, she frequently uses devices she has worked out beforehand to "handle" the parent. Teachers feel lower-class parents are the easiest to deal with because they do not have the time or interest to complain as higher-class parents would.

The internal organization of the school may be regarded as a system of defenses against parental intrusion. Teachers accept the principal as the supreme authority in the school, even when the position is poorly filled. A main function of the principal is to back the teacher up in any conflict between a parent or a child and the teacher. Principals who do not do this are severely criticized. The withholding of support by the principal may be purposeful as a gesture of disapproval and punishment. The undermining of the teacher's authority is one of the most extreme and effective sanctions the principal has. The extent of the principal's authoritarianism determines how the students will behave. When a principal is known to support his teachers, students will generally behave. When a principal is not sufficiently "tough," there will be a restless atmosphere in the school.

Principals are expected to supervise teachers — though always respecting their professional independence — and to give legitimate criticisms in private. The principal can be professionally helpful, but not snoopy. He can use sanctions such as allocating good or bad rooms, students, equipment, or extra work to a teacher. Teachers, on the other hand, can apply sanctions to a principal by ignoring him, by requesting transfers to another school, by collective passive resistance, or by creating sentiment against him in the community.

Teachers expect their colleagues to cooperate in defending them against authority attacks, and to refrain from endangering each other's authority. Because teachers have the privacy of individual rooms, opportunities for intervention seldom occur. Teachers generally feel they can depend on one another because of mutual needs and fears.

Becker concludes that the school is a small, self-contained system of authority and social control. Principals and teachers can in various ways control each other, and work toward preventing outside interference from parents or the community who would not be subject to the system of control.

"Programs for the Educationally Disadvantaged"[9]

> A variety of programs for the educationally disadvantaged children in our schools have recently been developed and put into effect in New York City, Chicago, Washington, Detroit, St. Louis, Wilmington, and other areas. A concise review of a number of these programs may be found in the Bulletin, Programs for the Educationally Disadvantaged.

Some of the main themes of action that are are common to almost every program developed by major cities for the educationally disadvantaged are the following.

1) *The improving of the child's self-image, and stimulation of motivation.* This has been done in a variety of ways: through classroom approaches, through the development of new readers and educational materials, and by using successful minority-group professional persons who may act as models for young people. Impressing on teachers the potential of each child has helped to elicit a more enthusiastic response among the students. Important in fostering the motivation of young people is the attempt to change the negative values that the peer group often holds to positive ones.

2) *Promotion of values in the classroom.* A variety of approaches have been tried to instill in disadvantaged students, who are frequently alienated from the mainstream of society's values, the most esteemed cultural values. Decision-making, courtesy, group relations, enrichment of skills, and moral standards are subjects within this field of attack.

3) *Remedial and compensatory classes and exercises in reading, languages arts, and mathematics.* A great many students fall below their levels in these areas which are crucial to almost all other academic endeavors. Individual attention in the classroom, special coaching, and programmed teaching methods have resulted in comparatively rapid improvement in these subjects.

4) *Enrichment experiences.* On the premise that most disadvantaged children do not have the chance to enjoy some of the richest cultural experiences of American life, a program of classroom enrichment with increased emphasis on reading, special music courses, creative writing, and the like have been undertaken. Similarly, field trips to famous

---

[9] U. S. Office of Education, *Programs for the Educationally Disadvantaged*, Bulletin 17 (Washington, 1963). The Bulletin consists of a series of papers presented at a conference on "Teaching Children and Youth Who Are Educationally Disadvantaged," sponsored by the Office of Education. Excerpts and digest used by permission.

American landmarks, to operas, concerts, plays, movies, and music festivals have been taken. The Higher Horizons program in New York has put special emphasis on such activities.

5) *Increased guidance and counseling.* Increased counseling staff has frequently been added to allow more intensive interviewing and counseling with students and parents. Increased follow-up counseling opportunities for "problem" students are made possible.

6) *Curriculum redesign.* Reevaluation of students' needs have resulted in reorganization of courses and the development of new texts, general educational matters, and audio-visual aids.

7) *Special programs for older students and potential drop-outs.* Varied new vocational programs, special counseling and guidance, and job placement have been increased. In some areas drop-outs have been contacted and encouraged to return to school.

8) *Teacher training and retraining.* Both new and experienced teachers have undergone orientation courses and participated in seminars to become better acquainted with the backgrounds and needs of their students. In the Higher Horizons Program special program teachers give demonstration lessons, conduct in-service courses, provide audio-visual aids, assist in project planning and room decoration, and many other activities of this nature. Increasing the enthusiasm of the teacher for his work and his students is a necessary key to a successful program.

9) *Parent relations.* Most programs have heavily emphasized increased school-parent relationships. Letters informing parents of how they can best help their children in their school work are sometimes sent home. Special individual and group conferences with parents, as well as special meetings and group sessions have been designed both to give the parent a better understanding of his child, the school, and the teacher, and to give school officials the chance to become acquainted with parents and the community.

10) *Community-wide approach.* Some programs have attempted to get the support of community individuals and public and private agencies in inter-agency projects. The Wilmington Program emphasized this theme and geared its efforts to providing opportunities for representatives of schools, agencies, organizations, and the general public to become acquainted and to establish the kind of rapport that would lead to sound working relationships. They also initiated school-neighborhood action programs to be developed by professional leadership from schools and agencies as means of discovering and developing indigenous leadership. Various community organizations soon sprang up and cooperation between existing groups developed and increased.

11) *Evaluation.* Preliminary evaluation of program results almost universally offered ground for optimism. Students' programs and performance as well as teacher understanding and morale have substantially improved in every program reporting.

Perhaps the most publicized of the large city programs has been the Higher Horizons Program in New York City. Frank Riessman has discussed and criticized this program in his book *The Culturally Deprived Child.* Riessman suggests that the chief importance of the program has been in demonstrating that culturally deprived children can learn and can excel. He criticizes the program, however, on certain specific grounds. For instance, he asks whether possibly the achievements of the program were merely a by-product of special treatment, chiefly brought about because a group had been singled out for special treatment? He questions which aspect of the special treatment produced the good effects: the smaller classes, the carefully picked teachers, the special efforts to involve parents, the trips? He contends that it is especially important to isolate approaches that can be used on a large scale in the everyday school setting, where enormous amounts of money, resources, and energy cannot be poured into a relatively small area as they were in the Higher Horizons Program.

His chief criticism of the program is that it fails to take cognizance of the positive aspects of the life of the so-called lower-class culturally disadvantaged child. He senses a patronizing attitude in the Higher Horizons Program which does not put any blame on the school for ignoring or alienating this population group, but which tends to blame the cultural poverty of the child for his problems in the traditional school system. Akin to this is the desire to educate the child primarily in the artistic-literary area, with consequent lack of emphasis on the social and physicial sciences. There is the desire to expose the child to "good" music and plays without considering how congruent these "enrichment" experiences might be with the existing culture and values of the child. Likewise the program does not emphasize minority group traditions or contributions. In general, it does not seek out or stress the culture, the coping mechanism, or the positive elements of the underprivileged culture.

One of the participants at the conference on the educationally disadvantaged was John Niemeyer, who reported on the experimental projects and research of the Bank Street College of Education (New York City.)[10] Excerpts from his report are given below.

---
[10] John Niemeyer, "Some Guidelines to Desirable Elementary School Reorganization," in U. S. Office of Education Bulletin 17 (Washington, 1963), pp. 80–85.

"Some of the experimental projects and research which Bank Street College has recently been conducting will be briefly described here, because they seem particularly pertinent to the topic before this conference and because they may suggest various lines of new action and thought. . . .

"Since 1943, Bank Street has worked cooperatively with the Board of Education of New York to improve a number of elementary schools, many located in crowded, low socioeconomic neighborhoods in the city. In 1957 the superintendent of schools invited Bank Street to try to help a cluster of three integrated elementary schools to strengthen their programs in various ways so as to (1) check the drift away from these schools of white middle-class families; (2) attract to the nearby middle-income housing development then under construction middle-class families with children who would, hopefully, enroll their children in these public schools. . . .

"The most important outcome of this project for Bank Street was the development of our hypothesis as to the cause of low achievement in schools of this kind and a general conclusion about what needs to be done to correct the situation.

"Our hypothesis is that the chief cause of the low achievement of the children of alienated groups is the fact that too many teachers and principals honestly believe that these children are educable only to an extremely limited extent. And when teachers have a low expectation level for their children's learning, the children seldom exceed that expectation, which is a self-fulfilling prophecy. A logical concomitant to this hypothesis is the conclusion that problems of these schools will not be solved simply through 'more services' or 'changing family backgrounds' *but through a functional, and probably structural, reorganization of the schools themselves.* [emphasis supplied].

"The following areas should be scrutinized for needed reorganization:

1. The child, his teacher, and the teaching-learning program

"An effective way to start would be for a school to take a hard look at everything it does and every aspect of the curriculum. It cannot do this productively without looking at the children and asking the question: 'What are the interests and needs, the motivational forces for learning, the learning-pattern with which these children come to school? Is it not possible that these children have resources for the educational program which do not depend on books, or the arts, or intellectual conversation in the home? May it not be that these children have a deep foundation for educational growth in their day-to-day social experience in urban life? And how can the school, without relinquishing its long-range goals, change its approach so as to take advantage of the true educational potential of these children?

"A few of the projects which Bank Street is engaged in at this moment seem particularly relevant to this first area of reorganization:

"*Multiculture 'readers' project.* — One specific way in which schools have unconsciously augmented feelings of alienation is by introducing children to the world of reading and books through readers which hold up as an exclusive model the culture pattern of the white middle-class suburban family. . . . Consequently, Bank Street has a team of writers working to produce readers which will use stories and illustrations to reflect back to children the positive aspects of the variety of community and cultural settings which constitute American society. These will not be books written specifically for minority or low-income groups, but will be books for and about all children. . . .

"*School entry study.* — This is a research project studying the relationships among such factors as home background, method of entry into kindergarten, the type of kindergarten program, and apparent success of adjustment to the school world on the part of the child. Both middle and lower social class children are involved, and the public school kindergartens which serve as locations are very different in character. From this study should come helpful hints for curriculum changes at the kindergarten level.

"*Classroom processes study.* — In four public schools offering contrasts in racial and socioeconomic settings, the classroom life of four second-grades and four fifth-grades has been examined to clarify mental health implications for children. The report from this study . . . should reveal possibilities for beneficial changes in school practices. It will also probably provide a new procedure by which schools can analyze a classroom in terms of its learning climate.

2. *The school's role vis-a-vis parents and community*

"This is the second area for reorganization. . . . Each school operating in a deprived neighborhood needs to work cooperatively with all of the agencies in that neighborhood. Further, certain schools will need to take on some of the responsibilities which usually are thought of as belonging to social agencies and not the school. One elementary school in Philadelphia, for example, has won the cooperation of police and milkmen to the extent that the school learns early in the morning of any child who has been locked out of his home for the night. Such a child is greeted by the principal, given a hot shower and breakfast, and put to bed for several hours. . . .

"All persons speaking at this conference have reported somewhat the same findings that Bank Street has gained: namely, that nearly all parents, even those who are severely alienated or defeated, look upon the school as the one source of hope that their children will have better lives than they have had. Nevertheless, the problem of how the school can help parents help their children in school is not an easy one to solve.

"Even though these parents look to the school with hope, many of them are fearful and confused in relation to the school. Furthermore, the school has difficulty in communicating with these parents. Sometimes there is an actual language barrier, but more often the chief barrier is stereotyped thinking on the part of both teachers and parents. There is also the communications barrier which separates different social classes. One mother speaking of a previous Parents Association meeting, said, 'In that there meeting the principal and all the teachers called us dopes — poor slobs that don't know what the kids are getting from school' To which the principal immediately countered, 'Why, Mrs. ——, you know very well that no one said anything of the kind in that meeting,' and the mother in question replied, 'Maybe you didn't say it, but that's what the atmosphere said.' However correct or incorrect this parent was in her perception, it is clear, that communication between her and the professional staff would be difficult. Two of Bank Street's present projects may be of interest here.

"*The Teacher-Parent Communication Study.* — . . . In the first phase of the project, most of the kindergarten and first-grade teachers, faced with the necessity for holding periodic conferences with their pupils' parents, worked with the Bank Street team to try to understand the obstacles to effective communications. They evaluated all contacts between the school and parents. . . and the Bank Street team attempted to affect the attitude of the teachers by broadening their cross-cultural understandings. In the second phase of the program, which is now in progress, the attention of the Bank Street team was turned more to the total school situation. Depth interviews have been held with 44 parents. An effort has been made to study the implications of pupil turnover and all the subtle and overt ways in which the school deals with parents.

"The plan for the coming year will also include experimentation with a research educator and licensed teacher in the role of assistant to the principal in improving the communications between the school and the parents of the school's children.

"*Study of a parent's association in relation to the total system of a school.* — In one of the projects located in a school within a low socioeconomic neighborhood, the attempt is to facilitate change by working with classroom teachers, the principal and the parents. A research educator with much experience in schools has been assigned to work with the very active Parents Association. The leadership of the association, mostly Negro, is troubled, as is the school principal, about the fact that only a small proportion of the parents participate in the activities of the association. The researcher has assisted the parent committee and, having won its confidence, is now interviewing other parents to ascertain their attitudes toward the school and the Parents Association. . . . One of the purposes of the total project is, of course, to devise better ways for the school to stimulate the kind of participation which gives positive support to the learning of the children in school.

3. *The internal organization of the school as an entity and as a part of a system*

"A third area calls for scrutiny. The school in its effort to educate the 'disadvantaged' must begin to study itself as a social system. An individual school is a small culture in and of itself; as such, it may operate in certain ways which prevent many of its pupils from realizing their true learning potential. Here is one very practical example: many schools unconsciously seem to put out an 'unwelcome mat' for parents. A parent who comes to one of these schools enters the school office and is faced with a long counter, behind which there are three or four secretaries. No one is set up as a receptionist. No names are in evidence. The parent may stand for a long time, shifting from foot to foot, before anyone comes to inquire as to his or her mission, let alone to extend a welcoming hand and smile. Yet the secretaries in question are friendly, warm people, devoted to the school and their work. What has happened is that somehow, subtly, there has been built into the system of the school a deep impersonality in terms of relationships between the school and the parents. Another example, much more serious perhaps, is the condition which exists in most school systems by which each lower rung on the bureaucratic ladder is led to believe that its purpose is to serve the rung immediately above. Somehow, down at the very foot of the ladder is the child in the classroom. . . .

"Equally important to knowing what changes should take place within our schools is knowing how change can be brought about in the schools and particularly in the school systems of our large cities. We are all familiar with many of the ways in which educators have traditionally worked to bring about change. Among these methods are inservice courses, the study of children and children's behavior by small groups of teachers, conferences and workshops, assistance to teachers, demonstration schools and classes, bulletins of curriculum bureaus, dicta issued by the superintendent, and so forth. A recent report done for the Commissioner of Education in New York State takes the position that change can be brought about in a school system only if those in high authority require the change and if they simultaneously provide teachers with demonstration units which offer proof that all of the teachers can do what the demonstration unit is doing. This is not a new approach to the process of change in education, even though the author of this particular report would have the goals for change established through research. The prevailing method being used in the programs attempting to upgrade schools in the economically depressed neighborhoods of our big cities is to saturate these schools with all kinds of 'special services.' It remains to be seen whether the chief change which will result will be upgrading of children's learning or the elimination of the responsibility of the classroom teacher for the learning of each pupil.

"The truth is that the process of change is baffling to our large school systems. This process is one which Bank Street is studying intensively. Our hypothesis is that the most productive kind of change process is that which involves intervention at many points in the social system called a school. This calls for actual experimentation. In the school mentioned above in relation to our study of the Parents Association, Bank Street is quite obviously attempting 'to intervene,' as the researchers say, at all levels of this particular school. Principals in schools like these who wish to bring about change are often baffled by what seems to them to be teacher indifference, if not opposition. The teachers, on the other hand, frequently feel that the principal is interested in his pet projects but does not pay attention to the changes which they, usually as individuals, wish. The parents, or at least the active parents, finally feel obligated to participate in the school but usually do not know why they are participating, and unless they are middle-class parents, for whom having an organization in itself is a satisfying aim, they do not know how to proceed vis-a-vis the principal and the teachers. In a school such as this it is quite apparent that the traditional procedures for attempting to bring about change or to introduce innovations may not be effective. The Bank Street effort to work for change in all phases of the school simultaneously, therefore, may well open up productive new approaches to the problem. . . . ."

PART IV
ADOLESCENTS AND ADULT AUTHORITY

INTRODUCTION

Many of the stories in this manual deal with junior and senior high school students, that is, those in early and middle adolescence. It is well to remember that these young people are undergoing certain marked psychological processes typical of this period which greatly affect their behavior within the school. (See the excerpts from an article by Erik Erikson at the end of Part IV.)

Adolescence falls roughly into two periods, each with its special concerns. In early adolescence youngsters wonder: Will I make it with my peers? Am I like others my age? Hence, the tremendous dependency on peer approval, and the tendency to join with other adolescents in admiring or, more often, in opposing certain adults. The young adolescent either idolizes uncritically, or rejects completely. There seems to be little or no middle ground. Teaching this age group, more than any other calls on the teacher as a total person, for he is going to be reacted to as a total person. As the young adolescent, in his own confusion, looks for security, he wants his adults to be all of a piece, and, above all, not to make him feel more insecure than he already is. This does *not* mean that the teacher needs to have all the answers, but it does mean that adolescents trust that person who "comes clean" with them. Hypocrisy is the main danger in relations between adolescents and adults. It stands to reason, therefore, that the youngster who, in his elementary school days has lost confidence in his own ability to learn and communicate with others, will be the adolescent who most easily feels left out by his peers and snubbed by adults. He is apt to react either by withdrawal, truancy, sullenness, or by aggressively covering up his insecurity with open hostility and taunting. To the further confounding of adults, some youngsters alternate between both patterns.

Whereas the early adolescent is primarily concerned with peer approval and with adults as heroes or villains, the older adolescent is worried about his place in the world of adults. Will he be able to earn respect? Will he be able to get a job? Will he be ready to start a family? An adult community which claims it has the answers when it often does not further alienates the youth who, earlier, has already begun to doubt his own powers to cope with the world. In our present educational set-up, we have too few signposts which clearly spell out to young people that they are on the right track. Hence, their insistent questioning of what and how we teach them. Is it really going to prepare them for the tasks ahead? Any teacher who works with high-school age youngsters has to come to grips with such questions.

Although the teacher may want to rebuild the personalities he encounters into reasonable facsimiles of his own ideal self, he will find this impossible. His most appropriate strategy is to develop a variety of systems of communication that work within limits acceptable to both the student and himself, and that permit him to convey comparatively neutral ideas and information to the student. This will permit the adolescent gradually to orient himself, with his personality only slightly modified, in a way that is socially acceptable.

Whatever tight little schemes the teacher devises he must be prepared — because of the complexity of all children — to have his schemes break down, and often when he least expects them to. Perhaps the inconsistent behavior that most confounds the teacher is when the meek rebel. Their rebellion ought to be a warning against stereotyping the members of a given class. Generalizations concerning adolescent reactions to adults can help the teacher to understand and to establish communication with those who seem reluctant to learn, but rigid stereotyping of a particular child can only feed the animosity between teacher and child and prevent the teacher from taking advantage of unanticipated but promising deviations from a generally consistent pattern.

A number of the school anecdotes in our stories derive part of their drama from conflict between student and teacher. Occasionally, the conflict seems almost deliberately provoked by the teacher. Although deliberate provocation of a student by a teacher is probably rare, unintentional provocation is common and could be equally destructive of the learning situation.

An acceptable, as well as a fairly common definition of the role of the teacher sees him as possessing knowledge, skill, and understanding that are valuable and that he is willing to transmit to others on his own terms. The teacher derives part of his power to dictate the terms through his possession of this valuable knowledge, skill, and understanding. He also stands guard at the major access routes to the more desirable vocations and especially controls access to the further education that must precede entry into many of these vocations. Although he wears no uniform, he does carry a powerful weapon — the gradebook. The power of the teacher tends to be neutralized if the boy or girl placed in his class does not value what the teacher has to offer and has no desire for entry into a vocation that requires further education.

Even though the child may value knowledge and want further education, he undoubtedly has many other wants and desires, and their insistent clamor may deflect his attention from goals that are necessarily distant. Teachers make use of punishments such as withdrawal of approval, isolation from the group, and threats of unfavorable reports to parents to counteract the immediate demands made by the student which teachers see as inimical to learning. By so doing, a teacher hopes to direct the attention of the learner once more to distant goals, and by restoring the situation to one conducive to successful learning to provide the student with an opportunity to sense the immediate and intrinsic rewards of increased knowledge, understanding, and skill. Unless the child has established within himself a strong awareness and acceptance of such distant goals as a good job or further education after high school, the teacher does not wield enough authority in his relationship with the child to use punishment as an inducement to learn.

He may use it to maintain order in the situation so that others may learn, or he may use it to maintain his status as a figure of authority.

Although both withdrawal and aggressive behavior are disturbing to the authoritarian teacher, he is unlikely to want to punish except for aggressive behavior. Before he decides to do so, he should consider a wide variety of consequences. Adolescents from all social groups engage in deviant aggressive behaviors when they are provoked. However, children from lower-class cultures sometimes engage in aggressive behavior as a habitual personal response with little or no provocation. Such behavior leads to the solution of problems deriving from their inclement social environments, and problem-solving anywhere is intrinsically rewarding. Among such behavior might be the use of profanity and other nonintellectual means of verbal domination such as shouting; physical aggression directed against peers, or as a last resort, against the teacher, with or without the use of weapons; insolent use of the body such as swaggering by boys or wearing very tight short skirts and tight sweaters by girls; laughter, at inappropriate times or in an inappropriate manner, raucous and derisive; and, perhaps hardest of all to withstand, intellectual verbal domination deriving from special knowledge of technical or a foreign language, or semi-intellectual domination such as repartee. The last mentioned may appeal so strongly to the "good" class members that they temporarily desert the teacher by becoming neutral or even indulging in treasonable laughter.

The teacher can either ignore aggressive behavior, punish it or somehow make use of it. Successful teachers often try to ignore it if it is not too shocking or too long continued. Most profanity seems, since World War II, to be slipping into the category of being not too shocking. Female teachers appear to become more upset by its use than male teachers. It should be recognized that children who come from lower-class homes often have been raised with words commonly considered "profane" as part of their natural home environment. Thus, these children do not realize the impact that their use of these words has on school personnel and others outside of their home and neighborhood. The teacher will want to discuss the use of profanity with the class from time to time for the sake of maintaining a standard of conduct, but the time for discussion is not when some uncouth child has tried to rock the class and upset the teacher by coming out with it. To meet an outburst of profanity with dead silence can be most effective. But this also requires that the teacher have a repertoire of techniques with which to recapture the attention of the class. Announcement, in an even voice, of the details of an impending examination, discussion of a concert, play or athletic contest, assignment of homework, or seatwork, or other significant change in the current classroom activity may be successful. The occasion when the teacher can actually capitalize on the occurrence as Betty Klar does in "Tough Guys," a story in this Part, is likely to be rare.

On the other hand, the class will find it difficult to support the teacher in ignoring the incident if they see that the teacher is genuinely put out by the profanity. Perhaps teachers should be trained in not displaying signs of agitation. Serene poise seems to be one of the attributes of the experienced teacher. In Kipling's *Stalky and Co.*, the students at Sandhurst, the British Military College, decided to use the cadet corps for just this kind of training. The uniformed boys lined up and took turns giving each other the worst tongue-lashing they could invent. The first to turn red was considered to have lost the encounter. The boys (Stalky and Co.) were children of military men and knew from experience that this kind of training would protect them from attacks by sadistic officers. Kipling did not emphasize the peculiar verbal skill the boys would develop for themselves when they, in turn, were assigned authority over others.

In all encounters with aggressive students, the cooperative teacher has striking advantages over the authoritarian teacher. In the first place his need to punish students is less insistent. He can withstand far more aggression from unwilling learners without losing face with the rest of the students, because he has no façade of authority that can be undermined. This does not mean that he is unlikely to have authority so far as the students are concerned. But it will more likely be an authority achieved as he helps students to cope with perplexities that they themselves perceive, rather than a legal authority deriving from his status and position as teacher.

All teachers use cooperation and all teachers exert authority. Some are more cooperative than authoritarian, and vice versa. An acceptable role for the teacher would see him cooperating with the student in a quest for knowledge and understanding. This role is currently less fashionable than the role of the teacher as authority, because a number of people, presently vocal, see authority as a prerequisite of school learning.

The cooperative teaching role is much more difficult to play than the more traditional authoritarian one; it is therefore not surprising that it has been played badly perhaps more often than it has been played well. Much of the current disrepute into which "progressive education" has fallen can be traced to sentimental and even fatuous portrayals of the role. Pandemonium in the classroom, sharing of ignorance, and other ways of "wasting the taxpayers' money" can all occur when what the teacher thinks is cooperation turns out to be *laissez-faire*.

A consideration of the teaching role as cooperative can lead to a more effective teacher interaction with children from cultural minorities. The goal of such interaction is a commitment on the part of the student to educational development.

The suggestion that teachers begin "where the pupils are" has been received in a variety of ways. Provisions such as ability grouping, grade placement, entrance examinations, and a range of electives are only partially successful in reducing the range of differences confronting a given teacher. Successful teaching requires that the teacher determine the development level of each student. If the student perceives the teacher as one who is helping him to do what both agree to be important, more frank reporting can be expected from the student than when he sees the teacher as taskmaster.

Beginning where the pupil is does not mean following the lead of the student. But the approach of patient explanation of alternatives, clear elucidation of consequences, and demonstration of links between what the teacher proposes and the pupil's past experience is quite different from that which asks the student to work in order to please the teacher whom he loves, or hates.

In many schools the cumulative folder follows the student through each grade making his past record available for the teacher's perusal. Such records can greatly help or hinder the student depending on how they are used. If the student's past experiences only serve to label or stereotype him, much damage may be done. If such information is used as an indicator of problem areas to be worked on, then the records may serve a very positive function. The uses of I.Q. and other test scores have already been discussed. (See Part II.)

A factor that weighs heavily in the evaluation of teachers is the ability to maintain order in the classroom. It is generally assumed that learning cannot proceed if the level of noise and movement is beyond the control of the teacher.

When children are uncommitted to the work of the classroom, the teacher must use power to maintain order. Different teachers use different weapons. Probably all teachers make some use of a charisma deriving from their students' affection for them. This effect can be expected to satisfy certain needs on the part of both the students and the teacher, but is at best a prop with which to initiate learning. It may be irrelevant, and at worst, it can prevent the student from becoming independent. Sooner or later, the student must work quietly and diligently at his studies because he wants to achieve mastery and not because he loves, or fears, his teacher. The teacher who works side by side with the pupil in a quest that both regard as significant may be in a position to see when to withdraw and when to interfere. The relationship to the pupil must be such that he is able to withdraw. The teacher must generate an interest in his students for learning itself. Special activities and propects can help promote such interest in the subject materials. Sincere enthusiasm on the part of a teacher is quickly recognized by students.

If the teacher sees the need to maintain himself as an authority for disciplinary purposes, he is likely to pretend to greater knowledge than he commands. This can be done subtly as well as crudely, especially by the teacher who is genuinely well informed. Already, his achievements may seem beyond the reach of all but the best of his students. The teacher working beside individual students on a broad range of problems quickly learns the futility of building an ideal image. By giving the student a more realistic view of scholarship, he may encourage him to continue working.

The chief argument put forward for cooperative as opposed to authoritarian teaching is that in a world of flux one of the major goals of education is to enable children to reflect upon their experience and to build new interpretations leading to fresh choices. Even those who see man's actions as arising largely from his feelings must admit that there is scientific evidence available to show that feelings can be modified to some extent by means of contemplation and rational thought. In choosing between the roles of authoritarian and cooperative teacher one should consider which capacity will best enable pupils to engage in reflective thought. The best teachers will probably play a variety of roles, depending on which method works with a given child.

Carl Werthman[1] has discussed attitudes of gang members in a San Francisco high school toward the school and teachers. These students do not *a priori* accept the authority of any teacher. They base their judgments of the legitimacy of the teacher's authority on four main criteria:

1) They evaluate the jurisdictional claims, and will accept the teacher's right to veto certain actions that he considers detrimental to classroom progress if he can give "good" reasons for his position.
2) The teacher must not give attention or differential treatment on the basis of the race, dress, hairstyles, or mental capacities.
3) Teachers who *request conformity* are more likely to be accepted than those who consistently use the imperative, *demanding submission*.
4) The chief criterion of the legitimacy of the teacher's authority is his manner of grading. Students survey and compare grades to see if they agree with the evaluation. Grades must be given out fairly. If this is not done, they feel that the teacher has perhaps tried either to bribe them for better deportment, punish them for malconduct, or just treat them randomly.

The lower-class youngster does not resist authority as such because he has experienced and accepted authority within the primary structures of the family, and frequently, the church. He does, however, resist authority within a formal and impersonal bureaucratic power structure, especially when such authority appears to be arbitrary, random, or unfair.

Many persons who have dealt with hard-to-reach adolescents have pointed up the necessity for the authority figure to be noncoercive in regard to values, playing "straight" — being honest and one's self, and not promising goods or services one cannot honestly give. If the teacher plays a role, it must be consistent and true to himself, as well as to his students.

In the following story, "Mistake," the lack of planning and the anticipation of unpleasantness at a school dance turn it into an unfortunate affair for both students and faculty.

"Psychology" depicts the situation of a capable girl who must take much responsibility in her home, but who is not given it by a teacher who feels that her class is not ready for the realities of the subject of

---
[1] Carl Werthman, "Delinquents in Schools: A Test for the Legitimacy of Authority," *Berkeley Journal of Sociology*, VIII (1963), 39–60.

psychology. A foil for this teacher is presented in the person of an imaginative mathematics teacher who is creative in his teaching and gives his students projects which offer them substantial opportunities for growth.

"Tough Guys" illustrates the variety of teachers' attitudes toward a hard-to-reach student. One sensitive, devoted teacher reaches him through her consideration of his interests and needs, and her ability to cope with his aggression.

"MISTAKE"

"When the jungle begins to take over, put a stop to it!" Miss Hardin tossed her grey head in the direction of the auditorium floor where several dozen junior high couples were stamping and whirling rhythmically to a lively record of shrieking music. There was a controlled smile on her lips, but her jaw was very firm and her voice determined.

"We'll keep an eye on the monsters," said big Tom Trayner, laughing good-humoredly. He really hadn't the slightest intention of interfering with the students' dancing, and the choice of records was up to the student committee, as far as he was concerned.

"Things'll be okay," added Marge Milding, "we'll keep the lid on." The third teacher assigned to supervise, Art Hobble, turned away to station himself at the far side of the room. Miss Hardin, with hesitation and reluctance, walked to the door and left the auditorium just as another group of excited youngsters burst through, some wiping the last trace of their lunch from their lips.

"Hardy is afraid Africa will take over every time we let them have a noon dance," Marge laughed, her grey eyes sparkling. (Tom found her neat blue coat beautiful against her blonde hair.)

"So they get biological when the beat gets bold and the blood is up! Has nothing to do with race. Caucasian kids like body movements and friction just as much as the others. It's hot youth, trying to stay that way in this chilly old auditorium." Tom looked down at Marge; their eyes met, and she looked a little embarrassed. She threaded her way over to the table where the student body secretary was operating the record player. She set her bag down, smiled at Judy, took out a coin and got herself a Coke from the machine. The room was crowded with young people, only some of whom were dancing. Of the hundred-odd students, about a dozen were Negro. There were a few Orientals, and the rest were Caucasian. Some were clean and well-dressed. Others were rather shabby. There were at least twice as many girls as boys, and most of the girls were much taller than their partners. Some girls danced together.

On the far side of the room, Art was marching up and down, overseeing the students very closely. Tom, on the other hand, was leaning against the wall chatting with a cluster of girls. Marge took a big swallow of Coke and caught herself moving smartly to the quick music. She'd like to dance a little herself.

"Keep your hands off me!" Marge heard the angry exclamation and saw a commotion at the far side of the room. Art was holding the arm of a tall, thin Negro boy who was struggling and whirling around the big teacher. Art moved him to the door, but the dancing broke off as other students pushed around to watch. Before Marge could do a thing, Judy stopped the record and stepped to the microphone.

"All right, people, let's have your attention!" Her voice was serious and confident. She waited until she had silence. "Miss Hardin has been worried about the way we dance. . . . " A chorus of groans and snorts of disgust interrupted her. She waited. "Well, anyway, Miss Hardin thinks we don't know how to dance properly." A couple of guffaws. "Let's prove we can. Now, the next record."

The dance went on. Marge moved over to the circle of students around Tom and worked her way to him. When she spoke, the students withdrew, and some began dancing.

"What was the fuss with Art?" she asked. "No big thing," Tom shrugged. "He didn't like the way Larry was moving. Grabbed him, and that set Larry off. As far as I could see, he was dancing about like everyone else. So, maybe his id was a little active, and his libido was running loose. Art's a little tight, you know, but Hardy wants us to get the ones like Larry."

"Larry's all right, he just dances a little wild. . . ." Marge's voice trailed off. She was sorry Larry was in trouble again. She didn't think he deserved to be. Just then Art came in the far door, a little red in the face. With a determined stride, he crossed to the front of the room, ignoring Judy. He stopped the record in the middle of the dance and shouted into the microphone:

"Boys and girls, we're not going to have any more Congo Crawling. We'll dance like ladies and gentlemen, or we won't dance at all." A number of girls caught their breaths indignantly, and several boys booed. One near Tom shouted, "Horse crap!"

Heavy silence fell. Then over the mike, Art shouted to Tom, "Nab that meatball!"

Before Tom could do anything, a tall blonde boy walked over to him and stood patiently, his hands in his pockets. "It was me," he said simply. Tom tried to hide his annoyance at Art's order as he turned with the young man toward the door. "Come on," he said.

"Now," said Art, and paused, "we can have a dance, I said *dance,* or we can go on out and wrestle on the playground or in the gutter somewhere. We won't have any more nonsense in this auditorium! Which shall it be?"

Judy, the red-haired mistress of ceremonies, stood beside the record player forlornly, her hands dangling awkwardly at her sides. Marge tried not to look at any of the students who knew her. There was a long silence. Several boys quietly slipped out, some by one door and some by another. Then Art turned to Judy, "Go ahead and play them some decent music, and let's see if they can dance decently."

Judy's voice quaked a little as she announced, "Okay, people, here's. . . ."

Just before the end of the dance, Miss Hardin came in to check. Now only about fifty students were left in the room, with perhaps ten boys among them. All of the Negro boys had gone, but several Negro girls remained. Two were dancing together. Tom was back, looking despondent. Art stood near the mike and watched the students closely. Two other teachers were also on hand, but there was no need for them. They were seated in the back, talking to themselves and laughing. Marge thought of her bag, went to pick it up, and then, checking, was shocked to find her coin purse missing. In dismay and disbelief she told Miss Hardin.

"That does it!" Miss Hardin's eyes flashed fire. "Animal cavorting and petty thieving. We've had enough for one day. This is the end of noon dances." She rushed to the microphone and declared, "Something has been stolen! No student will leave the room until it has been found! The dance is ended. Take seats and sit quietly until the stolen property is returned. There will be absolutely no talking."

For several minutes the students sat in silence while the teachers and their vice-principal talked in low tones near the microphone. Judy had been sent to sit among the others toward the back of the room. She was not under suspicion, really; still, she was the only student who had been near the bag all the time. No other student seemed to have been there except fleetingly while dancing. There was a great deal of anxiety on many faces, and some anger. Judy, social secretary of the student body, finally came up to ask Miss Hardin what had been taken and if the student government could do anything about it.

"Never mind, honey," Miss Hardin said, sweetly, "we'll handle the matter ourselves." More firmly. "The thief knows what he has taken. You go ahead and sit down with the others."

For the tenth time, Marge searched her bag furiously, but in vain. The coin purse was gone. She was sorry to lose the five dollars, but she was even more unhappy to see the student dances end in such a negative, unnecessary way. She was ashamed to look at the cluster of students in the back of the room, their pale faces registering silent humiliation or suppressed fury. She knew several of these girls.

"Take the boys to Room 10 and see what you can get out of them," Miss Hardin directed Art Hobble. He moved away briskly to perform his task.

"Let me see what I can do alone with the girls. You can get back to your work. I have a free period next anyway. Let me try," pleaded Marge, who felt miserable at what she had set in motion. Miss Hardin agreed to let her try. As the other teachers left, Tom turned to her with a pained look and cheered, "Good luck!"

Marge spoke briefly to the students. She was sorry about what had happened. She wanted to help them repair whatever damage had been done, to make future dances possible and to continue and improve the good feelings and relationships among students and between students and the faculty. If someone had taken something, would they return it? If they would, she promised nothing further would be done or said about it. She would leave the room. While she was gone, each student, individually, would file through the cloak room, at one end of the auditorium, and leave anything she had taken in the basket on the table. Judy, as student body social secretary, would be in charge. There would be no reprisals. When Marge had finished, she slipped through the door hiding her face in her handkerchief. She was near tears. The girls were very serious and still.

Ten minutes later, when Marge returned, the girls were tense with expectation. Judy stood before them, her face a mixture of pride and shame. Marge checked the cloakroom. Four articles were in the wastebasket. A black Parker pen, with a broken clip. A new tube of vermilion lipstick. One new notebook of the kind the school issued to students. And a brand new package of crayons. There was no wallet.

As Marge turned to leave the cloakroom, Alice slipped inside. She was a gentle little girl, shy, not very able, but very cooperative, a member of Marge's third-period social studies class. Now she looked at Miss Milding, with a tear coursing down her dark cheek.

"I'se very sorry, Miss. I took that notebook and colors. I took them from your desk before lunch. I snuck them into my folder. I los' my notebook and wanted to do good this report card time. I was gonna use the colors for maps and things. I'se sorry, Miss, really sorry."

Marge shook her head, trying to wipe away the whole incident as well

ADOLESCENTS AND ADULT AUTHORITY

as to tell the girl she was forgiven. "It's all right." was all she could say. She jammed her hands deep into her coat pockets and turned aside as Alice backed away. Marge's left hand struck something familiar, but unusual, something out of place. Then she remembered. In her excitement when Art caught Larry, she had dropped her coin purse into her coat pocket.

* * *

QUESTIONS FOR WRITING AND DISCUSSION

1. Comment on the attitudes shown by Miss Hardin, Tom, Marge, and Art. From their behavior at the dance, what kind of teacher would you expect each to be? What kind of relationship with their students would you expect?
2. How do you feel about holding school dances? What is their purpose? Do you see a way in which this difficulty over the types of dancing can be handled with less conflict? If so, how?
3. What do you think of the way the supposed theft was handled in general? What do you think of Marge's method with the girls? How would you have handled a similar situation? What are your ideas about the handling of theft in the school?
4. In Marge's position, what would you have done after discovering there had been no theft? Is there a conflict between what teachers in such a position *should* do and what they could reasonably be expected to do?
5. What image do many of the faculty seem to have of the students? What are their fears? What basis do their fears appear to have in fact?
6. What do you gather about the racial and socioeconomic make-up of the school? Does this enter into the peer student-faculty relations? How?
7. How does self-image enter into this story? What do you suppose the students reactions are to the dancing limits, to the "theft"?
8. What do you see as the basic conflict in this story: divergent cultural values or adolescent vs. adult values? Explain.

COMMENTS

The incidents in this story cast a disturbing light on the way in which negative student-teacher relationships evolve. The lack of advance planning, the underlying sexual overtones, and the evident disrespect for differences of values are all contributing factors.

Five aspects of this story stand out as requiring a closer look: (1) the purposes of extracurricular activities; (2) rules for organizing extracurricular activities; (3) the role and function of teachers and administrators in extracurricular activities; (4) the attitude of school personnel toward the students; and (5) the problem of stealing in the school.

Extracurricular activities such as athletics, school dances, or special interest clubs provide an opportunity for the child to put into practice the ideas, theories, and facts he has been exposed to in the classroom. By participating in these activities the student is able to put into action principles of good citizenship and democratic procedures. To study the United States Constitution and to read of the great heroes of democracy may have very little real meaning to the student; but to be able to test these ideas, under good supervision and guidance, gives the students a better understanding of their importance and function. In student government, clubs, and team sports, many decisions have to be made. In these student-centered organizations, self-reliance and self-direction, and independent thinking and action are encouraged.

Often teachers are not familiar with the cultural backgrounds and value systems of their students. A better understanding of these may help the teacher to select teaching techniques which will bring the best results from the students. Often the classroom does not allow adequate opportunity for both teacher and student to view each other as social beings. The extracurricular activities program provides this opportunity.

Once a school has clearly defined the aims and purposes of its extracurricular activities program, the next step is to establish rules for the organization of these activities. These need to take into account the idea of student-centered organization. The aim of the program in general and of each specific activity should be made clear to the teachers and the students. The selection of activities should be based on the real interests and needs of the students; as many of them as possible should be involved.

If in "Mistake" some of these steps had been taken the unfortunate central incident might not have occurred. The teachers had no clear understanding of their duties at the dance: Tom Traynor "really hadn't the slightest intention of interfering with the students' dancing. . . ."; Marge Milding was willing to "keep the lid on"; Art Hobble "was searching up and down, overseeing the students very closely"; and two other teachers were "seated in the back, talking to each other and laughing."

Very little planning, if any, had been done. Setting up the rules, selecting a theme, records, methods of discipline — all these things should have been agreed on before the dance and should have been well-known to student leaders, teachers, and participants. The planning of activities should be a cooperative venture. It should encourage student leadership and not faculty dictatorship. If a theme for the dance had been chosen beforehand, it would not have been necessary for Art to intervene, because the type of dancing would already have been established. If the records had been selected, preferably by the student leadership and subject to teacher review, then Art's statement "go ahead and play them some decent music, and let's see if they dance decently" would be out of order.

Formulation of rules of conduct and mode of dancing help to give both students and teachers direction. If "Congo Crawling" has been decided upon as an acceptable way of dancing, then the students should be allowed to perform it. If it has been declared unacceptable, then those students who prefer it probably would not attend. Teachers should be aware, however, of the current subcultural fads in dancing, and be tolerant of dance forms that may have been called alien, bizarre, or even obscene, in their day. The same relativity is called for in evaluating dances as in viewing adolescent dress or language.

Extracurricular activities can provide opportunities for development of better understanding and mutual respect between students and teachers. The reference to the students as "monsters," "meatballs," and "jungle denizens" by the faculty supervisors at the dance suggests that they do not hold the students in high esteem. Similarly, teachers must be sensitive to nuances in terminology referring to race or minority groups.

The attitude toward the students in this story is a somewhat confusing one. If the school had been predominantly Negro or predominantly lower class, one could explain the distrust by lack of understanding of varying racial or cultural values. But only a dozen of a hundred students at the dance were Negro, and many were described as middle class. What then led to the concern over the "jungle taking over," "Africa taking over," and "Congo crawling"? One possibility is that this is a changing neighborhood and so a changing school, and that the beginning of an influx of lower-class whites and nonwhites has threatened the security of the principal and some teachers. This period of changing student body make-up is frequently a difficult one. It is also possible that there is basically a lack of communication and understanding between the generations, an adolescent-adult conflict rather than a racial or cultural one.

Stealing is a knotty problem for the school teacher because each case may be unique. Students' motives for stealing may be very different, as well as reflecting differential concepts of regard for property. Some children who come from poor homes with large families are accustomed to freely using the property of others. They also expect others to use their possessions, meager as these may be.

On the other hand, some children who have a clear concept of what they are doing in taking another's property may do it deliberately for a variety of reasons. Some are "acting out" in compensation for problems at home. Some poor children steal so that they can have as much as their fellows, if they in fact do not. Others steal in order to give presents to their friends. Some steal to "get even" with other students or with the teacher. The causes are many and teachers should take this into account in dealing with theft. Some teachers who are able to ascertain the underlying reason for a theft will find a way to recover the lost article in such a way that the child who took it will not be identified. Since the school system may regard stealing as a very serious offense and since punishment may be severe to the point of suspension or dismissal, the teacher may wish to avoid reporting the offense to the office, but will, of course, discuss the matter carefully with the student, cautioning him about repeating the act. The actions of some students may warrant reporting.

"Mistake" includes an especially uncomfortable aspect to the stealing problem, since students have been publicly humiliated over a theft which actually did not occur. It is impossible to state what Marge should do. Art or Miss Hardin would undoubtedly dismiss the error with a comment to the effect that the students had probably stolen plenty of times when they hadn't been caught and that this was poetic justice. But Marge is shown as sensitive to the feelings of the students. Would she be able to see them punished by the loss of their noon dances for a crime she knew had not been committed? On the other hand, will she have the strength to admit that she has made an accusation of theft, with all its resultant unpleasantness, which was not warranted? To what extent is it necessary for a teacher to be right in order to maintain the respect of students? If the incident had taken place within her own class it is likely that Marge could tell the students of the mistake and apologize for having suspected them. It would be infinitely harder to do this when so many were involved, but if she could bring herself to do so, it is likely she would actually gain respect in the eyes of the majority of the students. One wonders, however, whatever Marge's decision, whether a Miss Hardin would allow her to let the students know that the whole episode had been unjustified.

"PSYCHOLOGY"

"Where's the mush?" A plump boy of eight perched on an unpainted stool before a battered red kitchen table, pounding rhythmically with a big tablespoon grasped in his little brown hand. "Where's. . . . ?"

"Patience, Hon. It's coming!" A buxom girl of sixteen slipped behind Tony to the gas range, patting his head as she passed. She brought a large aluminum saucepan over and ladled out big gobs of yellow corn meal mush to Tony and his sister Pearl who sat beside him. Pearl looked up at her older sister, her brown eyes full of thanks. Alice ladled herself a bowl of cereal and sat down beside them.

Tony was shoveling the mush down with concentrated determination. Bits of cereal missed and clung to his lips as he tried to maneuver the over-sized spoon. "You look nice, Hon," Alice turned to Pearl, and straightened the blue bow on her pigtails. Pearl didn't say a word, but her eyes were shining.

"How's Mom?" Tony halted his attack momentarily and turned to Alice.

"She'll be all right," said Alice, "I'll fix things up for her by her bed before I leave. You be sure and see her when you come home, before you go play. She might need something. Be sure."

"I will," said Tony, very seriously. "I will, too," said Pearl.

"Now, off with you, and don't get mussed up on the way to school." Alice made a last check of the pair. Tony's brown corduroys were thin and worn, and his blue shirt very faded. But his tennis shoes were clean, and the strings were tied. She grabbed a towel and wiped a smear of corn meal from his cheek. Pearl stood away from Alice, hands on hips, and posed for her inspection. She tossed her head prettily. Her pink dress was spotless and unwrinkled. Her smile was full of health and joy and the wide-eyed hope of a seven-year old. "Off with you, and check Mom when you get home!"

"We will, we will," chanted the pair as they tripped down the steps, past the rusting chassis of an old Ford, and along the path by the curb that served for a sidewalk. Standing in the doorway, Alice answered their last wave with a smile, then, closing the door, turned toward the bedroom where her mother lay. Her expression had become sober and thoughtful.

"Today, I think we'll start a new unit." said Miss Limon to her second period, tenth-grade homemaking class. Her voice sounded excited and eager, but faintly insincere. Students knew her as "sweet Limey." "We'll go over child care and on into basic principles of health and diet. Part will be review, but. . . . " Miss Limon was tired of explaining recipes and smelling burnt cookies. It would be a rest to shift to paper work. These girls clearly needed to know something about child care. Some of them would obviously be mothers soon. But it might be tough. They couldn't or wouldn't read much. Might be hard to hold their interest. Discussions tended to get out of hand. Still, they weren't so bad.

"Hey, can we have some of that psychology jazz Miss Jane gives her kids?" shouted one girl in the class.

"I hadn't thought we'd do anything with that." Miss Limon hesitated.

She didn't want to try psychology with this bunch. They didn't have enough ability in the first place. Brightest one here was Alice. She was verbal, *too* verbal in fact, but the records showed she had an I.Q. of only 99. Discussions of psychology could easily get out of hand. Too provocative. She hadn't any text for the subject. It wasn't part of the curriculum. They could get it in the twelfth grade. No. Not psychology for these. "We can talk a little bit about child development." Miss Limon tried to sound confident and determined, but she felt unsure.

"Shoot, we want psychology like the others get!" chirped another, a chubby girl with a big grin, who turned to work up support among the rest.

Miss Limon felt she must stop this immediately. They were not raising their hands. A class could get out of control *demanding* something. Two hands went up. Now was her chance, she could get them back. "Alice, what was your idea? Let's wait until they give you their attention."

"I think psychology would be interesting. It's related to child development. I was reading an article the other day about. . . ."

"That's enough, Alice. I'll decide." Very firmly. "We're going to drop this. We won't do psychology for several reasons. We haven't any materials on it. If we had, they'd be too hard for you to read. You'll get a chance to study psychology in the twelfth grade, if you stay 'til then. That's a good reason to work hard and stay in school. Besides, you're not ready for psychology. It's a mature subject." Limey stressed "mature" with a certain haughtiness.

"Miss Jane don't have no materials. She just makes up things. They talk. Shoot!" Other voices interrupted "We mature." This last set off giggles and snickers.

"That's *it*!" The "it" shrieked through the room. The twenty girls sat up straight. Limey was off again. No use making things worse. A few low whispers, then perfect silence. Limey stood motionless, her fiery eyes darting about the room, her fingers grasping the desk top behind her so tightly that her knuckles turned white. After a long minute, the class gradually relaxed and surrendered. Alice felt a little sorry for Miss Limon. She didn't care much about what unit they studied, really. Alice had already read half the paperbacks on psychology her college boy friend had given her. Miss Limon had handled things wrong. She just didn't know how to work with girls.

"Now, girls." Miss Limon spoke slowly, with studied confidence and deliberate sweetness, "Let's do a little reading first, about the needs of the child."

Third period Alice had Mr. Benedict for general mathematics. She had left three years of boring junior high school mathematics with a vague understanding of fractions and decimals, no more. Then something changed — taking care of the family, maybe, or Mr. Benedict, or Carl. Anyway, in three months she had mastered decimals and percent. Now she spent her evenings learning areas and volumes, working ahead on her own. Sometimes Mr. Benedict helped her after school; but mostly she was getting it herself. He had told her she had a mind for numbers. Now she was beginning to believe it. He was a wonderful man!

"Gang, first of the period," said Mr. Benedict, "let's work in teams. I'll explain some things to Harry's group, here at the blackboard. Janice's team go ahead working the examples on the board. If you get in trouble, Tom or Helen can help you. Let's keep the noise down. Alice's team in the back of the room, go ahead and see what you can do learning the circumference of circles. Alice knows. I'll be back after I get Harry's group to work. OK, gang?" Mr. Benedict was a big, good-natured, confident fellow, who seemed to assume everything would work. It usually did, in a casual way. The students liked him. Alice thought he was the best teacher she had ever had.

There were several minutes of turbulence, then things settled down. At the blackboard, Benedict was showing that 2/5 was the same as 40/100 by dividing up a diagram of a rectangle (a box of oranges) into five equal sections, with 20 oranges in each. Janice's group were working the blackboard examples. There was a lot of whispering and chatting. Some were obviously comparing each others' answers. Helen was helping a big boy with an athletic sweater. Tom finished the examples and buried himself in Mill's *Listen Yankee,* shrugging off another boy who asked his help. In the back, Alice tried to explain to the other five students.

"Well, you know, they call the distance around the circumference, and the distance across the diameter. Well, the formula is C, or circumference, is equal to pi, that's the thing you make like this, times the diameter. . . ." Alice turned from the board to her friends. "Huh?" grunted a big, smiling Mexican boy. "Tell me more!" said Pee Wee, a voluptuous blonde, with dreamy blue eyes.

Alice was exasperated. She had no idea how to go on. It was clear to her, but it was not clear to them. Was it C, or d, or pi, she wondered? Or, "formula"? Maybe none of them meant anything to her friends. Then she had an idea.

"Look, there's something crazy about any circle. You want to find out what it is?" They were not very interested, but they liked her because she was friendly, and her very excitement interested them a little. Alice ran to the front of the room, got the wastebasket, a tape measure, and a large round metal platter from the top of the filing cabinet.

"Now, look," she said, animatedly, "let's measure how far it is around each of these circles, both ends of the wastebasket and the platter. Then how far is it across each circle. Divide the distance across into the distance around. See what we get?" They huddled into two groups and started figuring, as Alice grinned to herself.

A few minutes later, when they compared their answers, they found they were all about 3.1. "That's the way it always is," Alice said triumphantly "and that's the way it always will be. Every time you do it with any circle, it will come out the same. Always 3.14. That's the nature of a circle. Well, the Greeks called that. . . ."

Suddenly Alice sensed someone behind her, towering over her. Mr. Benedict was grinning proudly. "OK, teach," he said, "now, what's a formula?" He was laughing, and the whole group laughed with him.

"Recipe for arithmetic!" Alice quipped. Mr. Benedict pulled up a chair and joined the circle around her.

QUESTIONS FOR WRITING AND DISCUSSION

1. From the opening scene what impression do you get of Alice's home life? At this point of the story, what would you expect of her as a student? Were your feelings later borne out or not?
2. Which things about Alice's home do you feel represent lower socioeconomic living? Which do not?

3. Discuss Miss Limon's handling of the change of units. Why did she reject her class's request to discuss psychology? Were her reasons sound? Was her attitude, both as a teacher and a person harmful to Alice? To the class as a whole? Why or why not?
4. Discuss Mr. Benedict's method, both in terms of teaching technique and relationship with the class. What do you think of his techniques for an average to low group? What drawbacks might there be, what advantages?
5. Discuss the importance of Miss Limon and Mr. Benedict as adult models for adolescents. Which of their attributes were especially good or bad for this age group?
6. Does the fact that a class consists of slow learners or children from a predominantly lower socioeconomic background limit the kinds of teaching methods that can be used? Illustrate your answer with reference to Miss Limon's and Mr. Benedict's approach to the same group of students.
7. To what degree do you feel the teacher should have control over the curriculum content and methods used; what decisions should be made by administration; should the students have a part in deciding?
8. Where do divergent cultural values, self-image, school process, and adolescent relationships each play a role in this story?

COMMENTS

Many of the culturally deprived children in our schools are the children of America's impoverished. But along with the many needs and lacks of the poor there are also considerable strengths which help to sustain their lives as they move and operate on the periphery of American society. Often, one of these strengths is a deep sense of family unity and family ties.

Alice is a girl from a very poor home who has managed, with help from her mother and family, to overcome some of the obstacles which stop so many young people like her. She has accepted responsibility, in both home and school, without developing negative attitudes. Homes with large numbers of children usually are so arranged that the older children are assigned vast amounts of responsibilities for care of their siblings, and for upkeep of the house. Some children resent these duties and view them as encroachments upon rights and freedoms which they should have. These resentments are likely to foment socially unacceptable behavior, while the responsibilities push them into adult roles which they are neither emotionally nor mentally ready to accept. Others, like Alice, take on an added maturity from such responsibilities, accepting them easily, and carrying the maturity over into other areas including their school life.

A great many children in the population group we call culturally disadvantaged have grown up in homes where there is often only one parent — more frequently the mother — and many brothers and sisters. There are certain advantages to growing up in a large family. Such children become self-reliant at an earlier age than children from small families and take on obligations within the family. There is a greater numerical potential for "togetherness" because children must play together and a paucity of money for toys often gives them the impetus to be creative in making up games and diversions.

These children may also have a variety of adults other than parents living with them: grandparents, aunts and uncles, or married siblings and their families. Yet the role of these adults as authority figures, vocational models, and sources of demonstrated affection and love is often meager. School guidance workers have pointed up the fact that many children coming from such homes are actually starved for relationships with adults. In their early years children want and need supplemental attention and love from adult authority figures other than their parents. But many of these children, denied such relationships, are often learning in an emotional vacuum as well as the intellectual vacuum they inherit from their home life and anti-intellectual subculture. In this regard smaller classes allowing them individual attention from the teacher would give them a closer relationship with an adult, as well as more concentrated academic training.

After the fourth grade, this receptivity to personal relationships begins to wane, and by the junior high level many of these children are emotionally withdrawn and sullen, compounding the problems of academic deficiencies. The avenues of personal approach are closed. After this point the importance of the peer group as the main social and psychological reference group increases. The often negative attitudes of the peer group toward authority figures, the school, and academic achievement militate against the establishment of individual relationships which could lead to constructive and supportive communication between teachers and students. Methods of getting to students to motivate them individually require sensitivity to the situation and the student, imagination, and often subtle strategies on the part of the teacher. Obvious overtures toward a student may put him at a disadvantage with his peers.

Some teachers have made subtle approaches to students by calling them in for extra instruction or to help with classroom chores after school. Over long periods such unobtrusive demonstrations of interest in a student's progress and future can do a great deal to motivate him. Other teachers state that the only model that can be effective at the junior or senior high level is an authority model outside of the school, or if it is one within the school, the attraction must be to the particular personality, athletic abilities, or special talents of the teacher. In this respect some Negro students have indicated that they would have been more at ease with Negro teachers and counselors if they had been available and willing to give extra help.

An alternative to attempting to develop one-to-one relationships at the higher grade level where this tends to be a difficult feat, is to create within the class an atmosphere of interest and warmth which both engages all the students in the subject matter and makes each one feel that the teacher has a special interest in him as an individual. Obviously the dynamics of this collective approach are difficult, and complicated by the fact that teachers frequently have very large classes which they meet for only one period a day.

The responsibilities of being a teacher, particularly in today's world, are great. In the past it was felt that the primary duty of the teacher was to teach the subject matter. The teacher of today has to "be many things to many students": a friend, a model to emulate, a disciplinarian, a parent substitute. Teachers meet these responsibilities in varying degrees according to their capacities and the demands of the particular situation.

The two teachers in "Psychology" are examples of different personality types and different approaches to teaching. Miss Limon appears to be uneasy with teaching and afraid of experiencing any uncontrolled situation with the students. She shows little imagination and she fears failure. Her response to this situation is particularly unfortunate. The class was interested and most likely would have gained a great deal from an introductory discussion of psychology. An effort to respond to this enthusiasm might have sparked added interest in other units of study. Miss Limon seemed pathetically unaware of the sophistication and maturity of many of her students in the practical affairs of life. These students need specific, accurate knowledge in areas such as psychology and sexual hygiene taught systematically by a person secure in her knowledge of herself and her subject matter.

Most teachers are symbols to children, but every now and then they encounter one whom they see as a person as well. Mr. Benedict seems to be this kind of teacher. To Alice "He was a wonderful man!" Unlike Miss Limon, he was a "good-natured confident fellow, who seemed to assume everything would work." He does not need to stand apart from the children and is therefore able to establish good rapport with them.

The teaching characteristics which prove most effective in working with children in general and with culturally deprived children in particular are many and varied. Some teachers say going strictly by the established curriculum plan is the best method of teaching. Others feel that the best way is to supplement the established curriculum with added materials as needed. Still others use the formal curriculum merely as a guide, and prepare a great deal of their own material or search out suitable material from other sources.

One reason Miss Limon was hesitant about teaching psychology to her tenth-grade homemaking class was the fact that "she hadn't any text for the subject. It wasn't part of the curriculum." Another was her low estimate of the ability and maturity of the students. If the teacher is unenthusiastic and has negative attitudes about her work and about the children, these attitudes are conveyed to the children.

Mr. Benedict, on the other hand, could operate without being bound by the limits of the formal curriculum plan. He could use extemporaneous devices and student study and work teams. His trust and sincere interest in the children created the kind of climate which encourages high achievement and high levels of aspiration. The problems involved for this type of teacher in the inherently conventional school system have already been discussed in Part IV, "The School Process." Since teachers in general need the support of their administration before feeling free to develop and use new styles of teaching, a great deal of in-service work with administrators in the area of the culturally divergent is needed. It is difficult to give up traditional methods, but since these methods have not succeeded with approximately one-third of our school population, nothing can be lost by trying new techniques. If they fail, schools are no worse off, and it they work, progress has been made. There would be many more Mr. Benedicts if his type of teaching were sought out, recognized, and encouraged.

The administration's role in supporting the teacher is not only in the trying of new techniques but in allowing him to fail with the confidence that he will not lose face and will be able to try again. Many successful teachers of culturally disadvantaged children began by having a very difficult time with discipline. But with support and understanding from their superiors who continued to stand by them through this difficult beginning period — which might last anywhere from a few months to a couple of years — they ultimately developed techniques for effectively maintaining control. After that point was reached, they became highly successful in motivating and teaching their classes, usually utilizing a definite structure and consistently enforced limits, within which boundaries an atmosphere of warm concern and permissive techniques flourished. Other new teachers have been let go because their superiors could not see beyond their inability to maintain discipline, even though they were highly motivated in working with these children, genuinely liked them and had faith in their ability to achieve, and had unusually good rapport with parents. In other words, through lack of encouragement by their superiors, teachers who had every potential for becoming the kind of teachers the disadvantaged need most were lost to the system.

We must not suppose, however, that Mr. Benedict's techniques are the only ones successful with the disadvantaged. Teachers must find and develop those methods which are most congenial and congruent with their own personalities, and there are numerous types of personalities who can work successfully with these children.

Frank Reissman[2] has described several of these types — each successful because of different elements in the teacher's personality and thus in teaching techniques.

One is compulsive, detailed and fussy, and tends to repeat the same thing over and over. The resulting structure, order, and constant repetition are elements to which disadvantaged children respond. Another is the strong, aggressive, self-confident person who sets distinct limits early and lets the children know he intends to teach them. He may not be popular but his students do learn, probably because his confidence in them helps their self-image. All too often they have received the impression in other classes that they can't be expected to learn anything.

Reissman also mentions other types with potential such as the person who is himself constantly inquiring, examining fresh ideas, and has a lot in common with young students, and whose eagerness carries through to them; the informal, earthy person who is physically expressive and so conducts his classes in the physical fashion lower-class children respond to; the quiet, sincere, calm teacher whose very dignity controls the teaching situation in a positive way; the colorful, dramatic person with a sense of humor, who can laugh with the class, involve them, and let them know that their opinions count; the relaxed, informal individual who lets them know that a teacher is human and can talk with them as one human to another; the true intellectual who is deeply interested in all kinds of knowledge, has broad horizons, and whose interests include many of those of his students.

---

[2] Unpublished paper, "Teacher Institutes: A Five Point Plan," July, 1964.

In short, no teacher who is sincerely interested in teaching the disadvantaged and who truly wants to understand them need worry that he isn't the "correct" type to work effectively with them. Most teachers can find elements in their own personality which can be adapted to teaching the educationally alienated child. One prerequisite to success, however, is a sympathetic understanding of the child and his background. Benedict's success in his classroom precedure points up the potential for teachers who attempt to use creative designs in teaching methodology, and the necessity for administrators who allow teachers to lay aside the standard books and use supplementary materials and techniques as discretion demands.

"TOUGH GUYS"

"They ought to throw his tail out of this school!" Jack Barry thrust the stub of his cigarette violently into the stale coffee in his saucer and twisted his lips angrily.

"Miss Goode wouldn't go along with that!" Bert Miller's voice became heavy with sarcasm. "We have to reach him, understand him, adapt."

"I tossed him out second period, and you tossed him out fourth. Maybe Goody will get tired of catching him on the bounce and send him home."

"Suppose he's one of the 'culturally deprived.' Needs special attention, spoon feeding, even if we have to neglect the others." Bert looked nervously around the teachers' lounge to see if they were alone. They were.

"Deprived? You mean depraved!" Jack responded. "Did you see his mother when she came last year? The father's worthless, never works, used to be a carpenter but finds it easier to lie around living off welfare. When his mother came to see the counselor, she was dressed to conquer. Dick was scared. Kept the door open the whole time, afraid she'd rape him."

"I remember her. She could support the family without moving a finger, but she might have to move something else a little."

Both laughed. "Who's that?" asked Ted Johnson, the big, burly shop teacher who had just come in and was pouring himself a cup of coffee.

"That Brewster kid's mother," said Jack. "We both had to toss that meatball out today!"

"Colored?" asked Ted.

"No, white, Shanty Irish, I guess. Lives down by the docks. Father alcoholic, mother makes a bit on the side. We've had others of that brood."

Just then Betty Klar came into the room, nodding a friendly greeting. As she put down her papers, Bert got up to get her coffee, which he served with a gallant flourish. She thanked him and lapsed into silence waiting for the men to continue their conversation. She had taught only a year. Originally from the slums of an eastern city, she had worked as a secretary at a naval base for a couple of years, saved her money, and worked her way through college. She was a vivacious and vital girl and attractive as well. Her charms were not lost on the faculty men.

"We were talking about Tom Brewster," said Bert, "but why spoil a beautiful afternoon with him. What did you. . . . ?

"Tom's an interesting young man. I have him for social studies sixth period." Betty's tone was noncommital.

"No!" exclaimed Jack, "*You* shouldn't have to put up with him. He should be given only to men teachers."

"Tom's no great problem." Betty said, but Jack interrupted her, his anger returning.

"Oh, yeah? He's about as smart as a moron, noisier than a clown, and dirtier than a pig. Ever read his record? I.Q. about 88. Expelled from elementary school for stealing. F's all through the seventh grade, promoted for size! Truant a dozen times since entering junior high; profanity, bullying, involved with some other boys in 'peeping' over at the housing project."

"I thought his I.Q. was 118." Betty was soft-spoken, gentle, somewhat tentative. "I think he has several scores ranging all over. He's big for his age, but still very young. He's had a lot of sickness, you know. Polio or something, that weakened his back. Lots of absences. Reads well, broke the test, but doesn't like the others to think he is able to do good school work. Wants to be an athlete, pretends to be strong, but his back stops that. He's noisy and rough, but it's mostly bluff."

"Don't make excuses for him, Betty." Jack's face was red. "He threw a compass across my math class and just missed striking a girl in the face."

"Well, he's on the warpath today," affirmed Bert. "Tried to carry a still across my science room and dropped it, breaking about fifteen dollars worth of glassware, then laughed, 'Easy come, easy go!' You'd better be ready for him!"

"Thanks. I'll keep an eye out," said Betty. "Say, did you get to the party last night? I couldn't make it, but I'm dying to hear how things went."

A few minutes later, Betty started down the hall to her sixth period class. She was no taller than the junior high school students. Only her smart suit and the reserved styling of her beautiful red hair distinguished her from the rest of the throng in the hurrying hall traffic. That and her big bundle of papers. Today they would go over Jackson's administration. She wasn't optimistic about interesting these students in that long ago era. She'd give them some study time, and she might be able to get something going about the reform movements — women's rights, slavery, prison reform — that might interest them.

There was a commotion up ahead, and she hurried along to see what was disturbing hall traffic. There was Tom, steaming through the others like Dewey through the Spanish torpedo boats, knocking everyone aside, and sometimes adding insult to injury by patting a boy on the head or jerking a girl's hair. Betty couldn't get to him, but his head was a foot taller than the others', and she could mark his path by the confusion, dismay, and anger that showed on students' faces. When she finally got to her room Tom was already there, in the middle aisle, waving his arms and shouting. Two boys were listening to his descriptions of a car he was helping a friend remodel, but the girls turned away in disgust at his untidiness, boisterousness, and conceit.

Miss Klar settled the class down, but had to caution Tom three times to quiet him. He respected her, but his respect did not curtail his noisiness. He liked her, but he was embarrassed to acknowledge it in any way. A student monitor took the roll, homework was passed forward and collected by another monitor, and the students went to work copying their assignment from the front board. While they were doing this, Miss Klar stepped to Tom's desk and kneeled down beside the blonde boy, who turned nervously toward her. His hair was unkempt, his face not quite clean, his shirt and jeans soiled and wrinkled.

"What is it, Miss?"

"Would you take some things to the library for me? That big box up by my desk?"

"Sure, sure!" Tom blurted, jerking himself to his feet and ceremoniously rolling up his sleeves.

"Thanks, Tom."

When Tom returned to the classroom, Miss Klar had already begun her discussion of the Jackson administration. He slipped to his seat quietly, and she smiled her thanks for the errand, then asked:

"What kind of a man was Jackson?"

Tom's hand was up, and Miss Klar called on him, sure that he would have a useful answer that would help develop the discussion.

"He was a tough bastard!" Tom shouted.

Dead silence fell over the class, as all eyes turned first to Tom, then to Miss Klar, then back again, awaiting the storm.

Betty's face registered nothing. In a very even, controlled voice, she asked, "How do you mean?"

Tom hesitated, glanced swiftly around him at the other students, then back to Miss Klar's expressionless face, then added nervously, "He was a very hard man."

"Why do you say that? Could you give us an example?"

Relief showed on Tom's face, and he replied in an eager, hurried tone.

"Like that time he had a duel. He waited until the other man fired first, and he was hit bad, but he stood firmly, aimed carefully, and shot the other man dead. When they asked him why he let the other fellow fire first, Jackson said he didn't want to spoil his aim, so he let the other fellow fire, then killed him. That meant the other fellow got to hit him, but he said, 'I'd have killed him even if he'd shot me through the heart!' He was one tough hombre."

"I think you're right," said Miss Klar. "Now who can tell me. . . . ?

Later Miss Klar gave the class a twenty-minute work-study period. Most quickly began their homework. She moved about the room checking their work, assisting them, and giving encouragement. When she came to Tom, she found him buried in Carlyle's *Heroes and Hero-Worship*, a library copy more dusty than worn. As she bent over him, Tom explained defensively that he would do the homework later, but he had to finish the chapter he was on. "He writes kind of funny," he said, "But I like his idea of history. Thinks it's a few big men that make the difference. I'm on Cromwell, Jeez! He was stern!"

"What made him that way?" asked Miss Klar.

"Well, he had an idea that God stood behind him all the time, approving everything he did. That way, he didn't stop at nothing."

When Miss Klar dismissed the class at the end of the period, Tom lingered. When the teacher began closing the windows, Tom helped, and finally, began straightening the desks and snatching up a few pieces of paper from the floor. As they finished Miss Klar turned to Tom and said smilingly, "Thanks."

"I'm sorry, Miss Klar, the way I acted, what I said, you know?"

"Did you say something that bothered you?" Her tone was bland, deliberate, but interested.

"Yeah, what I said. I was trying to be tough," said Tom and looked down at his shabby shoes.

● ● ●

QUESTIONS FOR WRITING AND DISCUSSION

1. What is your reaction to the coffee room conversation? How typical is it of teacher room conversation? What values or dangers do you see in teachers blowing off steam in this way? If you feel that outside-of-

class, teacher-to-teacher discussion of school problems is beneficial, do you see other ways it could be handled?
2. Do you think Bert and Jack are justified in resenting what they see as the pampering of a constant behavior problem? How representative of their attitudes toward other students do you suppose their attitude toward Tom is?
3. What do you think of Betty as a teacher? What indications of her teaching ability do you have other than her handling of Tom? How do you feel about her kneeling by Tom's desk, ignoring his use of the word "bastard" during class?
4. How do you feel about the use of cumulative folder material by a teacher in the specific case of Betty and Tom's record, and in general? In what ways is it beneficial? In what ways could it be detrimental?
5. What reasons do you see for Tom's behavior? What special problem of adolescence does he have? What limits do you think should be placed upon his behavior, even of you consider the behavior understandable?
6. How much effect on Tom's total school adjustment do you think the one period with Betty will have as compared to the ones with Jack and Bert? How much influence can one teacher expect to have? Do you see him as a potential dropout? What special positives does he have to work with? Are there parts of the school structure that could deal more effectively with Tom's total adjustment than Betty alone can?
7. Where does the element of cultural divergence enter into this story? How might it account for the different approaches of Betty and the men?

COMMENTS

There is a variation in philosophic orientation that divides teachers. On the one hand there are those who want to solve their problems by imposing an artificial simplicity on their environments — "get rid of the slobs" — and on the other there are those willing to deal with unending complexity. This is probably more a matter of feeling than it is of cognition. Some teachers are willing to take chances, others are not. The Jack Barrys of the profession seem willing to work only with the easy, conforming, disciplined child. The Betty Klars seem willing to gamble a bruised ego in trying to shield a growing youth. It appears rather clear which kind of teacher will work most effectively with underpriviledged children.

Jack Barry and teachers like him are not to be hated as people. He has difficulty liking anyone — children, parents, or principals — so he is not simply voicing negative judgments of the "lower class." It may be that another choice of profession would have been beneficial to him as well as to his students. As it is, both he and they may be victims of his mistaken choice.

As part of her effort to understand Tom, Betty made a careful study of his school record. Teachers are generally divided on the wisdom of this. Some say that it leads to prejudgment of a child. However, knowledge of the range of test scores taken on Tom, of his health difficulties, of his reading ability, and of his basic personality must have been useful to Betty. Creative intuition in any situation seems to come only after prolonged study. The use of the numerical I.Q. may again be questioned, but as this subject has been discussed in detail in an earlier section, it will not be taken up again here. It may be worth repeating that the idea of tacking a number on a child and then handling him in terms of that number is rejected by many thinking educators. Intelligence tests are known to be incompletely valid and not always reliable, especially for those students other than the white, middle-class group on which most tests have been standardized.

The story makes a clever juxtaposition between a successful and an unsuccessful use of a student to carry something. A child may want to be helpful, but be so eager, or inexperienced, or poorly coordinated, that he drops and breaks an article of value. If the child is obviously overcome with shame, most teachers seem to think the best method is to ignore the trouble as much as possible. However, if the child is deliberately careless, as implied by the "easy come, easy go," then he needs to be won over. Punishment in such a case cannot be expected to affect behavior if the child takes pleasure in being hurt.

Coercion of students can only be regarded as partially effective in the life of the school, even when these students show compliance either through their need for what the school has to offer, or for rewards, such as entrance to college. Successful coercion is only possible if loss of status in the school community is seen as a threat. Where the student disregards the school community, there can be no threat and so no coercion. Many teachers regard the use of punishment to persuade students to learn as ultimately helpful, but there is a genuine difference of opinion at all levels of the profession concerning this.

Peer status is probably important to a boy like Tom Brewster, and indeed to all boys and girls. However, evidence is available to show that children who have accepted adult values, either in whole or in part, are less influenced by the mores of their peers and presumably less in need of peer status. However, peer status seems far more important to Tom Brewster than school status which indeed makes no apparent appeal to him. Coercion, at least by punishment, is therefore out of the question. The possibility that he is being coerced or at least manipulated by Betty Klar must not be overlooked, for one can be a slave to love as well as to fear. This raises a nice point: unemotional teaching is a contradiction in terms, but to what extent should the personality of the teacher intrude between the student and his lesson?

The question of foul language in the classroom has already been discussed in this manual. A very worried teacher might expect the walls of custom and authority to be crumbled by a single vocalization of "bastard." Some teachers would think Betty was right to overlook the use of the word in class. Others might think she ought not to have continued to do so when she and the boy were alone. But did she overlook it after all?

One might think it was possible for Betty to work with Tom only because he had a foothold on learning. He liked to read and he read at a fairly difficult level for an eighth grader. With many unruly boys there seems to be nothing to use as a base for contact, but an imaginative and sympathetic teacher like Betty would probably have found a way to get through even to them.

Teachers and principals occasionally find themselves as opposed in their views as they have been depicted in our story, with some of the teachers favoring a vigorous system of expulsion for unruly children and the principal willing to keep on trying. Sometimes the roles are reversed with the principal favoring a "tough" policy. Either way, the child can usually stay in school if the teachers want him, as a principal rarely expels a student until several teachers have complained.

This story concerns a Caucasian boy from a poor home. Children who just can't get along are not unknown in well-to-do families, but the plain facts are that more poor boys than rich ones get into serious trouble, first in school and then with the police. While it is important to remember that delinquency is not reserved for the lower classes of American society, nevertheless, probably because poor people and Negroes have been more often badly treated, the categories of "poverty," "Negro," and "trouble" do to some extent overlap.

The conversation in the teachers' lounge is an important element in this story, indicating the extent to which attitudes and perhaps behavior may be influenced by the informal talk about students and their families which takes place there and then spreads in its effects throughout the school. The tone of the conversation in the lounge, as depicted in the story, can occasionally be detected in any teachers' lounge. Teachers sometimes use their colleagues for a variety of therapeutic purposes. Teachers need some place to salve their psychic welts. Their usual armor of poised serenity is costly to the spirit. This lack of a safety valve for frequently irritating problems often leads to rather overstated and even melodramatic gripe sessions in teachers' lounges. There are usually few formal discussion situations which would give teachers the opportunity to discuss their classroom problems candidly and to exchange constructive ideas or stratagems for the solution of problems.

In-service training programs are progressively being developed across the country to meet the needs of teachers to blow off steam in a more constructive manner than in teachers' room discussion, where all too frequently the negative ideas are propounded most loudly and new teachers may get a one-sided view of students and conditions in the school. Planned, candid give-and-take discussions about common problems and ways of coping with them can serve many uses. For some, there is the definition and clarification of previously hidden feelings and prejudices. Others are stimulated to summon untapped personal resources and to develop ways to cope with difficulties. For many there is relief in knowing that others share their classroom problems and concerns.

Such in-service training is designed so that the teachers can discuss their reactions to their problems under the direction and guidance of a leader. Hopefully, the teachers reach a deeper understanding of the reasons for their attitudes. As they see the part they play in the relationship with the student, they find it more possible to change their behavior and deal more effectively with students.

Such discussions cannot be divorced from new information. If they are, the talks may tend to remain in the same groove, with participants feeling merely frustrated by the whole experience. The following in-service training program developed in one California school district is an example of how this combination of needs may be met.

A first semester course is offered, filled with information on the characteristics of lower-class subcultures, problems of self-image, the causes of lack of motivation of our alienated students, and the factual conflicts between the culture of these children and that of the school. Speakers, films, panels, tapes, role playing, readings and discussion methods are all used. While the emphasis is on information, the discussion sessions do bring in the teachers' reactions to the information.

A second semester course is then offered in which the emphasis is on group discussion, and where the school personnel become active participants rather than just recipients of new information. Expression of all kinds of attitudes is encouraged. With the information gained in the first semester as a basis, the group tends to be willing to examine ways in which teachers may need to change, as well as the things about the children which disturb them. As these discussions continue, a need for further information becomes apparent and the group asks for more speakers, bibliographies, and the like. These are provided, but grow out of the teachers' own desires and vary with each group.

Some graduates of the two semesters have become so committed that they continue to meet without in-service credit, and to work on plans for involving those school personnel who do not take the courses. Also, since a great many schools in the district now have had from one to six of their faculty involved in the courses, teachers' room discussion is beginning to be influenced by the teachers who have had this training.

Tom Brewster is shown to be aggressive in school, even in Betty's room. Some children become aggressive when treated badly by adults and can't be expected to be more discriminating than adults. Teachers can expect to be on the receiving end of a certain amount of undirected aggression whether they are the ones provoking it or not. Some teachers who have been unusually kind to a child are bewildered if he turns on them, but this does happen. Worse than an aggressive child, from the point of view of his own eventual adjustment, is the child who takes it out on himself. In the face of Tom's aggression, Betty actually kneels beside his desk. Some would consider this a sacrifice of the teacher's dignity which might be questioned as a matter of classroom procedure; others will see this not as a sacrifice, but as the natural gesture of a warm person.

Betty gives of herself to her students, and in doing so may offend the preconceptions of some as to what kind of behavior is dignified and proper to a teacher. But at least in the case of Tom Brewster — a "hard-to-reach" student of the worst order — she was successful. Perhaps one reason for Betty's success is that she is not the typical middle-class teacher herself. It is mentioned that she was originally from the slums of an eastern city and had had to work two years before she earned enough to enter college.

On the other hand, professionals who make the transition from lower- to middle-class are especially sensitive about their background, and in an effort to leave it behind are exceptionally critical of the lower class. Such teachers may be even more detrimental to disadvantaged students than a teacher of middle-class background, and this demonstrates the fallacy in assuming that a Negro teacher will necessarily be more effective with Negro students. It is possible that a Negro who becomes a teacher — and thus one of the relatively few of his race to reach middle-class status — will reject and be rejected by lower-class students. There are those individuals of all races, however, and Betty seems to be one, who are able to move upward socioeconomically and still retain their roots. Such teachers have a special understanding of their students' problems from personal experience and are able to work with them easily and fruitfully.

DIGESTS OF SOCIAL SCIENCE READINGS

"Identity vs. Identity Diffusion in Adolescence"[3]

> Erikson, a psychiatrist, addresses himself to the problems of identity as they are experienced during the crucial adolescent years. He reminds us that the problems of identity are always worked out within a social context. Significant others, such as family or peer group members are important factors in the maturational drama. Erikson discusses, too, the main components of identity diffusion.

"Ultimately each component should be discussed in connection with adolescence as a normative life-crisis; in connection with individual pyschopathology; and finally, in connection with social pathology, such as delinquency.

"First, I speak of a sense of *time diffusion*. This ranges from a *desperate urgency* (to act right now) to *utter apathy*. Phenomenologically, such diffusion is typical for all adolescents at one stage or another, but becomes pathologically marked in some. The tremendous changes in time perspective in adolescence (backward and forward; infinity or fantasy, and immediate long-range commitment) are aspects of this diffusion. The original trust of the world is here challenged, again, for emotional autonomy must now become complete. Time diffusion can reawaken *basic mistrust*, and thus call on very primitive mechanisms.

"*Identity consciousness* means preoccupation with discrepancies between the self-image (or images) and one's appearance in the eyes of others. The vanity and sensitivity of adolescents belong here, and also their apparent callousness to suggestions and their lack of shame in the face of criticisms. Again, these are primitive defenses, upholding a shaky self-certainty against *doubt* and *shame*.

---

[3] Erik H. Erikson, "Identity vs. Identity Diffusion in Adolescence," in *New Perspectives for Research on Juvenile Delinquency*, ed. Helen L. Witmer and Ruth Kotinsky, U. S. Children's Bureau (Washington, 1955). Excerpts reprinted by permission.

"Connected with this, there is often a provocative experience with a *negative identity*. Adolescents, at one time or another, for longer or shorter periods, and with varying intensity, suddenly decide to try to be exactly what significant people do not want them to be. It is here that what we analysts call compensations can suddenly crumble, causing inner anarchy and either paralysis of initiative or that psychological initiative which is crime. Young people in extreme conditions may, in the end, find a greater sense of identity in being withdrawn or in being delinquent than in anything society has to offer them.

"Then *paralysis of workmanship*. Here you have merely to note the deep difference between 'completing a job,' in the sense of creating a value or a commodity of any kind, and 'doing a job' (that is burglary) or 'making a good job of it' in the sense of completing a destruction. From here it is only one step to another obvious consideration; namely, that young people must have learned to enjoy a sense of workmanship in order not to need the thrill of destruction. Schizoids and delinquents have in common a mistrust of themselves, a disbelief in the possibility that they could ever complete anything of value. This, of course, is especially marked in those who, for some reason or other, do not feel that they are partaking of the technological identity of today. The reason may be that their own gifts have not found contact with the productive aims of the machine age or that they themselves belong to a social class (here 'upper-upper' is remarkably equal to 'lower-lower') that does not partake of the stream of progress. I shall come back to that later.

"*Bisexual diffusion* in adolescence needs little explanation. It fuses with identity-consciousness in the adolescent's preoccupation with the question of what kind of man or woman, or what kind of intermediate or deviate, he might become. An adolescent feels that to be a little less of one means to be much more of the other — or, rather, to be a little less of one means to be *all* of the other. If at such time something happens that psychosocially marks him as a homosexual or a tomboy, as a mannish woman, or a 'longhair,' he may develop a deep fixation, connected with a negative identity, and true *intimacy* will seem dangerous.

"By *leadership polarization* I mean that the adolescent has to learn both to lead and to be led. He has to find out what the pecking order feels like. If this is short-circuited, he develops some kind of *authority diffusion*. Even leaders must be corporals first. On the question of who can tell whom, and what, the delinquent remains stuck.

"Finally, there is *ideological polarization*. Young people must be given meaningful ideological opposites from which to choose (or to think they choose) a clearly marked group-identity, and a clearly rationalized repudiation of other identities. Otherwise, *ideological diffusion* will make a well-sustained identity formation impossible. Offhand, it might seem that the present division of the world into two worlds provides such clearly marked opposites. But I would think that any analysis of the effect of the cold war on youth (probably on both sides) would show that this is an ideological war between people in late middle age, and that youth is not only not ideologically involved and committed but has become somewhat suspicious of the whole thing."

"Delinquents in Schools"[4]

In this paper Werthman shows how delinquents react to their teachers' attempts to maintain authority over them. He analyzes attitudes toward grading and stresses the importance of "fair" treatment by teachers.

Data collected by observation and interviews over a two-year period on the educational performances and classroom experiences of lower-class gang members suggest that there seems to be no relationship between academic performance and "trouble" in school during middle adolescence. Gangs contain everything from honor students to illiterates. Also, difficulties occur only in some classes and not in others. Good and bad students alike are consistently able to get through half or more of their classes without friction. It is only in particular classes with particular teachers that incidents leading to suspension flare up.

For events in high school classrooms to proceed smoothly students must grant teachers some measure of authority. Most students accept the authority of teachers to pass judgment on practically all behavior that takes place in classrooms. This is why most students do not question the grades they receive. Gang members do not *a priori* accept the authority of any teacher. They first discover whether authority is being exercised on suitable grounds and in a suitable way.

Gang members make decisions to accept or reject the authority of teachers on the basis of four criteria. Some teachers not only insist on the physical presence of students but also expect a measure of "attention" as well. First of all, gang members do not grant teachers the right to punish misbehavior, although good reasons for ceasing such activities as sleeping, reading comic books, talking to neighbors, chew-

---

[4] Carl Werthman, "Delinquents in Schools: A Test for the Legitimacy of Authority," *Berkeley Journal of Sociology*, VIII (1963), 39–60. Digest used by permission.

ing gum, etc., are often accepted. Second, under no conditions can race, dress, hair styles, and mental capacities receive legitimate attention. Failure on the part of teachers to ignore these irrelevant items often contributes to the denial of their authority. Third, gang members are extremely sensitive to the style in which authority is exercised. Use of the imperative is perceived as an insult to those addressed this way. Teachers who "request" conformity are more likely to achieve desired results. Ultimately, however, the decision to accept or reject the authority of teachers is made on the basis of what grounds they use to assign grades.

If a boy concludes that he is either being discriminated against, bribed, or treated randomly in the way he's assigned a grade, he does *not* modify his behavior. He will not conform to the teacher's demands for obedience to get a better grade. He is prevented by his sense of morality; the tactic is considered illegitimate.

When gang members decide a teacher's claims to authority are illegitimate, they are careful to avoid all behavior that recognizes this authority. Of all techniques used by gang members to communicate rejection of authority, the most subtle and annoying to teachers is demeanor. They use body movements that communicate a casual and disdainful aloofness; this is referred to as "looking cool." They may wear clothing to enhance the effect, such as a hat if the scene takes place indoors.

Yet when gang members are convinced that the educational enterprise and its ground rules are being legitimately pursued, that the teacher is really interested in teaching them something, and that efforts to learn will be rewarded, they consistently show up on time, stay until the class is dismissed, raise their hands before speaking, and stay silent and awake.

PART V
THE SCHOOL AND ITS RELATION TO LIFE EXPERIENCE

THE SCHOOL AND THE WORLD OF WORK

The sociological investigations stimulated by Robert K. Merton have emphasized the values we as a nation hold in common. Values are the goals we share: those things which people hold dear and by which many profess to live. They are transmitted through the family, through the schools, and through literature and mass communications. Merton observes that one of the main values espoused by Americans is economic success. His inquiries have led him to conclude that this value is diffused throughout the total society and all its subsystems. Thus while our nation is composed of many income levels, there is general agreement that getting ahead economically is very important.

It has been suggested that an emphasis on economic success and achievement is a necessity for Western industrial society, for it must locate and train the most talented persons in every generation. We cannot know in advance who these persons are, hence all must be motivated to strive so that the most able and talented will be the victors in the competitive struggle. Therefore, emphasizing success is a way of ensuring the survival of industrial society.[1]

The obvious question which this raises is what happens if everyone aspires to this goal although the opportunity to attain it is not open to everyone? The process which is designed to ensure order at the same time produces a disorder in which many talented people are excluded from the conventional avenues to success. This results in such persons, as the victims of the process, turning to antisocial acts or to illegal means of securing both the social status and the livelihood which they desire.

Merton suggests several kinds of adaptation, depending on one's position in the social system, which occur when this kind of opportunity blockage takes place:

1. One may decide to be an innovator, and continue to accept the goal of economic success yet eschew the accepted means to attain it. In this group we find the robber barons, embezzlers, delinquents, and other adult criminals.

---

[1] Richard A. Cloward and Lloyd E. Ohlin, *Delinquency and Opportunity: A Theory of Delinquent Gangs.* (Glencoe, Ill., 1960), p. 81.

2. One may decide that economic success will never be attained and, hence, by some kind of inverted thinking, lose interest in the value and focus ritualistically on the means to achieve success. Here we find the petty bureaucrat, more interested in the rules of the game than the aim for which they were designed.

3. One may decide to withdraw from the struggle completely. These are the individuals who follow the path of the hobo, the beatnik, the mystic.

The important group to focus on in this analysis are the "innovators," especially among the working or lower class. If these young people constituted only a small percentage of the school population, we could look on them as students with individual problems, but since they make up 30 percent or more of the student body we must give the problem considerable attention.

All youth finds itself enjoined to succeed but working-class youth has much more limited access to the means for success than middle-class youth. Hence, for the former the pressure to engage in disapproved behavior becomes very great.

We all seem to agree that in our society education is critically important to social advancement. Why, then, do a substantial portion of lower-class males avoid higher education? Lower-class males come from backgrounds in which schooling is either not valued or in which an educational tradition (emphasis on reading and speaking) is not nurtured. The other major barrier to obtaining a higher education is an economic one — necessity dictates early employment.

The young person who would like to get ahead but can't usually perceives his situation accurately. Nationwide surveys have made the point that those at the lowest rung of the economic ladder intuitively sense or consciously perceive that they can't make the grade. Moreover, they experience this failure in terms of some lack in the social order rather than in themselves. The psychological impact of this circumstance is one which bodes ill for the school and for the formal learning process generally. The feeling of unjust deprivation weakens the motivation for accepting conventional norms as legitimate, "It's not what you know, but who you know." This increases the sense of alienation. The visibility of barriers to opportunity, especially if the youths are Negro, speeds up the process of alienation. The most troubling aspect of the alienation from the school's point of view is when it occurs in a context where others are in a similar situation. The disadvantaged youngsters interact with one another and define the situation for themselves. This increases the likelihood of delinquent behavior.

The foregoing analysis of the problem suggests some general points of attack by the school in reducing the alienation of their students and attempting to bring them into the mainstream of American life.

1. We can make sure that those who manage to get through school can find employment. This means paying more attention to quality in our education. A high school diploma should be more than a certificate of attendance.

2. We should provide students with the kinds of skills which can be generalized to other areas. Even though specific jobs may not exist in the future, we should be providing students with broader skills which will apply in a wide variety of situations in our automated economy.

3. We can address ourselves to the student's alienation (caused to a large extent by discrimination and prejudice) partly by assuring him in myriads of small ways that he is wanted and needed.

4. All levels of the school system must cooperate in providing work incentives for the future. We have to get knowledge about the world of work down to the elementary school.

5. All levels of the school system must explore ways to capture the child's interest through courses constructed around hobbies and interests, or through concerns for employment such as courses related to part-time work. Interest in English and mathematics and other subjects can then be sparked out of the student's practical need for them.

6. The school must work to educate parents for their role in motivating their children. Parents should also be informed about any practical programs that are initiated for their children so that they too can have a sense of the relevance of school to practical life experience.

THE SCHOOL AND PREPARATION FOR COMMUNITY LIFE

The preceding section discussed the alienation of lower-class youth from the economic opportunity structure of this country. The same situation prevails in other areas inextricably connected with our economic life. Various systematically disadvantaged groups, and Negroes in particular, have for many years effectively been closed out of desirable housing, egalitarian social interaction, and interracial religious participation. It has only been within the last few years that any basic attempt has been made to improve in these areas. The school can now help its students by pointing out new opportunities opening to them and by preparing them for new roles in community life.

In a number of ways the school can help prepare young people for adult roles in the working world and as family and community members. It is imperative that the school furnish the most current information available concerning employment and vocational opportunities for young people. Counselors should be continually alert to changes in the labor market. Groups of junior high students could be taken on field trips to employment offices, union halls, and large industries. Students should get practice in filling out employment forms and in conducting themselves and communicating in a socially acceptable manner in employment interviews. Some schools have experimented with "Pro" or "Semi-Pro Day," on which they bring in persons of varied minority groups representing different professions from whom young people can get "straight" information.

The school can help prepare the lower socioeconomic group child for his place in family life by well-planned social relations and marriage courses. Instruction on the family can be given without emphasis or approval of specific family form, because forms vary among different ethnic groups, and specific details which explicitly or implicitly legitimize one family form may deprecate that form in which most members of a class have been reared. Students could profit from instruction in such consumer skills as marketing, budgeting, and nutrition; and in the kind of practical know-how that more affluent persons frequently take for granted: where to go for legal advice, for help in finding housing, in getting loans — from credit unions instead of from "loan sharks," for example — in family planning, and for medical or mental health assistance. Community clearing houses of information and referral services should be developed to familiarize lower-class persons with the services which often can be easily obtained through community resources.

The school must realistically come to grips with the problems of early marriage and extramarital relationships which exist for many youth. It should be borne in mind that sexual activity may have different implications from one subcultural group to another. These differences pose difficulties for the school which attempts to deal with these problems, but they must be faced. Many children, however, lack an adequate understanding of the actual biological processes and social consequences of sexual behavior, and are often in need of specific facts and advice. Several school systems are attacking this topic by instituting a special program in the early grades, and then extending the new curriculum gradually into the higher grade levels. Other schools have introduced special classes, for example, "social living," for high school juniors and seniors, as an elective class. These innovations may be regarded as only a beginning.

Social studies and civics courses have a great potential for motivating and stimulating minority group children although, unfortunately, the potential is not often realized. The achievements of all ethnic groups and their contributions to American life can be brought out more easily in this area of instruction than in others. Here the development of racial and ethnic consciousness and pride can be most effectively fostered. However, the teacher should be aware that most lower-class children of minority background need ethnic role models with whom they can easily identify. A local Negro citizen of prominence may be a more effective instrument toward this end than would a Negro of international reputation. Citizenship and the privileges and responsibilities of community participation can be taught through discussions of community organization and the social movements currently developing. Recent advances in indigenous ethnic and community leadership and groups can be discussed. The enduring integrity of the differing groups within the great American melting pot can be shown as a continuing strength of a democracy.

Finally, social studies classes can include information on prejudice and discrimination by discussing anthropological and genetic factors as they relate to ethnic and biological differences.

Imaginatively planned and forthright classroom discussions on current events in areas of opening community opportunities can be very helpful for junior and senior high school students. Students who are effectively engaged in such discussion will be more motivated to strive for continuing education to reach these opportunities. Speakers from outside the schools, especially those whose roots are in the subcultures from which the students come, and successful professionals who can serve as models with whom students can identify, should provide motivation and interest in continuing education. Discussions and talks which are informative and engaging for young people in the schools will also spread information throughout the community. Subjects broached and explained in the school may be brought home and discussed with parents, relatives, and friends. Thus a wider audience than the student population is reached by discussion of problems of immediate significance.

Negro youth of high school age are well aware that the "struggle" is not over. The ghetto disturbances of which we have become so "shockingly" aware in the last few years attest to the inequities within American society. We should hope the school would be honest enough to admit that inequities do exist within our social structure and are likely to persist for some time. The school should show, however, that students and teachers by their own actions as citizens can contribute to their eventual elimination.

The fact that nonwhites live in a white world with advantages and gains geared for whites is a fact learned early by the nonwhite child, be he Negro, Mexican-American, or other, and this fact is frequently reinforced in the schools. The school can be highly significant in indicating to the minority group child what he can expect from his community and from life in general. Important in this is whether the school system operates on an egalitarian or differential basis in the classroom, the principal's office, and in extra-curricular activities. The attitudes and behavior of teachers both as authority figures and models are the immediate vehicles of the school system's attitudes and intentions. The importance of the total school environment in setting the prototype of the community experience for the child should not be underestimated.

The following stories illustrate some of the implications for life in the broader community that school experiences have for students.

In "Expectations" the widely differing life situations of a lower-class Negro boy and a prosperous Caucasian boy are contrasted. A dramatic event in the Negro student's family life, combined with his feelings of alienation from school and society, leads him to unprovoked aggression in school.

In "Skill" a class questions a teacher about the relevance of its school work to life's larger demands. The teacher cannot answer these questions in a meaningful way nor can he constructively relate the discussion about employment and automation to the needs of his students.

"Variety" describes the problems of an interracial student couple in high school.

"EXPECTATIONS"

"Try to keep away from the black boys, son. Give them a wide berth!" Dr. Eric Schreck put down his newspaper, raised his coffee cup, and looked out the window over the city which lay spread before him from hill to waterfront, shrouded here and there by the early morning fog. Then he turned back to his son, Paul, who sat opposite him eating cornflakes and cream topped with bananas. Paul spilled some cocoa as he put down his cup and replied, "Dad, they don't bother us, really. Lots of them are good fellows. There are three in my history class who are whizzes. Don't worry about it." He thought better of telling his father that he had just joined the Interracial Understanding Club at Center High.

"I know colored people. I've treated them all my life. I've hired them, too, and some did a pretty good job. There wasn't any problem in this area until the riffraff from the South came in. The old colored stock here never caused a bit of trouble. They stayed in their areas and kept out of trouble. It's the new ones whom the reds have stirred up. Demands! Equality! Absurd! Equality is not something you demand, you know. You earn it by hard work and respectable behavior, like the rest of us did! Try to keep out of their way, son. I wish we'd put you in private school as we planned."

"Hon," said Mrs. Schreck gently, coming in from the library with the doctor's bag, "things are going all right down at Center. Mr. Harrington, the principal, talked to the PTA last week and told us how they are building the kind of friendly, integrated school atmosphere we all want."

"I know, dear," said the doctor, patiently, "but you don't do that by inviting Negro rabble rousers to speak at assemblies, now, do you?" His smile was kind and his voice condescending.

"Why, Lomax made a fine talk, Pop. Didn't say anything radical. Just made the point that we have to fulfill the American Dream, put our ideals into practice."

"I know that line, son, and where it came from. Some of us at the club were talking the other day about the disturbances at Center and your principal's ideas about the race problem. You're at school to learn your fundamentals, to prepare for college and get a good position. Keep away from the troublemakers. Don't get involved. I just want you to get out of Center with a clean bill of health." The doctor was rising and had obviously finished the conversation. Paul ducked his head to his cornflakes again, and his mother slipped into the kitchen. Paul hurried to finish so that he could get a ride down the hill with his father.

"They taken him away! They done taken him away!" his mother moaned. Reggie took another big bite of French bread and peanut butter, chewed violently, and then pivoted his head around to peer at his mother. Then he pounded the table top before him with his fist.

"Annie call. She tol' me. They took him last night. Three of them come, with they guns. He didn't even fight, he just went."

Reggie chewed furiously, a picture of wrath and frustration. Just then his sisters hurried by, turning as they went out the door to call goodbye to mother and brother. Their pigtails were tied with blue ribbon. Their smiling faces suggested that they did not know, or did not understand, that their older brother had gone away to prison.

Reggie pressed the palm of his right hand against the sharp corner of the unpainted pine table top, then jabbed his arm several times viciously against the corner, scratching the flesh. He turned away from his mother, who sat opposite him, and stared out the window at the dirty gray apartment house next door. He couldn't say a word. She said nothing more, but tears were running down her cheeks, along her nose. They sat speechless for several moments, then Reggie rose.

"This the last day for me in their school!" he asserted with fierce determination. "I'm goin' get my stuff outa that locker fifth period an' blow!"

Reggie caught up with his friend Dash a few blocks from school. He told Dash what had happened and that he planned to quit school. Dash tried to talk him out of it.

"Things are shapin' better for blacks," he argued. "There'll be jobs if we train. Like Lomax say, we gotta get ready for the future that black fighters are winnin' for us. Won't do no good at all for you go make a fuss. Your brother's gone now. Your job is to stay on here and make it."

"Lomax making it, Harrington making it, them teachers making it. They don't give a damn about us, long as they get theirs. Long as we say what they want, we fine. Otherwise, they got the fuzz for us. Shoot, man, I've had it."

"There are some good ones," urged Dash. "Some of the whites are changing. Paul, that doctor's boy, you know him, he understands. We were talking the other day."

"Who's he? Who cares what he say? This place nothin' but a jail. Everybody do what teachers say, whether they wrong or right. I been pushed long enough. I cuttin'."

The halls were crowded with hurrying students. Negro and white, Oriental and Mexican. Well-dressed and demonstratively polite, ill-dressed and careless. Some laughing and gay, some harried and ill-tempered. Some sullen, silent and alone. Inevitable collisions. Some apologies, some curses.

Paul Schreck and his chum Barry hurried to their American history class.

"Had another clash with Dad this morning," Paul reported. "Same old thing, the wicked blacks, the conspiring reds, the whole treatment. Mom stood right up for integration, though. Even the PTA seems to have gotten the message."

"You'll never change the old generation," sighed Barry, philosophically. "It's the youth who have to straighten this out."

"Honest, man, how many of the youth really *want* to?" asked Paul. Barry shrugged.

In American history, Reggie sat through fifty minutes of unrelieved torment and mounting wrath. There was a brief discussion of current events, including a report on technological unemployment and its special implications for youth and minorities. "Where my job?" he thought. Then a thirty-minute test, essay, with one item:

"The Negroes were more disadvantaged during Reconstruction by Northern politicians, who duped them, than by Southern landowners, who previously had made them slaves."
Support or attack this proposition in a brief, well-organized essay, giving reasons for the position you take.

Reggie thought of his brother Bennie, of his sad-eyed mother. He thought of their shabby apartment at the end of a run-down, pock-marked street. He thought of his sisters, who probably didn't know yet what it meant to be considered a "dirty, worthless nigger." He fingered the fifty-cent piece in his pocket. He noticed that blood from his hand had stained his neat, light-grey trousers, his only good pair. He glared at his shoes.

He was supposed to write an explanation of how white men had been able at first to enslave and then to dupe his people. And he wondered, "Am I a slave, or am I a dupe?" He wrote nothing, but fixed his eyes on a cloud far away over the hills which looked like a soldier with a bayoneted rifle. He clenched his right fist furiously and wadded the paper he had borrowed from Dash and threw it wildly across the room. The teacher sat at his desk correcting papers and either did not notice or pretended not to. When the period ended, Reggie and Dash bolted for the door, Reggie muttering, "Bastards, white-bellied bastards!"

As Paul and Barry left the same class, Barry remarked, "Pretty good test! Gave us a chance to consider the overall picture of how totally the slave and Reconstruction periods put the Negro into a position of subjection from which he is only now recovering."

Paul smiled at the pedantic way his friend expressed himself and wondered how Negroes would feel about such a test. "Yeah, good test," he said, as they hurried down the hall. At the end, the current of traffic had to funnel through a narrow door, and at that spot Paul collided with a tall Negro student. The Negro let out a shout of rage and threw a wild right, his whole body behind the blow, striking Paul full in the mouth.

Dash threw his arm around Reggie's shoulder and pulled him away quickly. "You shouldn't have done it, man, you shouldn't have done it!" There was anguish in his voice. "He's a good guy, the doctor boy, a really good guy!"

Crammed up against the lockers, Paul slowly got to his knees. Then he took his hand away from his mouth. Shining through the handful of blood were two white objects. Tears poured from his eyes and he sobbed, not at the pain, but at the loss of his teeth. Barry patted his shoulder helplessly, as other students crowded around. A male teacher shoved his way through the group, shouting orders.

At the end of the corridor, Reggie left Dash and started to leave the building. As he pulled the heavy metal door open, he sensed someone beside him — a tall, large man. Mr. Harrington laid a gentle, but very firm, hand on Reggie's shoulder. Wearily, "All right, Reggie, you've made your play! Now come with me!"

* * *

QUESTIONS FOR WRITING AND DISCUSSION

1. Do you see any way Dr. Schreck indirectly contributed to his son's injury? If so, how? Can you suggest why Paul does not share his father's feelings about Negroes?
2. Compare the kinds of preparation for school Paul's and Reggie's homes gave them. What would you guess Dash's home to be like? Why?
3. The guilt or innocence of Reggie's brother is never discussed. Do you

think this would have been relevant to Reggie's reaction? Why? In what way were police and school equated in Reggie's mind?
4. What things give you a picture of the school and its general racial policy? What are some of the results of this policy? How would you expect Harrington to handle Reggie after the story ends? Why? Do you expect the school to take any further notice of this episode other than specifically in regard to Reggie?
5. In what ways was Lomax, as a nationally known Negro, a good choice as a speaker; in what ways a poor one? Support your answers by material from the story.
6. What do you think of the choice of the test question for this very divergent class? Evaluate Barry's, Reggie's, and Paul's reactions to it. Do you think the teacher should have handled Reggie's obvious hostility to the test directly, or was it best for him to ignore it?
7. Do you feel the attack by Reggie on Paul will have any effect on the previous racial attitudes of either? If so, in what way? Do you see it affecting such students as Barry, Dash, and others? How?
8. Was the development of events inevitable, or could some change along the way have prevented it? Could it have been anticipated? Do you think it was an unusual event in this school?

COMMENTS

The descriptions of the morning breakfast scenes, the general home situations, and the accompanying conversations, vividly depict the polar differences in way of life between the prosperous Caucasian doctor's son on the hill and the Negro boy from the flats. The contrast gives material evidence to the different worlds experienced by the two boys featured in the story.

The values and perceptual differences in the homes also come through with force. Paul's father represents a certain kind of racial moderate who maintains his own prejudices and lines of segregation primarily when his personal interests are at stake. He compliments the Uncle Tom complacent "good old colored stock" while condemning those Negroes who demand their rights.

Dr. Schreck reminds his son of the right kind of future cut out for him — college training and a good position in life.

In contrast to this is Reggie's breakfast scene — a hastily eaten meal in the midst of an emotional situation concerning his brother who was taken to jail the night before. Reggie's anger and frustration dangerously threaten to shape his future, as they have no doubt contributed to the fate of his brother. Perhaps Reggie feels greater anger and more frustration because the police have taken away his brother than would a Caucasian in the same circumstances. As a Negro, rightly or wrongly, with or without justification, Reggie is more likely to see the policeman as an enemy who will pick on him primarily because he is Negro. Years of harsh treatment in the South and discrimination in the North, coupled with misunderstanding and rejection of newly arrived minority groups, have shaped the Negro's identification of the policeman as an enemy whose actions can never be justified rationally.

There was no father in Reggie's domestic circle to encourage educational and professional aspirations. The chances are that Reggie, like many other Negro children, has grown up in a home where social and economic circumstances limit the possibility of there being a stable male authority figure. Some of the implications of growing up in the mother-centered household were discussed in detail in the earlier story "Citizenship."

The general subject of whether to stay in school or to quit and get a job which may provide some immediate gratifications is brought up. The dropout as an unskilled laborer faces a variety of problems in an increasingly automated society. The Negro dropout is even more disadvantaged by reason of overt and covert discrimination and lack of know-how in getting and keeping jobs.

The importance of professional Negroes who may be influential as role models by speaking in schools can be noted by the mention of Lomax whose appearance affected the characters of the story in very different ways. Apparently Dash, although coming from the same socioeconomic and ethnic background as Reggie, nevertheless had begun to get a deeper understanding of the race problem in America. As we stated in our introduction to this section, it may often be more effective to utilize locally known leaders with whom ghetto youth can more easily identify. The level of intellectual sophistication must be correctly judged in these matters by the educator who, like Mr. Harrington, is trying to create a better self-image among Negro students.

The importance to Caucasians as well as Negroes of having an opportunity to mingle with one another as individuals in classes and clubs was illustrated by Paul's giving examples to his father of Negro "whizzes" in his classes and personal friends he had made. Dash also tried to point out to Reggie that some whites were understanding and sympathetic to the Negro cause and problems.

Mr. Harrington has obviously made attempts to really integrate his school, rather than simply accept the physical presence of different races. It is not clear whether the history class was heterogeneously grouped, or was composed of students at college prep level — as the essay test question might suggest. Reggie's general class performance is not indicated, although he understood the question being asked but did not answer it because of his wrath at the moment. However, it might be guessed that Reggie's anxiousness to quit school and his failure to see that education and the sort of advice given by Lomax were applicable and might work given the chance, reflect his lack of the sort of middle-class educational and vocational aspirations that are generally found among students in the upper groupings, attitudes that are usually requisite to the persistence needed to excel in grades. If Reggie and Paul are achieving at the different levels one might expect, it appears that Mr. Harrington has done away with the type of grouping which so often results in segregated classes within an "integrated" school.

He also has sponsored, or at least allowed, formation of an Interracial Understanding Club at the school, has talked to the PTA about the advantages of a "friendly, integrated school atmosphere," and has invited Lomax — a fiery Negro spokesman — to speak to the students. Although the school has not been able to compensate Reggie for what society has done, it does seem to be making efforts beyond those normally found.

The class discussion of technological unemployment and its implications for minorities apparently did not engage Reggie's personal interest or identity, perhaps because of his particular emotional state that day. The teacher who is sensitive to the needs and backgrounds of his students can find a level of discussion which would particularly appeal to the interests of students of minority group status and disadvantage. A sensitive teacher would have already spotted trouble brewing in Reggie's action during the test and would have made attempts to reach him outside of class. If he had taken cognizance of Reggie's wadded paper thrown across the room, he might have been able to control the situation by talking to Reggie privately or by some other action that would have precluded the violence that followed.

Reggie's rage and hitting out at Paul were the cumulation of his pent-up anger and frustration. Many children who come from crowded homes and overstimulating situations come to school in a state of hyper-irritability and are ready to react violently at slight provocations. In this way they may handle a myriad of anxieties by "acting out" in situations unrelated to their specific problems. That Reggie's wrath was expended on a boy who was particularly interested in trying to alleviate the problems that Reggie, his family, and his friends face, was one of the tragedies of the story.

THE SCHOOL AND LIFE EXPERIENCE 183

The title of the story has implications on a number of levels. Chiefly it reflects the fact that if a social situation is of such long-standing, encompassing and pervasive a nature, vivid expectations can indeed be self-fulfilling prophecies in terms of both immediate daily behavior and in the limiting of potential future goals and opportunities. The existing evils of a system are further reinforced by "expected" behavior, thus providing more grist for the mill of those who predict the worst, like Dr. Schreck, while those such as Mr. Harrington, Paul, and Dash who are trying to change a difficult situation find advances blocked and progress wiped out. No doubt Dr. Schreck will indeed have his day now and say both to his son and to his friends at the club, "I told you so."

"SKILL"

"Mr. Biddle, what skill we learning in here?" Tom cocked his head to one side, and his brown face was a mask of wonder. His dark eyes were bright and alive, but Mr. Biddle couldn't tell whether mockery or confusion smouldered there. Tom hadn't raised his hand, but that was all right. Friday was "current problems" day and he wanted an informal class for this. With this particular group of only thirty-two students, 11th grade American history, it was better to let them talk at times, even if they weren't very courteous. If you got too strict about raising hands, they'd clam up and the class would die. But what was Tom getting at? Like most in the group, Tom was not very bright, and sometimes he was pretty coarse, but occasionally he came up with a good idea.

"Skill?" began Mr. Biddle. "Well, when we write a test, that's a skill. Or when we read our text or the newspapers, that's a skill, reading, a very important one. . . . "

Tom's face changed gradually from perplexity to indignation. He turned and looked around at the other students, trying to pass on to them his query and challenge.

"Shoot, man, Ah knows that. . . . " Tom's voice filled with exasperation, searching for words to express what he meant. "Ah means, what skill is history?"

Mr. Biddle felt more confused than before. Should he explain the skill, the science, of historiography? Tom and his friends wouldn't know there was any, and it would be way over their heads to explain. Citizenship? That sounded a little silly sometimes, and students didn't always take it very well. Citizenship was a delicate subject, right now anyway, in a class with many Negro students. Sure, citizenship was one goal of American history. But the class had been discussing automation and unemployment. Should he get off on citizenship?

"Like, I mean, what you teachin' us to *do*?" Tom's voice was now a clear challenge, on the edge of disrespect. What had gotten into him?

"Do you mean how does an understanding of history help citizenship?"

Tom snorted, shook his head in disgust, waved a hand before his face, and then seemed symbolically to throw away the whole idea.

THE SCHOOL AND LIFE EXPERIENCE 185

The discussion was dead now, Mr. Biddle thought, and everyone was a little confused. Sometimes the "current problems" day was the best in the week, but sometimes it was the worst. Then, directing his attention to the rest of the class, "Now, we were supposed to have reports from some of you who were going into the background of America's employment problems. Who is ready?"

A hand went up, Karen's, a slender, light-skinned Negro girl, with a shy face and a delicate figure. "Karen?"

"I have a report on Harrington's book called *The Other America*." She hesitated. "It will take quite a while. It's about poverty. Did you want me to go ahead with it, or. . . . "

"Oh, my yes, Miss Book Bug. You just get your skinny little butt up there and tell us all about it. We just dyin' to hear," Nelly Thomas whispered loud enough to be heard.

"Nelly!" Mr. Biddle's voice was a gentle admonition. "That's enough!" He knew that the buxom girl was a bomb with a short fuse. "Karen, would you go ahead? Come on up!"

Karen glanced quickly at Nelly, then turned away, her eyes a little fearful. Karen had worked hard on her report under the watchful eyes of her father. She didn't know why Nelly hated her, but she didn't want to have any trouble. She knew Nelly's reputation.

Murmurs of disgust broke from several students at the prospect of Karen's report. Others looked disapprovingly at the disrupters and turned to the teacher to demonstrate their loyalty. As the hubbub rose, Mr. Biddle took the matter in hand.

"Listen, kids, we've been having a serious discussion about the problems of our city civilization, our machine age, the growing scarcity of work for those who lack a proper education and a high level of skill. This is important for you, for what you do in school — what you learn, the grades you earn, whether you are graduated or even go to college — will determine whether you get a good job later or even any job at all."

Tom roused himself, then flung his arm to the side of his desk toward the other students.

"Maybe you get a job, maybe not. You clever enough, maybe you get a job. You clever enough, you don't want some jobs, reading stupid things like this book got." His eyes flashed. "You takes your chance. My old man, before he got busted. . . . "

"You gets a job you lucky enough or you clever enough!" exclaimed Teddy, "Or if you stupid enough to want some jobs around. How come you teach?"

"Maybe Karen get a job, all right, but she sure as hell never get a man.

She better learn how get her kicks from 'cyclopedias, 'cause she sure as shit ain't gonna get no jazzing!" Nelly spoke angrily and she came to a sputtering halt, glaring first at Karen, then at Biddle, then exchanging a glance of agreement with Tom.

"All right, class! All right! You want to make a comment, raise your hand and tell us what you think. But let's cut out this personal stuff. We're going to be courteous here. We don't have to agree, and let's say what we think, but we can be respectful. Harry?"

"What I gonna, gonna say, Mr. Biddle," Harry began, fighting a nervous stutter, "What I gonna say, like, I gonna ask, right now, there millions young people ain't got no jobs, can't get no jobs, they can't get no jobs, now, what I gonna say, and what I gonna ask, is, they finish high school, they all have jobs?"

"Okay," said Mr. Biddle, "now I'm not sure I understand Harry's question, but the aspect of the problem you people have to be concerned with is jobs for young people. That depends upon education, on finishing high school. . . ."

"Mr. Biddle," Karen interrupted, then clapped her hand over her mouth in embarrassment that she had spoken out. After a pause, meekly, she went on, "Well, Mr. Biddle, did you want my report today, or later on?"

"Let's get it over with!" Teddy chirped from the rear.

Mr. Biddle threw a disapproving glance, then nodded to Karen. She rose, hesitated, looked around the room, back to Mr. Biddle, then started toward the front. Tom groaned in agony and slipped down into what would look like sleep. Several students toward the front sat up straight, took out their pens, and too conspicuously got ready to take notes. "Now we gonna get educated," grunted Nelly.

When Karen turned to face the class, she saw in front of her some faces filled with interest, genuine or assumed; others disinterested but neutral; others, like Nelly, displaying hostility and disgust by posture, gesture, and facial expressions. Mr. Biddle sat behind her at his desk and gently encouraged her to begin.

Karen ended her talk about four minutes before the bell. "Questions?" asked Mr. Biddle.

"What's they to ask? She told everything. She a genius! She go to bed with Webster's Unabridge," Nelly stated coolly.

Karen walked to her seat quietly, trying not to see Nelly's scorn and Tom's pained disgust. Fred raised his hand, and Mr. Biddle, hoping for a change, quickly recognized him.

"I think Karen's report was O.K. Do they have a plan or a program or kinda scheme to wipe out all those poor she told about? Like drunks, and farm workers, and old people, and the unemployed, and then young people?"

"It's a big, complex thing," said Mr. Biddle, beginning to straighten up the papers on his desk. "What we have to focus on is education, getting the training and the skills we need for jobs, the kind of jobs machines require. It's smart to stay on in school as long as you can."

Mr. Biddle was unhappy about the period. Never had a day quite like it before. It should have gone well. The subject was a matter of relevance to these young people. But the conflict between the girls, completely unexpected, had been distracting. And for some reason, several of the fellows didn't take a positive interest in the issues — Tom, Harry, some of the others.

As the bell rang, Mr. Biddle stepped to the door to open it, at the same time announcing, "Dismissed!" The door swung out crazily, jerked, and fell sideways onto the hall floor with an ear-splitting bang. Several girls screamed as Mr. Biddle jumped back in panic. Simultaneously a roar of laughter burst from the boys. Amazement flashed across Biddle's face, surprise mingled with dismay.

"Brainy operator!" someone exclaimed. Mr. Biddle turned, his face filled with consternation.

"Some smart guy!" said Tom, smiling, as he brushed quickly past the teacher, stepping onto the fallen door.

"Some skillful son of a bitch sneaked out the hinge pins sometime during the period," Teddy whispered to Nelly as they walked off arm in arm. Then, shaking his head, laughing, and speaking loud enough for all to hear, "Some *skillful* son of a bitch!"

• • •

QUESTIONS FOR WRITING AND DISCUSSION

1. What question do you feel Tom was really asking in regard to skill? Do you think he was trying to provoke Biddle or really wanted an answer? Do you feel Biddle actually could not grasp the question or did, but was afraid of handling it? How do you feel about a teacher admitting to a student that he doesn't understand him?
2. How might Biddle have made the discussion of jobs, and the relation of the course to jobs, meaningful to the students?
3. How do you feel about Biddle as a person and teacher: is he rigid,

naive, understanding, inadequate? Do you feel he lets the class use obscenity and generally behave as they do as part of a deliberate plan or out of lack of any plan?
4. Do you feel the class would gain or lose by more structure? What kind of structure do you feel necessary; how enforced? What behavior in this story would you absolutely prohibit, and where would you be flexible?
5. What do you feel is actually involved in the interplay between Karen and Nelly? Do you think it would have been wise to have handled it more directly or to try to ignore it?
6. What are some of the meanings in the unhinging of the door? What do you suppose were the motives of the "offender"? What about the response of the students?

COMMENTS

Biddle appears to have two basic problems in handling his class. One is his inability to understand the actual concerns of his students and to admit this to them; the other is that he has no clear idea of class structure and the limits within which he and the class are operating, with the inevitable result that he is unable to enforce any consistent and effective discipline.

The question of "skill," brought up by Tom and misunderstood by Biddle, has many levels of meaning in this story, pointing up at least four extremely timely and important problems:
1) The matter of relating academic subjects in a meaningful way to culturally diverse students without parents who can motivate their interests in abstruse or abstract matters, or with parents who consciously or unconsciously deprecate or destroy their interest in such pursuits.
2) The problems of the teacher in confronting and explaining the realities of employment and life opportunities on a level that engages students' interest and gives them a framework within which to place the events of their experience, the conversations they hear at home and in their communities, and what they may read about national problems.
3) The interests and expectations of Negro females in the traditional school activities.
4) The fact that concepts such as skill and intelligence must be considered to be relative and that they are manifested differently in different population groups.

THE SCHOOL AND LIFE EXPERIENCE 189

The goal of teaching history to develop skill in a mode of inquiry has not been strikingly successful in the high school. Justification for tasks assigned in school is sometimes difficult to provide. Perhaps a simple statement of goals such as the following may prove useful in motivating students to study history. At the very least it may draw the attention of the teacher to practices that may make history more palatable, especially to reluctant learners.

a) The story of the past may be made very engaging and worth listening to and reading about through the use of imaginative devices by the teacher, such as selecting provocative subjects as the focus of the course and of the themes assigned. Reading and listening skills can also be practised in this way.

b) Identification with heroes of American history, among whom were representatives from a wide variety of nations and races, excites feelings of pride and satisfaction. Especially for Negro youth, who have traditionally been exposed to little or no literature or other teaching materials about the achievements of Negroes, materials about recognized successful Negro figures will be important and may provide incentives and feasible models for emulation. Practice in the expression of these feelings stimulates growth in the ability to talk and to write.

c) Current political and social problems have roots in the past. A knowledge of the past is helpful in understanding current events. Here the teacher must be imaginative in bringing out the historical basis of current matters of interest.

The successful planning and carrying out of "current problem" discussions requires a good deal of professional and personal competence. Negro youth are especially sensitive today to the problems of employment. They are highly sensitive to racial discrimination in employment. It is no wonder that they are cynical and critical of discussions of these subjects which try to circumvent the actual issues or to cover them up with glittering generalities about "education," "staying in school," and even "skills." The teacher who can successfully present the issues on a meaningful level and keep in hand articulate discussion on this subject must be knowledgeable about the group dynamics of this volatile population. He must maintain better relations with the class and a more sophisticated approach to his subject materials than Biddle appears to have been able to do.

With these qualities present, a teacher can admit his weakness to the class. It is a fact of our ever-increasingly complex world that there are few people who have all the answers to the important questions of life and, few teachers, therefore, can be expected to have a comprehensive grasp of the social and technological problems confronting our country. The teacher who attempts to hold a general discussion period must realize that he may be unable to give full answers to students' questions and so be able to admit to the class where his knowledge ends. Biddle begins an open-ended provocative discussion that he cannot handle. Yet, he cannot tell his students that he does not have the abilities to handle it, and they, in turn, cannot respect him either for his knowledge or his competence in managing his class.

A confident and respected Biddle might have had much the same problem in handling Tom's questions, but he would have been able to say something like, "Tom, I'm just not getting your point and that's probably my fault as much as yours. Your question has some meaning to you that it doesn't have to me. I'm sorry. Will you try again to get it across to me? Maybe some of the rest of you can help." Teachers who want to can learn a lot from their students, and students do not look down on a teacher who misses their point if he is willing to admit it and shows interest in learning.

Many of Biddle's problems with the class would have been avoided if he had established a definite structure and limits within which it operated, and which he consistently enforced. All children need limits, but the culturally disadvantaged seem to work especially well within a definitely structured situation. Uncertainty, argumentiveness, and testing of limits will not occur in individual circumstances if the class knows from the beginning that certain ground rules exist and will be enforced without favoritism. Teachers will differ as to what these essential ground rules are, but there would probably be general agreement that such things as obscene or profane language, deliberate defiance of the teacher, or fighting, should not be tolerated under any circumstances, and some sort of rules should cover tardiness, bringing in proper equipment, and homework assignments. For the last category, it might be effective to have the class make decisions on the rules and punishment for infractions. In some schools a Student Council might have responsibility for working out such rules. Self-discipline is always more effective than imposed discipline, but since our culturally divergent students have had little training in self-discipline in their homes, they need to know there is an authority above theirs which is consistent and fair. Such students have expressed respect for the teacher who "let's us know just where we stand," and is "real strict but fair with us."

Structure and definite class limits do not have to be rigid however. The criterion should always be the effect of these on a constructive learning situation, and when an exception is made to established rules the students should always be aware that the learning situation *is* the criterion. For example, there may be a rule that hands must be raised and the speaker recognized during discussion, but if a good discussion should get going without this, the teacher can declare a temporary suspension of that rule as long as the meaningful discussion continues. There may be certain rules to maintain a quiet study atmosphere, but there are times when productive learning may be going on in the midst of what might seem to be bedlam — especially during committee work or individual projects. At such times the teacher makes it clear again that this noise is being permitted because everyone is working, but that it is to be stopped immediately if horseplay enters into it.

Maintaining discipline among young people while using creative, active teaching methods is a difficult combination to achieve successfully. Many of the potentially best teachers of the culturally disadvantaged are lost because of their inability to maintain discipline, but if the essential ingredients of warmth, understanding, and skill in teaching are there, the discipline techniques effective for each individual teacher can be developed.

The interplay between Karen and Nelly is important for two reasons:

1) Nelly's language would not have been allowed under the ground rules just discussed.
2) Karen and Nelly represent two polar attitudes. Karen is interested in school and wants to achieve in her scholastic activities. Nelly, on the other hand, is more interested in getting male attention and feels that sexual interests are more important in realistic life experience. Karen was helped at home by her father. It is possible that Nelly's attitudes and lower expectations are the expression of adverse feelings about the school in her home and community, combined with a futility resulting from years of discrimination. As social conditions become more favorable we may hope the school will encounter more students like Karen and fewer like Nelly.

The relativity of different forms of skills and intelligence must be appreciated and reevaluated to seek out the positive strengths that all persons possess. Many individuals of the lower socioeconomic groups have great skills and abilities and show amazing ingenuity in activities not traditionally recognized by our social order as being desirable. Negro youth, especially, see hypocrisy when the abilities and know-how of their parents and associates in the Negro community are deprecated, while persons with skills demanding lesser intelligence are given prestige in the larger society. The fact that skills may vary in kind, although always having a clearly defined and comprehended goal, is portrayed dramatically by the unhinging and falling of the door at the close of Biddle's class. The unfortunate thing is that in this incident the abilities have been channelled destructively to emerge as dexterity and craftiness rather than constructively as skill and intelligence.

"VARIETY"

"Homo sum; humani nihil a me alienum puto — Terence." The motto in shining brass arched over the broad double doorway, a relic of another era. Beneath it on the worn marble steps nearly a dozen youth, boys and girls, lingered. Most were dark skinned, Negro and one Mexican, but two were Caucasian. The friends clustered here often before school. Sometimes they ate together in the park across the street at noon time. Most came here again for a few minutes after the day was over. The group was held together by a vague fellowship. They talked but little for they already knew one another's opinions. They watched the world around them, sometimes sneering, often laughing, but always with a sense of security that came from their association together. They felt a friendly warmth in this fact which was difficult to explain.

"Shoot, there goes the soldier again," Ricardo remarked casually. The group of friends watched the duty teacher patrolling the sidewalk area a half a block away with his walkie-talkie. "Watch out, you nut," he called in mock warning to a jaywalking girl, "or the general will shoot you!" Snorts and laughter broke from the group.

Now attention shifted from the teacher to a police car, driving slowly by, its occupants sharply watching the little knots of students moving toward the main door. "Fuzz!" several called out. Scornful guffaws.

"I don't know why they run this school like a damned jail!" Douglas Carter was a tall, handsome youth of dark complexion but with sharp Caucasian features. His eyes mirrored confidence. The others nodded their agreement with obvious respect for their friend.

"I wish we had classes every other day like up on the hill," Ricardo ventured, motioning with his head in the direction of the city's junior college, several blocks away. And then, suddenly spotting a member of the gang approaching, "Hey, Doug, here comes Patty."

A slender, Caucasian girl with a pretty face and long hair came bouncing up the steps, her short skirt swinging. Douglas stepped down to meet her. He threw his arm around her shoulder and pressed his dark face into her chestnut hair.

"See you," he said to his friends. Then he and the girl turned inside the great doorway and started off down the hall.

"Honey," said Pat softly, looking up at her boyfriend, "Dad was a little upset about how late I got in. Didn't mind our going to the movie, but didn't see any reason for the coffee house afterwards."

"Did it get rough?" Anxiously.

"Not really, sweet. He's trying hard to be 'understanding.' But Mom," she hesitated, "that's another story. She just doesn't say much at all to me anymore since she found out about us."

"It'll be all right, Pat. It'll be all right."

In a corner of the teacher's cafeteria, five teachers were grouped around a table having morning coffee. Ben Mullings, the Latin teacher, bit into a doughnut. He was nodding his grey head in firm agreement with the course of the conversation. Opposite him sat Amelia Briddle who taught shorthand, typing, and office practice. At the end of the table, Alex Chardonay, a Negro, sipped his coffee while he tried to correct papers. He was the new social studies teacher.

"I tell you, Mr. Mullings, things are getting out of hand!" Miss Briddle tightened her lips until they became a thin line. Her eyes were full of angry determination. "I think we should go in a group to Mr. Jason and let him know what's going on."

Ben Mullings set his cup down and nodded affirmatively.

"We're not doing our job if we permit this kind of thing!" Amelia Briddle babbled on. "It's ruining our school, what with all these new students and everything. We really should be more careful than ever about controlling the lovemaking in the halls and on the school grounds. You know what will happen if some of the parents hear about it. We'll lose more and more of the decent ones, the achievers. Besides, it's the worst possible thing for integration. People will assume . . . well you know what I mean."

Mr. Mullings' hand on the table top trembled nervously. "Did you see Patty Madison this morning with ah-er . . . her boyfriend?"

"You mean Douglas Carter, I suppose?" Mike Jacobs entered the conversation. He had been half listening. He was young, forward, argumentative. Mike Jacobs had been teaching mathematics at Central for the last two years and was popular with students.

"Well, personally, Mr. Jacobs," Miss Briddle continued, "I think it's the principal's responsibility to prohibit those unnecessary displays on the front steps each morning. They give a distorted picture of our student body to the public."

"All I can say," said Mullings, in a condescending way, placing his hand on Mike's shoulder, "in the old days, the profession never tolerated flagrant petting and sexual expression in school." And then, reflecting a moment, he added, "Whatever the merits of integration from an educational standpoint, the Supreme Court decision certainly wasn't meant to encourage miscegenation as school policy, now, was it?"

Mr. Chardonay, in the corner of the room, raised one eyebrow in a slightly surprised manner. A smile flitted across his brown face. He quietly went back to his papers.

"Understand me," broke in Miss Briddle hurriedly, a little nervous as she glanced down the table toward Alex, "it has nothing to do with civil rights or their abilities." She stressed the word "their." "What I mean is we just haven't any business at all giving our approval to racial mixing. It'll prejudice the whole idea of integrated school facilities and bring no end of woe for the young people we're supposed to protect."

Mike's eyes flashed and a self-assured smile spread across his face. He took another swallow of coffee and then hit them.

"Now, you can't stop students from congregating, hell that's their right! As to mixing, 95 percent of all American Negroes are at least partly Caucasian in ancestry, and countless Caucasians, without knowing it, have at least some African ancestry. That's from 'passing.' Mixing has been going on for at least four hundred years in this country, almost all of it resulting from white men exploiting black women. Before that there was earlier, unrecorded, even prehistoric mixing of races. Take Douglas Carter. Obviously he's at least half Caucasian, genetically speaking. So, if his white father, or white grandfather, 'mixed' with a Negro woman, why not permit him to 'mix' with a white one?"

"You're not serious?" Amelia Briddle stiffened, hesitated. She blushed slightly, started to speak, then turned to Ben Mullings. He became grave and spoke very deliberately.

"It's not our professional responsibility to try to solve ancient evils nor to try to balance old wrongs with new ones. It is our responsibility to guide young people morally," he paused slightly, "and intellectually. We seem to be permitting our schools to be turned into amusement parks and carnivals. We are cheating our young people and letting them fall."

Mike took another, and last, big swallow of coffee, and then, very casually, "Well, Ben, I just want you to remember that some of these kids are on the honor roll. Both Douglas Carter and Patty Madison are, if I'm not mistaken."

During first lunch, Mike Jacobs met Pat and Douglas in the hall. Doug was on duty as hall monitor, and Pat had taken the opportunity to join him. They were eating their bag lunches together. They stood and held hands as Mike talked to them. They had met him at the coffee house a month before. Now they compared impressions of the foreign film which Doug and Patty had seen the night before and which the teacher had previously seen. After a few minutes, Mike left them. Amelia Briddle came down the hall. When she spotted the couple together, her jaw became set with determination.

"Pat, what are you doing in the hall eating your lunch? What business do you have staying here with Douglas?"

The girl was unable to repress a scarcely audible, "Oh, crap!" Miss Briddle's response was quick, her voice hard and cold.

"You'd better get to the office, young lady!" Douglas nudged Pat and smiled as if to say that everything would turn out all right and not to worry. Shrugging her shoulders gently, Pat turned to follow the teacher to the office.

At 3:30 in the afternoon, most of the gang were back on the steps, seated now in a circle in the bright sunlight. Pat was there, and she had just told the story of her difficulty with Miss Briddle. The vice-principal had reprimanded her for eating in the halls without authority and had mysteriously cautioned her about her "associations."

"She tried to be tactful, but the general idea was I ought to pick a new boy friend," said Pat.

"Shoot, they mess around with stuff that's none of their business," one of the boy's remarked.

"Briddle's a busted bag!" a white chum joined in.

"Don't worry, gang, Patty and I will work our way around them," said Douglas, as he took up his books, rose to his feet, and offered Pat his hand. Just then a police car passed, and attention shifted to that despised symbol.

"They looking for us to make trouble!" charged Ricardo.

"Oh, they're not all bad. Some of them just have that job to do. Keep out of their way is my advice!" said Douglas.

Minutes later, Douglas and Pat reached the sidewalk with others from the group. Ben Mullings was driving by and he caught sight of the pair out of the corner of his eye. Douglas and Pat were facing each other a few steps from the curb. Doug's big brown hands squeezed Pat's waist and then moved upward to her shoulders. She stood on tiptoe. Her eyes looked into his with tenderness and trust. They kissed.

Ben's face turned bright red. He was overwhelmed by a flood of fury.

THE SCHOOL AND LIFE EXPERIENCE   197

He jammed his foot onto to the gas pedal to speed away. Almost instantaneously, he heard the police siren behind him, saw the patrol car in his mirror. He pulled to the curb and, sweating, stumbled out to meet the officer. Nearby he heard the mocking laughter of Doug and Pat's friends.

"Mullings been fuzzed!"

* * *

QUESTIONS FOR WRITING AND DISCUSSION

1. Many minority group students exhibit a contempt for the school and for the police. How do you see each of the basic themes of this manual — cultural difference, self-image, school process, adolescent vs. adult authority, and the preparation for life after school — as pertinent to these students' attitudes?
2. Which school personnel in this story reinforce the students' negative attitudes? Why? Which teacher might do most to break them down? Why? Do you feel Amelia Briddle and Ben Mullings wish to see successful integration and are sincerely concerned that the student behavior in the story will jeopardize it? Do you feel Mr. Chardonay, the Negro teacher, could have taken any effective part in the teacher conversation rather than remaining aloof? Why do you suppose he remained aloof?
3. What do you think of Mike Jacob's facts on racial mixture? Do you suppose the other teachers were aware of these things? Did they believe Mike? Would such awareness make any difference in their thinking? To what extent does knowledge affect feelings?
4. Which aspects of the students' behavior bothered Amelia and Ben? Do you believe any or all of these things to be justifiable concerns of school personnel? Why? To what degree?
5. How do you think Mr. Harrington of the previous story, "Expectations," would have improved student morale? How would he have handled the matter of interracial romance?
6. In your experience, do school personnel become involved when interracial romances come to their attention? In what ways? Do you feel this is within the province of the school's concern? Why?
7. How is the matter of the school's handling of interracial dating connected with the school's preparation of the student for adult life experiences?

COMMENTS

"Homo sum; humani nihil a me alienum puto" — Terence. "I am a man; nothing human is alien to me." The story which unfolds after the noble Latin inscription above the doorway shows that today such mottoes are more often platitudes and exercises for translation than they are philosophical guides for youth morality. The changing teenage sex mores, when joined with the racial integration issue, make for an especially explosive situation in the urban school. It is clear that today's schools have a particularly difficult task in resolving this question. Unfortunately, in many schools it is not being satisfactorily dealt with. Racial prejudice, if not overt, is often mixed with moral judgments. Thus the hypocricy of teachers like Miss Briddle and Ben Mullings becomes quite apparent to nonwhite youth. This fact interferes with the primary task of the school, the learning function, and fosters antipathy towards the school, as a community institution. Furthermore, as was evident in this story, negative school attitudes may become shared with white youth when they too begin to experience discriminatory treatment or ostracism because of their associations with non-white friends. For a young person in love, such treatment can be particularly bitter and damaging.

There are really two issues involved in the story: dating and peer group behavior not considered appropriate for school facilities — interracial association and dating. Mr. Mulling's comment, "In the old days the profession would never have tolerated flagrant petting and sexual expression in school," is not a completely objectionable response if addressed to the first issue. However, when it becomes an excuse for discouraging interracial groupings or pairing off, then a double standard emerges which is transparently clear to many students as well as to other teachers like Mike Jacobs.

Both teachers, Briddle and Mullings, rationalize their disdain for close interracial association by saying, "It's the worst possible thing for integration," and "we'll lose more and more of the decent ones, the achievers." These statements illustrate that the two teachers, regardless of educational skills which they may possess, have no real understanding of, or commitment to the principle of school integration with which they say they are in agreement. Their statements about the interracial couple and the "gang" on the school's front steps belie their supposed convictions.

The fallacy of the arguments of both Mullings and Briddle can be considered in the following manner. If Negroes are conceived as equals in American society, not inferior to whites, then there should be no consternation when an interracial group congregates any more than when an all-white group of friends gets together before classes. Neither should there be consternation when a white girl accepts a Negro boyfriend. This is not to say that interracial dating should be considered lightly, given the emotionally tinged social mores of our culture in this sector. Rather, the point of the story is the unconscious dishonesty of the teachers who claim to desire "integration."

On a factual note it should be pointed out that the supposed "danger" of interracial dating leading to marriage is overstated. In California fewer than 1 percent of all marriages are interracial. Furthermore, social science findings indicate that it is not likely for this percentage to increase in the near future.

The responses of Briddle and Mullings, and the methods which they undertake to deal with the problem as they see it, only serve to alienate Negro youngsters and their friends. The action taken by Briddle towards Pat is typical of the techniques often employed in schools to discourage interracial relationships. Interracial romances are frequently discouraged by preventing actual physical contact between people of different races. Imagine what a Negro pupil feels towards the "system" when in gym, during social dancing, he is excused because there are not enough Negro partners to "go around." Schools have also handled interracial romances by having a faculty member, close to the Caucasian partner, approach the Caucasian and put pressure on him or her to sever the relationship. These methods suggest to a non white how inferior the school feels such students to be and engenders in him contempt for such educators.

There is only one legitimate reason for school personnel to be concerned with interracial dating. It is that the students involved may not have sufficient maturity to deal with the situation. In "Variety," Douglas Carter appears to possess this quality and perhaps Patty also. Mike Jacobs is the kind of teacher who is able to recognize that Doug and Patty are an exceptional couple. In the story he cites the fact of their scholarship as evidence, a factor seemingly overlooked by the two concerned teachers.

Mike Jacobs' relationship to "Variety" is a positive one. Given the response from him as compared to Briddle and Mullings, it seems obvious that the incidents which seem to alarm the more conservative teachers could be handled in a more positive manner. Frequently in these situations, a lack of clearly defined procedures governing student conduct can lead to differential treatment in practice. This appears to have been a factor in the story which, combined with prejudicial teacher attitudes, led to heightened student hostility.

DIGESTS OF SOCIAL SCIENCE READINGS

"Social Structure and Anomie"[2]

Merton's essay provides one explanation of why so much nonconformity, delinquency, and crime are found among the lower classes. What is distinctive in our way of life is the American dream of mobility. Conversely, the American nightmare is not getting there. Our social structure means that people at the bottom of the ladder have lofty goals, but limited opportunities for attaining success. When people are frustrated because of thwarted aspirations, they may try various ways to escape from the intolerable situation; or, their ambition may lead to illicit attempts to achieve success.

Merton distinguishes between two types of values. The first type governs the *ends* people pursue; that is, it specifies the goals they should seek. The second governs the *means* by which the socially approved ends are to be sought. In other words, we have norms, or rules, which spell out the allowable procedures to get us to our goals.

Merton is concerned with the extreme emphasis our society places upon accumulating wealth as a symbol of success. Most people believe that this goal should be sought only in socially approved ways. Thus, stealing is not a permissible way to acquire wealth. Rather one should increase this wealth through hard work and investments. But some people use whatever means are most efficient in attaining the socially approved value, whether legitimate or not. Crime bcomes increasingly common when people pursue the success-goal through the most efficient means.

Individuals may reject either society's means or ends, or they may accept or reject both. There are five alternative modes of adjustment or adaptation individuals can make. *Anomie* or deviance is not simply present or absent; there are instead different types.

---

[2] Robert K. Merton, *Social Theory and Social Structure* (Glencoe, Ill., 1949), pp. 131–160. Digest used by permission of the publisher, The Free Press.

THE SCHOOL AND LIFE EXPERIENCE

	Adaptation	*Cultural goals*	*Permissible means*
	Conformity	accepts	accepts
	Innovation	accepts	rejects
Types of Anomie	Ritualism	rejects	accepts
	Retreatism	rejects	rejects
	Rebellion	accepts/rejects	accepts/rejects

Persons may shift from one alternative to another as they engage in different activities. The categories refer to role adjustments in specific situations, not to whole personalities. A person may be an innovator in his economic roles (a thief) but a conformist in his family roles (a good father.)

Most members of every society accept both the culture goals and the approved means for their achievement. This *conforming* pattern is not anomie. *Anomie* here refers to rejection of either the accepted means or ends, or both.

The *innovator* wants the things emphasized by his group, but does not accept the socially prescribed means for attaining them. The criminal, for example, agrees with the rest of society that success is important, but uses illegal ways to secure it.

The *ritualist* rejects the ends of his society, but continues to accept the prescribed methods of achieving them. One type of ritualist is the man who performs his job diligently, but has given up hope for monetary and occupational success.

Retreatism involves a rejection of both the socially approved means and ends. It is the least common adaptation in every society. In this category are some of the activities of the mentally ill, vagrants, drunkards, and dope addicts. These people are not interested in monetary success and are not committed to a legal occupation.

Rebellion involves rejection of the socially approved means and ends. At the same time, persons adopting this pattern substitute new means and ends that they consider right and proper. Revolutionaries are an example of people who fit into this category.

Merton's analysis stresses that anomie or deviant responses are due to means and ends not being integrated with each other. Monetary success becomes important to the individual because of the emphasis placed on it in American society. There is the belief that success should be open to everyone, no matter what his position in society is. Yet the lower classes, who have the same incentive for success as everyone else, have disadvantages that others do not have (poverty, lack of education, etc.). We are taught that ambition is a virtue, but it is also the source of some large vices. Ambition promotes deviant behavior. Thus the American stress on success and ambition invites anxiety, hostility, neuroses, and antisocial behavior.

"Goals, Norms, and Anomie"[3]

> *Cloward and Ohlin suggest that lower-class persons experience relatively greater dissatisfaction with their present positions and also have fewer legitimate ways of changing their status. Thus they experience greater pressures toward deviant behavior.*

Many lower-class youths seek higher economic positions without wanting to change their life styles or associations. The lower class continues to be their reference group. While aspiring to more money, they do not aspire to a middle-class life style. Some lower-class boys, however, do strive for a change in the economic as well as the social spheres of their life, and so adopt middle-class means for their change.

"The literature on lower-class delinquent subcultures is replete with references to the conspicuous consumption of wealth: delinquents repeatedly remark that they want 'big cars', 'flashy clothes', and 'swell dames'. . . . These symbols of success, framed primarily in economic terms rather than in terms of middle-class life-styles, suggest to us that the participants in delinquent subcultures are seeking higher status within their own cultural milieu. If legitimate paths to their status become restricted, then the delinquent subculture provides alternative (albeit illegal) avenues" (p. 94).

There are cultural as well as structural and economic barriers to change in life style. For instance, lower-class youths encounter cultural and economic barriers to continuing education. Some are discouraged by a cultural tradition that deprecates school, but generally there are even greater economic problems. Many are struggling to maintain a minimal level of subsistence. It has been found that most adolescents who quit school did so because they needed and wanted immediate employment rather than because they did not value education as such. Moreover, the lower the social position of one's father the less likely it is that one can take advantage of educational opportunities.

"What we are suggesting is that lower-class attitudes toward education are adaptive; that is, expectations are scaled down to accord with

---

[3] Richard A. Cloward and Lloyd E. Ohlin, *op. cit.*, pp. 77–104. The Free Press.

the realistic limitations on access to educational opportunities. Educational attainment and related forms of goal-striving are thus eschewed not so much because they are inherently devalued as because access to them is relatively restricted. Although those cultural orientations, once crystallized, persist as major obstacles to the utilization of opportunity, it should be remembered that they emerged initially as adaptive responses to socially structured deprivations" (p. 103).

Young people will then alternatively respond to other channels of achieving high positions, such as in sports or entertainment fields which do not demand great education and change of life style as one of the means of achievement. These vocations symbolize the possibility of achieving success in conventional terms despite a poor education and low social origin.

It is suggested finally that tendencies toward delinquent practice in the lower class are modes of adaptation to structured strains and inconsistencies within the social order.

"Growing Up in a Class System"[4]

Cohen points out that in our democratic system children of different social levels are compared in terms of the same set of standards. Yet the ability to achieve these standards is distributed according to family background and social class. Children of the most disadvantaged classes are relegated to the bottom of the status pyramid because they lack the personal qualifications of middle-class children. The middle-class home trains the child to compete successfully in terms of the dominant American value system. The working-class child starts out with a handicap; he is found wanting because his family and neighborhood often fail to provide "middle-class" models for him.

Cohen summarizes the middle-class standards by which children and adolescents, particularly males, tend to be evaluated in our society:

1. Ambition is a virtue; one must aspire to reach goals difficult of achievement.

---

[4] Albert K. Cohen, *Delinquent Boys: The Culture of the Gang*, (Glencoe, Ill., 1955), pp. 73–119. Digest used by permission of the publisher, The Free Press.

2. One must assume individual responsibility, be resourceful and self-reliant, reluctant to turn to others for help. The middle-class ethic minimizes the obligation to share with others.

3. One should cultivate and possess skills and tangible achievements. Academic achievement and skills of potential economic and occupational value are especially applauded.

4. Great value is placed on "worldly asceticism," a readiness and ability to postpone immediate satisfactions in the interest of long-run goals. Industry and thrift are admirable in themselves.

5. Rationality is highly valued, that is, forethought, conscious planning, the budgeting of time, and efficiency.

6. Manners, courtesy, and personability are rewarded and encouraged. One should be able to "win friends and influence people." One needs patience, self-control, and the inhibition of spontaneity.

7. Physical aggression and violence must be controlled.

8. Recreation should be "wholesome." One should not "waste" time, but spend his leisure "constructively."

9. Middle-class values emphasize "respect for property." The owner has the right to do as he wishes with his belongings. "Things" are to be treated carefully.

The ability to conform to these standards comes easily when the child grows up in a world where they are emphasized and where he is trained in the necessary skills and habits. The middle-class home is more likely to train the child to meet these standards than is the working-class home. Middle-class socialization is conscious, deliberate, demanding. Parents are concerned with their children's achievement of age-graded "norms." They are geared to the future as well as the present. The child is aware of what his parents want him to be and become. Middle-class parents surround the child with educational books and toys. They supervise friends and activities. The middle-class home generates in the child a "need" for, a dependence upon, parental love to an unusual degree. It is something to be earned by effort and achievement. The child feels anxiety which is allayed only by good behavior and constant striving.

"Planning" and "foresight" on the part of parents are not as evident to the working-class as to the middle-class child. Working-class aspirations with respect to jobs and income are often well below what a middle-class person would consider necessary for respectability. Working-class parents do not evaluate a job in terms of its prospects for "advancement." In the working class the "ethic of reciprocity" means a readiness to turn for aid to others, and a sense of obligation to share one's own resources with them. The working-class person is more spontaneous, gives freer expression to his aggression. He is less likely to possess or value the sophistication, fluency, "good appearance," and "personality" so useful in middle-class life.

The working-class child may be more dependent upon his relationships to his peer group than the middle-class child. He is freer to explore in areas forbidden to the middle-class child. His learning is likely to be motivated by the solution of immediate practical problems. The effects of physical punishment, common among the working-class, are less lasting and less of a deterrent than the threat of the loss of love is in the middle-class family. In the working-class, fighting is likely to be viewed as a natural and legitimate way of settling disputes. Middle-class parents emphasize "reason" and diplomatic maneuvers. Physical prowess tends to be channeled into organized, competitive sports, governed by rules of "fair play."

The personalities of the children of these two classes are in general younger versions of the personalities of their parents. Ability, as measured by performance in conventional tests of intelligence, varies directly with social class. The results of these tests are an index of the ability of the child to meet middle-class expectations.

Working-class children are always at a disadvantage when they move in a middle-class world of children or adults. They do not have the money, clothes, or other material insignia of status of middle-class children. They cannot participate in activities which require material things they cannot afford. The writings of American educators imply that a major function of the schools is to reward middle-class ambition and conformity to middle-class expectations. When conformity is rewarded, the nonconformist is subtly condemned and punished. Working-class children are likely to be considered problems because of their relative lack of training in order and discipline, lack of interest in intellectual achievement, and lack of reinforcement by the home of the school's requirements. The failures in the classroom in terms of conduct and academic achievement are drawn disproportionately from the lower social class levels. Similar conflicts are seen between the middle-class values of adults in charge of settlement houses or other recreational agencies and the working-class values of the children they deal with. Such organizations feel they do a lot of good, but can't reach the children who need them most. Working-class children have the problem of adjusting to a middle-class world.

"The Religious Beliefs and Practices of Delinquent Youth"[5]

> Werthman discusses the attitudes of delinquent boys concerning themselves and their future prospects under present social conditions.

Fifty members of tough delinquent gangs in San Francisco (including Negroes, Mexicans, and Caucasians) were given a questionnaire to learn their attitudes toward the school, the occupational world, the family, and the nation as a whole. Every gang member in the sample was an adjudicated delinquent.

Older adolescents between the ages of seventeen and twenty-two responded quite differently to the questionnaire than did younger adolescents between the ages of thirteen and sixteen. Both groups are ambitious and both complain about racial discrimination. However, the younger boys do not yet perceive that obtaining a job will someday be a problem and that they may not have sufficient skills to obtain the jobs that do exist. Moreover, the younger boys appear to have the brains, motivation, and opportunity to get a good education, even though they are exceedingly critical of the teachers, principals, and counselors in the school itself. They are also great believers in hard work and in their country.

It is the older boys who have become social critics. Even though they admit to their lack of skills, they are bitter about leaving school and their inability to find jobs. They expect to end up as unskilled workmen someday. Belief in the value of education is replaced by a belief in good connections, and they believe that "you have to lie, cheat, and steal in order to get along in this world." In addition, they are not particularly patriotic.

The major difference between the younger and older delinquents studied is that the older boys have clearly failed, while the younger boys are in the process of doing so. Most older gang members have flunked out of school, failed to find jobs, and are still somewhat reluctantly living off their parents. They perceive that they have no future. Lack of education and lack of occupational skills mean that most avenues to a conventional life are closed. The delinquent gang is the only refuge they have from the failure.

Younger gang members, on the other hand, are still in school and have

---

[5] Carl Werthman, "The Religious Beliefs and Practices of Delinquent Youth," Unpublished paper. Digest used by permission of the author.

not yet had to face the job market. They can still live at home without guilt. At least formally they are still within conventional institutions, and, although they do not think much about the future, nothing happens to make them think that there might not be much of a future for them.

ACKNOWLEDGMENTS

General Introduction
1. From "Lower Class Culture as a Generating Milieu of Gang Delinquency," by Walter B. Miller, in *Sociology of Crime and Delinquency*, ed. Marvin Wolfgang, et al., © 1962 John Wiley & Sons, Inc.
2. From "Note on Race Relations in Mass Society," by Joseph D. Lohman and Dietrich C. Reitzes, *American Journal of Sociology*, LVIII, November 1952.

Part I
1. From "Lower Class Culture as a Generating Milieu of Gang Delinquency," by Walter B. Miller, in *Sociology of Crime and Delinquency*, ed. Marvin E. Wolfgang, et al., © 1962 John Wiley & Sons, Inc.
2. From *Delinquent Behavior: Culture and the Individual*, by W.C. Kvaraceus and Walter B. Miller (Washington, D.C.: National Education Association, 1959).
3. From "The Disadvantaged Child and the Learning Process: Some Social Psychological and Developmental Considerations," by Martin Deutsch, in *Education in Depressed Areas*, ed. A.H. Passow, © 1963 Teachers College Press.
4. From *The Culturally Deprived Child* by Frank Riessman, © 1962 by Frank Riessman; Harper & Row, Publishers.
5. From "Workers' Attitudes Toward Participation and Leadership," by Frank Riessman, unpublished Ph.D. dissertation (Columbia University, 1955).
6. From "Social Class Variations in the Teacher-Pupil Relationship," by Howard Becker, *Journal of Educational Sociology*, XXV (April 1952).
7., 8. From "The Separate Culture of the School," by Willard Waller, *Sociology of Teaching*, © 1932 John Wiley & Sons, Inc.
9. From *The Vanishing Adolescent* by Edgar Z. Friedenberg, © 1959 Beacon Press.

Part II
1. From *Crisis in Black and White* by Charles E. Silberman, © 1964 Random House.
2. From *Nobody Knows My Name* by James Baldwin, © 1961 Dell Books.
3. From *Racial Awareness in Young Children* by Mary Goodman, © 1952 Addison-Wesley.
4. From *The Cool World* by Warren Miller, © 1965 Fawcett.
5. From *Spinster* by Sylvia Ashton-Warner, © 1959; and *Teacher*, © 1963 Simon and Schuster.
6. From talk given at Conference on Disadvantaged Youth at UCLA by Harry Rivlin, November 1963.
7. From *The Mark of Oppression* by Abram Kardiner and Lionel Ovesey, © 1951 The World Publishing Company.
8. From "Racial Identification and Preference in Negro Children," by Ken-

neth B. Clark and Mamie Clark in *Readings in Social Psychology*, ed. Theodore Newcomb and Eugene L. Hartley, © 1947 Holt, Rinehart & Winston, Inc.

9. From "Social Status and Intelligence: An Experimental Study of Certain Cultural Determinants of Measured Intelligence," by Ernest A. Haggard, *Genetic Psychology Monographs*, XLIX (May 1954).
10. From "Teacher Comments and Student Performance: Seventy-Four Classroom Experiments in School Motivation," by Ellis Batten Page, *Journal of Educational Psychology*, XLI (August 1958).

Part III
1. From *From Max Weber: Essays in Sociology* ed by H.H. Gerth and C. Wright Mills, © 1946 Oxford University Press.
2, 3, 5, 7. From *Bureaucracy in Modern Society* by Peter M. Blau, © 1956 Random House.
4, 6. From *The Dynamics of Bureaucracy*, second edition, by Peter M. Blau, © 1963 University of Chicago Press.
8. From "The Teacher in the Authority System of the Public School," by Howard S. Becker, *Journal of Educational Sociology*, XXVII, (November 1953).
9, 10. From U.S. Office of Education, *Programs for the Educationally Disadvantaged*, Bulletin 17 (Washington, 1963).

Part IV
1, 4. From "Delinquents in Schools: A Test for the Legitimacy of Authority," by Carl Werthman, *Berkeley Journal of Sociology*, VII (1963).
2. From unpublished paper by Frank Riessman, "Teacher Institutes: A Five Point Plan," July 1964.
3. From "Identity vs. Identity Diffusion in Adolescence," by Erik H. Erikson, in *New Perspectives for Research in Juvenile Delinquency*, ed. Helen L. Witmer and Ruth Kotinsky, U.S. Children's Bureau (Washington, 1955).

Part V
1, 3. From *Delinquency and Opportunity: A Theory of Delinquent Gangs*, by Richard Cloward and Lloyd Ohlin, © 1960 The Free Press.
2. From *Social Theory and Social Structure* by Robert K. Merton, © 1949 The Free Press.
4. From *Delinquent Boys: The Culture of the Gang* by Albert K. Cohen, © 1955 The Free Press.
5. From "The Religious Beliefs and Practices of Delinquent Youth," by Carl Werthman, unpublished paper.

www.ingramcontent.com/pod-product-compliance
Lightning Source LLC
Chambersburg PA
CBHW021705230426
43668CB00008B/730